Implementing SAP R/3

Second Edition

Nancy H. Bancroft
Henning Seip
Andrea Sprengel

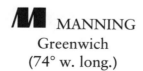
MANNING

Greenwich
(74° w. long.)

The publisher offers discounts on this book when ordered in quantity. For more information, please contact:

>   Special Sales Department
>   Manning Publications Co.
>   3 Lewis Street
>   Greenwich, CT 06830
>
>   Fax: (203) 661-9018
>   email: orders@manning.com

Library of Congress Cataloging-in-Publication Data
Bancroft, Nancy H., 1940-
        Implementing SAP R/3   / Nancy H. Bancroft, Henning Seip,
    Andrea Sprengel. — 2nd ed.
            p.   cm.
        Includes index.
        ISBN 0-13-889213-X
        1. Computer integrated manufacturing systems.   2. Client/server
    computing. 3. Reengineering (Management).   I. Seip, Henning. II.
    Sprengel, Andrea.   III. Title.
    TS155.63.B36   1997
    670'.285—dc21.   97-25858
                                                   CIP

⚫ Manning Publications Co.
    3 Lewis Street
    Greenwich, CT 06830

    Copyeditor: Elizabeth Martin
    Typesetter: Dorothy Marsico

Printed in the United States of America
      4 5 6 7 8 9 10 – CR – 00 99 98

Praise for the First Edition

"This book has already proven to be of value at Perrier and we're sure its importance will grow... thanks for your excellent publication."
— *John Gilmore, SAP Implementation Team, The Perrier Group of America*

"[This book] will be snapped up by members of large and medium sized companies implementing or considering using SAP software."
— *Frank Monteleone, Tenneco Packaging*

"I definitely recommend this book to anyone considering or going through SAP implementation. The emphasis on project teams is right on."
— *Steve Wells, Suburban Propane*

" ...a must read for technical and business people at all levels of the organization who are involved in the implementation of R/3."
— *Paul Sager, SAIC*

"I wish this information had been available to us when we decided to move to the world of SAP in 1994."
— *Lois Giese, Ciba Geigy Corp*

"This book does an excellent job describing R/3's strengths and weaknesses, changes that the client should make, and changes that will be required."
— *Peter J. Luise, President, Renaissance Solutions, Inc.*

"A good introduction to the issues that will be faced in an SAP R/3 implementation ... recommended reading for business owners of the project to help them avoid the pitfalls."
— *Andy Gaule, project manager, DiverseyLever/Europe*

" ...your SAP book is a big hit among our newer SAP implementation teams ... your overall message adds credibility to one I've been trying to transmit to my management."
— *Diane Schwarz, Manager, Information Strategy and Tactics, Steelcase*

"...most questions that I had about change management, training, etc. were answered in an effective manner. Congratulations—it's a great book!"
— *Miguel Gallardo, SAP Project Manager, Galvak, S.A. de C.V., Mexico*

PERMISSIONS

Some of the material contained within this book was originally created as a series of three articles coauthored by Nancy H. Bancroft and Erich Almasy. The articles bear the copyright of Symmetrix, Inc. The material is used herein with their permission.

SAP, R/3, and R/2 are trademarks of SAP AG, Systems, Applications and Products in Data Processing, Neurottstrasse 16, 69190 Walldorf, Germany. The publisher gratefully acknowledges SAP's kind permission to use its trademarks in this publication. SAP AG is neither the publisher of this book nor responsible for it under any aspect of press law.

CONTENTS

Permissions   *v*

About the Authors   *xv*

Preface to the Second Edition   *xvii*

Preface to the First Edition   *xix*

Who Should Read This Book   *xxi*

Overview of This Book   *xxiii*

SECTION   1   APPROACHING THE R/3 SOLUTION   1

     Introduction   *3*

       What Is SAP?   4

       Description of R/3   5

       Why Not Choose R/3? What Are the Risks?   5

          Risk 1: 1980s Technology   6
          Risk 2: Lack of Flexibility   8
          Risk 3: Complexity   9
          Risk 4: Possible Lack of Fit with Corporate Strategy   10

       The Bottom Line   11

   1   *A Tour of the R/3 System*   *13*

       1.1   Key Components of SAP Software   14

       1.2   One Database/One System   16

       1.3   Client/Server in R/3 Applications   17

1.4 Basis Technology 22
  The System Architecture 22
  Systems Administration 25

1.5 R/3 System Features 27
  The Data Repository 27
  Tables 28
  Business Workflow 29
  Correction and Transport System 30
  ABAP/4 Development Workbench 31

1.6 Overview of Modules 31
  Financial Accounting 32
  Human Resources 33
  Manufacturing and Logistics 33
  Sales and Distribution 34

2 *Basics for Configuring the R/3 System, Training, and the Users' Group* 37

2.1 R/3 Basics: The Window 38

2.2 Online Help with Configuring the System 40
  The Reference Model 41
  The Procedure Model 43
  The Implementation Management Guide (IMG) 47

2.3 Training 48

2.4 The Users' Group 51

3 *The R/3 Basis Technology* 53

3.1 SAP R/3 System in Depth 54
  Technical Architecture 54
  Objects and the ABAP/4 Repository 55

3.2 System Administration 56
  Computer Center Management System (CCMS) 57
  Correction and Transport System (CTS) 60
  User Maintenance 63
  Application Data Archiving 64
  Database Administration 65

3.3 ABAP/4 Workbench 66
  ABAP/4 Repository 66
  Application Hierarchy 68
  The Object Browser 68
  The Data Modeler 70
  ABAP/4 Data Dictionary 71
  ABAP/4 Programming Language and Editor 71

The Screen Painter 72
The Menu Painter 72
The Data Browser 73
Program Test Aids 73

4 Configuring SAP R/3 75

4.1 Configuration Concepts 76

4.2 The Client Data Structure 76

4.3 Architecture of SAP Applications 79

4.4 Tables and Data Types 81
Application Data 82
Configuration Data 83

4.5 Configurable Elements 85
Central Functions 85
Organizational Elements 86
Control Elements 90
Data Validation 92
System Control 92

4.6 Configuring an SAP Document 93

4.7 Working with Master Data 100

4.8 Working with Documents 104

4.9 Working with Reports 109

5 Plan for Reengineering 113

5.1 What Is Reengineering? 114

5.2 The Many Faces of Reengineering 115

5.3 Reengineering Process 119

5.4 The Case of Hill's Pet Nutrition 120

5.5 The Role of Information Technology in Reengineering 122
When to Reengineer—Before, during, or after R/3? 123
IS and User Role Changes 126
IS Implementation Process 126
Implementation Skill Becomes a New, Distinct Competency 127

5.6 Reengineering Is Organizational Change 128

6 Implementation Guidelines for R/3 129

6.1 The Case of Battco 130

6.2 Nine Critical Success Factors 133
Understand Your Corporate Culture 134

Begin Process Changes First   134
Communicate   135
Provide Superior Championship   136
Ensure the Project Manager Is Capable   136
Choose a Balanced Team   137
Select a Good Methodology   138
Train Everyone   138
Commit to the Change   138

6.3 Unique Aspects of R/3 Project Management   140
R/3 is not a Silver Bullet   140
R/3 Does Not Support Loose Boundaries   140
Customize, Don't Modify   141
Be Sure You Fit within R/3   142
Training Is Only the Beginning   143
Visionary and Detail Focused   144

6.4 Implementation Time Frame   144

6.5 Implementation Approach Choices   145

6.6 Communicate to the User Organization   146

SECTION 2   STEPS IN THE PROCESS: WHERE ARE THE PITFALLS?   149

7   Phase 1: Focus   151

7.1 The Steering Committee   152

7.2 Identify R/3 Modules   154

7.3 The Project Leader   156

7.4 Structure the Project Teams   157

7.5 Integrate the Team Findings and Decisions   159
Integration Mechanisms   159

7.6 Set Objectives   161

7.7 Develop Guiding Principles   162

7.8 Develop a Detailed Project Plan   163

7.9 The Case of Agrium, Inc.   164

8   Phase 2: Create the As Is Picture   167

8.1 Analyze Current Business Processes   168

8.2 The Case of a Systems Integration Company   170

8.3 Map Business Processes into R/3   171

8.4 Identify Data and System Interfaces   172

8.5 Inventory Existing Hardware/Software 173

8.6 Install R/3 174

8.7 Begin Project Team Training 175

9 *Phase 3: Create the* **To Be** *Design* 177

9.1 Develop High-Level Design 178

9.2 The R/3 Hierarchy 179

9.3 Gain User Acceptance 180

9.4 Detailed Design 182

9.5 Scenarios, Scripts, and Tables 182

9.6 Iterative Prototyping Using Tables 184

9.7 User Communications 190

9.8 Gain Final Acceptance 190

9.9 The Case of a Semiconductor Company 191

9.10 The Case of a Products Distribution Company 192

10 *Phase 4: Construction and Testing, and Phase 5: Actual Implementation* 195

10.1 Develop a Comprehensive Configuration 196

10.2 Populate the Test Instance with Real Data 197

10.3 Build and Test Interface Programs 201

10.4 Write and Test Reports 201

10.5 Test the System 202

10.6 User Testing 203

10.7 The Case of Felix Schoeller, Osnabrueck, Germany 204

10.8 Phase 5: Actual Implementation 205

10.9 After Implementation 206

10.10 Moving into the Future 207

10.11 The Case of Chevron 208

10.12 The Case of Hydro Agri North America (HANA) 209

SECTION 3 MITIGATING THE RISK 213

11 *Managing Change: The "Political" Challenges* 215

11.1 Why Companies Change 216

11.2 The Case of Monsanto   216

11.3 Key Principles of Change Management   219
    Leadership Enrollment   219
    Communications   220
    Training   221
    Organizational Roles and Structure   222
    Performance Management   224
    Management Practices   225

11.4 Change Management Learnings   225

11.5 Multinational Implementation Challenges   227
    The Case of Digital Equipment Corporation   229
    The Case of Samsung Heavy Industries   231

12 Team Formation and Development   233

12.1 The Essential Elements of Successful Teams   234
    Choose the Right People   234
    Provide Excellent Project Management   236
    Establish Clear Goals   241

12.2 The Gap between Strategists and Implementers   241

12.3 Setting and Maintaining Expectations   243

12.4 Team Training   244

SECTION 4   IMPLICATIONS OF THE "NEW" TECHNOLOGIES   247

13 Changes in User and IT Roles   249

13.1 The Four Challenges   250
    Reduced Need for Development Programmers   251
    Reliance on Complex Technological Architecture   252
    Higher User Involvement   253
    User Ownership of Data/System   254

13.2 Meeting the Four Challenges   254

13.3 The Case of NEC Technologies   256

14 Lessons Learned   259

14.1 The Case of Owens Corning   260

14.2 Summary of R/3 Implementation Issues   264

14.3 The Mature Installation   267
    The Case of RTL Television   267
    RTL and Its Relationship with SAP   270

Appendix A: Data Modeling Concepts   273

Appendix B: Content and Structure of the SAP Data Dictionary   277

Appendix C: The Development of ABAP/4   281

Appendix D: Relational Database Concepts   285

Bibliography   291

Glossary   293

Index   307

ABOUT THE AUTHORS

NANCY H. BANCROFT is president of Bancroft, Brite & Associates, Inc., a consulting firm specializing in the human and organizational impact of technological change. She is recognized as an industry expert in the area of implementing enterprise-wide systems solutions. Nancy has published *New Partnerships for Managing Technological Change*, *The Feminine Quest for Success*, and most recently *Implementing SAP R/3*. She has an A.B. degree from William and Mary and an M.B.A. from Clark University. She completed the Columbia University advanced program in organizational development/human resource management.

HENNING SEIP is chief executive officer/cofounder of The Consultants Network (TCN), New Canaan, Conn., a consulting firm providing post-implementation support to SAP's customers. With more than twelve years experience as an IT professional, he has worked in software development as a project manager for Mercedes Benz AG and Bertelsmann AG, the German multimedia giant. Before founding TCN as the director of management information systems, he managed the consolidation of the information systems infrastructure of Bertelsmann's largest publishing subsidiary, Bantam Doubleday Dell, in New York City and introduced SAP R/3 as the new core business system. Seip earned an M.B.A. in industrial engineering from the University of Hamburg, Germany.

ANDREA SPRENGEL is president/cofounder of TCN with more than eight years of SAP software configuration and teaching experience. She began her career in Germany with Jungheinrich AG as a programmer analyst implementing the SAP R/2 system. In the course of this project she also received extensive training at SAP headquarters in Walldorf, Germany. Later Sprengel contributed as a configuration specialist to the SAP implementation projects of Phillips

Consumer Electronics (Germany), the Timken Company (U.S.A./France), Siemens Medical (Republic of South Africa), Novacor Chemicals (U.S.A./Canada) and Schindler Elevator Corporation (U.S.A.). She continues to offer hands-on training and configuration support.

PREFACE TO THE SECOND EDITION

Following the success of *Implementing SAP R/3,* Manning Publications asked author Nancy Bancroft to prepare a revision, focusing specifically on the details of configuration and the experiences of companies outside the U.S. as well as those involved in multinational implementation projects. Additional information in several other areas has been added to the original text as well.

Accordingly, we located two experts in configuration, Henning Seip and his partner Andrea Sprengel. Seip and Sprengel recognized the need for high-end configuration support during the implementation and maintenance phases of the SAP system life cycle. Together, they developed a full-service help desk for SAP's customers, providing expert implementation and post-implementation support using remote consulting techniques. This innovative service has been recognized as filling a critical need to reduce consulting expenses by the Gartner Group, the leading IT industry research and analysis organization. Together, they have prepared the more technical additions to the original manuscript resulting in the chapters *The R/3 Basis Technology* and *Configuring SAP R/3.*

Bancroft began a research effort focused on locating companies outside of the U.S. Several of these case studies are added throughout the text. In addition, a section titled *Multinational Implementation Challenges* has been added to Chapter 11. Based on this research on enterprise-wide systems solutions, a monthly newsletter, *The ERP Insider: Enterprise Systems and Solutions*, is now available.

The authors would like to thank Karin Schemmer of RTL and Dinesh Gambhir of Ernst & Young LLP for their review of the manuscript and their advice on the technical chapters. We also want to thank Karin Schemmer for the story of the RTL implementation and Brent Glendening, Ashok Bakhshi,

and LLoyd Seltzer of Schindler Elevator Corporation for their support throughout this project.

We hope you will find this second edition of *Implementing SAP R/3* to be
even more helpful than the first.

NANCY H. BANCROFT

Evergreen, Colo.
bancroft@rmi.net

HENNING SEIP

New Canaan, Conn.
hseip@TheConsultantsNetwork.com

ANDREA SPRENGEL

New Canaan, Conn.
ASprengel@TheConsultantsNetwork.com

PREFACE TO THE FIRST EDITION

SAP's product R/3 has become an extremely popular choice for medium to large companies that need an integrated software product which will provide all the basic business automation. Implementing such a major change in any organization presents significant challenges. This book was written to provide guidance in that endeavor.

Late in 1995, I initiated a research study of R/3 customers—companies that are in the process of implementing R/3 or that have completed its implementation. I interviewed more than 30 individuals representing over 20 companies. Several companies were studied in greater depth than others because of the universal nature of their experiences. This continuing research was not sponsored by SAP, since it was felt that an objective view would be most useful. SAP has, however, been most gracious in providing experts in their technology and implementation process, as well as access to several of their customers. The study also included discussions with consultants in some of the "Big 6" consulting firms.

This book will present an implementation approach which emphasizes methodologies that deal with the challenges inherent in all large system changes. It will also identify the issues specific to the implementation of SAP R/3. Change management approaches that have been found to be highly effective in a variety of settings and that are being modified to respond to the unique R/3 challenges will be identified. I will identify the critical rules that cannot be broken for the implementation team, the sponsoring executives, the project team members, and the ultimate users of the system. The book includes clear models and diagrams, along with many examples taken from real-life situations.

There are many people who contributed to making this book possible and I am unable to mention them all here. I interviewed people in over twenty companies. All were helpful and forthcoming with details of their particular projects. Information about some companies was obtained from the trade materials, Sapphire (the annual SAP Users Conference), or conversations with outsiders. Some companies are mentioned explicitly in the book, while others provided contextual material.

I wish to thank several individuals who have been of particular help in this project.

At SAP, Claire Herm, Dennis Ladd, Tyrone Scott, and Michael Spaventa graciously spent many hours on the phone with me, and provided details of the system I could not obtain elsewhere. I also want to thank Peg Culotta for arranging numerous contacts, including my attendance at Sapphire 1995.

Symmetrix, Inc. provided early support in this project. Erich Almasy hired me to write the initial articles about SAP. Eli Hauser provided invaluable research help.

Hanley Brite, my partner and husband, provided editorial and content review of the chapters regarding teams, change, and reengineering. As always, I am grateful for his encouragement and support.

Finally, I wish to thank Marjan Bace and all the production people at Manning Publications for their enthusiastic and helpful response to this book.

NANCY H. BANCROFT

Evergreen, Colo,
bancroft@rmi.net

WHO SHOULD READ THIS BOOK

This book is intended for anyone contemplating implementation of or who is already engaged in implementing R/3 by SAP. It will also be useful for those involved in any highly complex, enterprisewide information systems (IS) project. The nature of such projects has changed over the past few years in several ways. First, responsibility for the system has passed to the user organization. Second, the user organization consists most often of a series of functional departments that represent an entire business process. Therefore, the most effective project teams are comprised primarily of people from the various line organizations. This presents a challenge to the team to achieve cohesiveness. Third, the IS challenges provided by the system, the interfaces, and the client/server technology require new skills and knowledge. Fourth, implementing an integrated enterprisewide information system is either driven by, or drives, corporate reengineering.

This book, then, will be useful for all levels of professionals from the IS department and the line organizations—including the CEO, the CIO, and the CFO, as well as executives of all the functional organizations involved. It is also intended for all project team members and user managers who must understand the broad issues of managing complex technological change. Knowledge of issues that complicate enterprisewide reengineering and information systems projects will alert management to the potential pitfalls involved. You cannot prevent the brick walls and roadblocks, but you can be prepared to successfully overcome them.

OVERVIEW OF THIS BOOK

This book is divided into four sections plus appendices. The reader may find one section more useful than another, depending upon his or her perspective or role in the implementation process.

Section 1 provides an overview of SAP and the R/3 system, and the key issues involved in a successful configuration. This covers the basics of SAP and its meteoric rise in the software world. It provides a tour of the R/3 system. Chapter 1 presents information about the basis technology, which is SAP's term for the technical premise for R/3, including the client/server architecture, the hardware, and the database engine. Chapter 1 also describes the available application modules. Chapter 2 continues with a description of what R/3 will look like to the user, and covers the three online tools that help the project team to configure the system. Chapters 3 and 4 are new. They present the more technical issues inherent in understanding and configuring R/3. In addition, they refer to four new appendices for greater understanding of the concepts of data modeling, content and structure of the SAP data dictionary, the development of ABAP/4, and relational databases.

Actual configuration will require even greater depth of knowledge; this deeper level is beyond the scope of this book. The technical reader will find that Chapters 1 through 4 provide an extremely useful overview of R/3. The less technical reader may wish to skim portions of these chapters.

Chapter 5 contains a discussion of reengineering (since implementing R/3 is a form of business reengineering). Chapter 6 presents implementation guidelines, including the nine factors critical to the success of an implementation project.

Section 2 is devoted to a discussion of the issues inherent in a successful implementation, followed by the step-by-step process you will need to follow to implement the system.

SAP and each of its project partners identify implementation steps differently. In each case, however, the basic concepts remain the same. We have divided the approach into five phases: focus (Chapter 7), create the *as is* picture (Chapter 8), create the *to be* design (Chapter 9), construction and testing, and actual implementation (combined in Chapter 10). Each chapter describes the work that must be done, the difficulties that may be faced by a project team during that step, and suggestions for overcoming roadblocks. Numerous real-life examples are included. These will provide the reader with ideas that may be used in his or her project. The revised edition has been expanded with case examples of implementation projects outside of the U.S. These examples include projects completed within a particular country and across borders.

Section 3, *Mitigating the Risk*, covers two key issues that must be successfully addressed to achieve the goals set for the project. Chapter 11 presents the key principles of change management. We found the words and concepts used by Monsanto compelling and succinct, and so used their structure in this chapter. Chapter 12 discusses how to form and develop a team that works well together. This chapter also addresses ways the team can creatively meet the challenge it has been given. The chapter also discusses the issues of setting and managing expectations across the corporation.

The final section, Section 4, contemplates the new direction in implementing information systems taken by SAP. Chapter 13 describes the changes in roles that have occurred in the IS and line departments of many companies. Chapter 14 summarizes the major themes found in the book.

Finally, as stated before, we have added four appendices to provide greater depth of understanding of significant concepts inherent in your ability to configure R/3. All are included to help team members, executives, and end users understand the general concepts that underlie the process of configuration. It is our experience that this information is often not available and is certainly not included in the available training for R/3. The appendices are:

A: Data Modeling Concepts
B: Content and Structure of the SAP Data Dictionary
C: The Development of ABAP/4
D: Relational Database Concepts

Approaching the R/3 Solution

Introduction

What Is SAP?   4
Description of R/3   5
Why Not Choose R/3? What Are the Risks?   5
The Bottom Line   11

The commercialization of client/server technology and its adoption by industry is demonstrated by the rapid growth of SAP and similar applications software. Increased global competition, new needs of executive management for control over the real economics and product flow throughout their enterprises, and ever more numerous customer interactions are driving the demand for enterprisewide access to real-time information. This demand, in turn, is creating a new wave of large-scale technology-based projects. These projects often have budgets in excess of $10 million, and project teams of 50 or more people. In total, their combined software, hardware, and consulting expenditures approached $10 billion in 1995.

Success of these projects requires a variety of business, communications, and organizational skills which are independent of the considerable technology demands. In addition, specific knowledge of the R/3 system is required and scarce. My research shows this combination of skills to be the key factor to success or failure. Enterprises that focus on technical implementation alone do so at great risk; those that consider and embrace the breadth and depth of the cross-functional implementation challenges they face will clearly be the winners.

What Is SAP?

SAP seems to have arrived on the scene fully developed and unconquerable. While a few industry observers tracked the company in the early 1990s, to most in the U.S., it has taken the market by storm only in the last two or three years. This is principally due to the client/server-based product, R/3.

SAP AG, the parent company, founded in 1972, is based in Walldorf, Germany. It employs over 8,000 people worldwide. SAP America, the largest of the international subsidiaries, is based in Philadelphia, Pa., and is responsible for sales and support throughout North and South America and Australia.

SAP leads the client/server software market worldwide and is the fifth largest independent software company. In the first three months of 1995, new product orders were up by 65 percent. SAP's revenue growth in 1996 was 38.1 percent with revenues of $1,049 million. SAP America achieved sales of $294 million. It is variously estimated that SAP wins between 50 percent and 70 percent of the business for which it competes. The company provides two basic products—R/2 and R/3. R/2 is a mainframe set of software modules; R/3 is built for the client/server market. More than 4,000 companies worldwide have installed R/3.

It is estimated that the R&D budget for SAP is larger than that of its top competitors combined. This is one reason companies are flocking to sign on.

To maintain focus on its core competency, SAP has formalized partnerships with a number of companies that provide services necessary for complete implementation. There are four classes of partners: alliance partners provide a variety of implementation services; platform partners provide the hardware platforms that are optimized for the system; technology partners work with SAP to integrate new technologies, databases and operating systems; and complementary software partners provide specialized add-on software products.

Description of R/3

R/3 provides a set of business application software modules designed for the client/server environment. The modules are integrated, and span most functions required by a major corporation, including manufacturing, finance, sales and distribution, and human resources. The modules are explained in greater detail in Chapter 1. Each module accesses over 1,000 business processes, each based on industry *best practices*. The system's configurability is made possible by 8,000 tables that manage the hierarchies of the company, encompassing everything from corporate structure to pricing discounts. The system provides true integrated real-time enterprisewide information system processing. No wonder it is a hot seller!

The latest release of R/3 is 3.1. The 3.x series contains 25 percent more application functionality than 2.2, its predecessor. And the functionality is growing. With 3.1G, which is available at this writing, R/3 has begun to provide improved interface capability. Release 4.0 (now expected to ship late in the third quarter of 1997 or early in 1998) will allow customers to better implement system enhancements. Pricing is flexible, depending upon the number of users and modules, and the type of relationship the companies wish to negotiate with SAP.

Why Not Choose R/3? What Are the Risks?

SAP's R/3 presents a number of challenges unique to the information systems world. Successful implementation requires business process reengineering, a client/server environment, the ability to manage the system's flexibility, and the ability to cope with high complexity levels. Trained technical people are scarce and expensive. In addition, successful implementation of R/3 projects requires superior skill in a variety of generic business, communications, and organizational skills, in addition to knowledge of the unique R/3 technology. Under these circumstances, traditional implementation approaches are not sufficient.

This book addresses these challenges. They are inherent in implementing any enterprisewide information system. Many experts in the information technology arena believe that, when successfully implemented, R/3 will be seen to be a major driver of significant improvement in the business world. At this point in SAP's young history, its customer base is generally pleased with the results of its investment, both in dollars and in committed resources.

But some are not so sure R/3 is the way to go. Why? There are four basic risks to evaluate in choosing R/3. They represent a set of reasons to evoke caution in evaluating vendors, but not necessarily to dissuade the company with a compelling need for total integration from buying R/3. There are arguments to counter each of the four points we will present—some more convincing than others. However I believe the risks remain issues to consider. Risk management is the ability to recognize a threat, accurately assess its implications, and develop approaches to mitigate the risk in a cost-effective manner. This section is offered in that spirit.

The four risks are as follows:

- 1980s technology.
- Lack of flexibility.
- Complexity.
- Possible lack of fit with corporate strategy.

Risk 1: 1980s Technology

R/3 is based on late 1980s client/server technology and functional capabilities. In particular, it does not use pure object-oriented design, which provides such exotic features as encapsulation, componentization, polymorphism, and inheritance to yield greater levels of reusability. R/3 has a huge integrated model that is contrary to the use of pure objects. True, it uses OLE (Object Linking and Embedding) from Microsoft; however, that does not mean R/3 is an object-oriented system. OLE is used in two ways. First, on the desktop, OLE provides the interface to system function calls. This allows SAP to make powerful graphical user interface (GUI) tools available for the user. The second use of OLE is as a part of the workflow process. Here objects are identified as a collection of elements such as screens or customers. The value of this approach is additional flexibility in workflow integration. The user can create multiple processes from the same components.

R/3 uses pooled data and flat files. The servers in the middle of the three-tier client/server design are treated as distributed mainframe computers. The desktop is treated as little more than a dumb terminal. Function calls are used to carry out requests made by the client to the server. (A client/server overview is provided in Chapter 1.) Stored procedures are generally preferred to function calls, since they provide greater protection for the data. Replication is a preferred approach to the problem of distributed data problems, over the two-phase commit used by R/3.

Should management care about these bits and bytes issues? It should, because they are the keys to the flexible distributed systems of the future. Bobby Cameron, Director of Software Strategy Service at Forrester Research Inc., divides customers into three categories. He says 20 percent of the market is made up of *incremental extenders*. These are companies that do not need to change rapidly and who are drawn to client/server technology as a means of providing better data access for decision makers. The bulk of the market (65 percent) is what he calls the *one-time transformers*. These are companies who are significantly constrained by old legacy systems that don't talk to one another, and who need integration and need it fast. Finally, the remainder of the market is comprised of true *reengineers* (15 percent), those companies whose leaders have recognized that their business requires rapid continuous change. Forrester advises one-time transformers to purchase R/3. Companies in the other two categories are advised, however, that R/3 will not meet their needs. Incremental Extenders will find that R/3 "frustrates leading edge use of client/server technology," and reengineers will discover that "fast-paced radical change with R/3 is difficult and costly." Cameron offers the opinion that even the bulk of the market may find that SAP has become the legacy system in the five-year time frame when the smaller vendors, none of whom can compete with SAP today with a full suite of offerings, have evolved into true competition.[1]

This opinion is supported by several other observers, such as Myers, who states, "Packaged solutions are not the answer. They are a monolithic response to a consumer that is sick of all the trouble involved in trying to integrate systems. The real answer is in business objects, and that is where the packaged-solution vendors should begin to differentiate their offerings."[2]

R/3 is based on the R/2 mainframe, unit-record mentality with a proprietary software language which limits its openness. Unless SAP initiates nothing less than a complete redesign of the R/3 approach, it will find itself constrained by its 8,000 tables and 1,000 predefined business processes in its ability to provide the flexibility the customer base requires. With its enormous research and development budget and its demonstrated ability to respond to customer demand, it is likely that this redesign is on the boards. As of 1997, it appears that such a rewrite is in progress; SAP has added considerable capability for the future. For example, the system is now somewhat componentized providing greater flexibility for users. Release 4.0 is expected to deliver some object-oriented code

Risk 2: Lack of Flexibility

How can a system that is advertised as flexible identify lack of flexibility as a risk? R/3 is flexible in terms of its ability to make table entries that allow the customer to operate it in an infinite number of ways. However, that detail flexibility is constrained by structural inflexibility. The system provides a centralized and structured approach to business processes and functions that may not be suitable for all companies.

Some potential customers have chosen alternative approaches to R/3 because they believe R/3 is not flexible enough to fit their company's unique needs. American Cyanamid Co., for example,

---

[1] See *The Software Strategy Report*, produced by Forrester Research, Inc., Volume V, Number IX, December 1994 and a presentation made December 12, 1995, at a conference on *Successful Implementation of SAP R/3* sponsored by the Institute for International Research, for example. The Forrester reports were supplemented with personal conversations with Bobby Cameron, Director of Software Service.
[2] Marc Myers, "The Trouble with Off-the-Shelf Apps," *Network World*, October 9, 1995, p. 37.

abandoned R/3 for a competitor's offering that was easier to modify.[3] Others have chosen one of SAP's competitors because they believed the structure of the technology (including the lack of pure objects) would ultimately prove too difficult for rapid continuous change.

The R/3-structured, centrist approach may prove effective for many customers, since it is useful for control. However if 35 independent business units are told to force fit R/3, it is likely they will find ways to operate around it, thus defeating both the purposes of true integration and any decrease in operating costs.

Businesses are increasingly more sophisticated in their ability to offer customization of products and services. Their systems must be able to support this. Many need, or will need, rapid modular repositioning of functions, a business need that is difficult to accomplish using R/3.

To counter this objection, SAP offers Application Link Enabling (ALE). A company may implement multiple versions of R/3 that can communicate with one another using ALE to obtain the benefits of companywide integration. Processes may differ in various business units; however, data elements must be defined similarly to take advantage of this approach.

The lack of flexibility of R/3 itself is seen in the discrete manufacturing arena in particular. For example, R/3 has recently added the ability to manage customized assemble-to-order capability in the sales and distribution modules; however, this functionality has not been driven down into the manufacturing modules. Nor can R/3 provide the capability to manage engineer-to-order, assemble-to-order, *and* ship-to-order manufacturing.

Risk 3: Complexity

The technical, business, and behavioral change necessary to implement R/3 creates a highly complex situation. The challenge to organizations to effectively manage these changes can be daunting.

The R/3 system frightens off some prospective customers, because they don't think they can learn it quickly enough. While the system requires some experience to comprehend its depth, the complexity challenge is due primarily to the combination of new technology, business reengineering, and change management.

---

[3] As reported in *PC Week*, June 12, 1995 in an article by Robert L. Scheier, "Tailor Made," pp. 19–20.

Technically, shifting to a client/server environment poses significant questions that must be resolved in terms of a substantial information architecture that will serve the firm for a number of years. Shifting to this architecture alone places significant demands on the entire organization.

Reengineering may be forced on a business as a result of the process of identifying the correct business structure. Implementing R/3 requires the business to evaluate and improve the business processes that are at the heart of how it runs. Many detailed business process decisions must be made prior to actual implementation.

Most people who have been through a major implementation report that the political or change management issues are the most difficult to identify and to solve. Simply dealing with changes in job roles and organizational structure are relatively easy compared with cross-functional issues, such as who owns which data or process and exactly how the company ought to run. Making these decisions in an environment of constantly changing business requirements will require a knowledge of the information systems peculiarities, the current and future business structure, and the strategic direction of the company—in other words, the wisdom of Solomon.

These levels of complexity will be dealt with in this book. They are difficult, but certainly not impossible to address. And they will apply to any similar change project.

Risk 4: Possible Lack of Fit with Corporate Strategy

R/3 works particularly well for companies that have a strong top-down organization or that are structured in the same ways that R/3 is structured. When this is not the case, the system must be modified through the normal system configuration channels, or via tack-on modules written by external vendors or the companies' system programmers. These modifications can cause major upgrade problems.

More significantly, some companies prefer to allow divisions to benefit from operating in unique ways. This will be difficult or impossible to accommodate using R/3. For example, one company needed to be able to process drop shipments to distributors from their warehouses, as well as to ship factory to factory and direct to consumers. Even within SAP there was disagreement as to whether it was possible to accommodate this need.

In another case, a company needed to operate stock rooms in independent and different ways because of a combination of hazardous and nonhazardous materials. One stock room was JIT (just in time), while in another the approach was to allow inventory to build up. In this case, the answer was to move the functionality into the stock room itself; however, R/3 did not have the needed capability.

Companies that embrace the strategy of using *best of breed* solutions to business problems find that the ability to integrate R/3 with a number of non-R/3 solutions is difficult to accomplish and maintain. Forrester Research advises its clients to isolate R/3 from other vendor's products using replication and messaging (not ALE).

The Bottom Line

There is nothing available today that provides the same enterprisewide integrated set of solutions as R/3. For the company that prefers to find a single vendor that can meet nearly all its needs, and that promises to keep up to date in the future, SAP is the answer. For the reasons set out above, some companies will make another choice.

Interviews with many companies that have implemented R/3 have revealed the normal amount of frustration with a large company that is the victim of its own success. Company personnel couldn't always contact someone who could answer a pressing question; the system improvements were late; the system couldn't be customized to accommodate some particular need. Companies that implemented early in the 1990s report more difficulty with such issues as technical configuration and functionality of the system than do those implementing today—nothing new there. However, most difficulties faced by companies implementing the system are not caused by SAP or by R/3, but by their own organizational resistance to change.

Companies that are R/3 believers have found ways to mitigate or manage the risks noted above. Most SAP customers feel the company will improve over time, as it has in the past. Even when required functionality is missing, believers will wait (albeit impatiently) for promised improvements. Nonbelievers will have more difficulty making the transition to R/3.

We believe SAP is a good choice for most companies. This book is based upon that premise. However, the system is not a silver bullet, nor will it implement itself. There are aspects of managing technological change that must be resolved before R/3 can be of optimum use.

CHAPTER 1

A Tour of the R/3 System

1.1 Key Components of SAP Software   14
1.2 One Database/One System   16
1.3 Client/Server in R/3 Applications   17
1.4 Basis Technology   22
1.5 R/3 System Features   27
1.6 Overview of Modules   31

In this chapter, we hope to give the reader a sense of how the R/3 system operates, and what it provides the customer. SAP R/3 is an integrated client/server software application. It has several special features that enable its ability to provide a centralized database and the related reporting and planning functions that accrue from such integration. They include the Business Workflow, the Development Workbench, and the multiple tables used to configure the system. To use these features, the project team must have an understanding of the system structure and architecture.

This chapter will begin with an overview of client/server applications. Next, it will cover the basis technology, including the business workflow, the R/3 tables, and the ABAP/4 Development Workbench. Finally, it will provide an overview of the several modules available. Chapter 2 will provide a tutorial on the basics of how to operate in R/3, including information on the three integrated implementation support elements, the Procedure Model, the Reference Model, and the Implementation Management Guide (IMG).

1.1 Key Components of SAP Software

The SAP R/3 software is one of the most complex program packages ever written for use in corporations. Its functionality goes far beyond typical software since it is geared to support all aspects of a normal operation of a company. In the past, custom-written programs were the foundation of corporate data processing. Traditionally these programs were developed by the staff of the MIS department and were enhanced and modified as the business needs changed. In most cases, programs were developed upon the request of the business department. Their view is naturally limited by their unique operative responsibility.

Each department also defines its data according to its own goals and priorities. For example, at one bicycle factory, the manufacturing department had far greater interest in raw materials than in the value of the product on the balance sheet. This was reflected in the software developed by the programmers of the MIS department. For the manufacturing department, a material master file was developed containing data such as the names of the raw materials (e.g., steel pipes) used for the products, their dimensions (e.g., length, diameter, thickness), physical attributes and so on. The sales department requested a system with the ability to process orders which also contained material master information but focused on availability restrictions. Sales needed to know when a certain bicycle type was available for delivery rather than what type of steel was used in the production process.

Thus, developing over time were software islands which had to be connected through batch interfaces pushing data back and forth between the departments. This connection generally happened at night when users were not online, and to control this interfacing of the different systems, a special control department had to run reports to reconcile the data. Because of the different views and responsibilities of the business departments and the lack of clear data definitions, the meaning of data fields with similar or same names was defined differently in different systems. Redundancy and confusion grew, leading to staggering inaccuracy. Users became highly frustrated since the data on reports generated from different systems for their business departments which supposedly showed the same results never matched. Figure 1–1 illustrates a variety of stand-alone applications connected through batch interfaces.

In the case of a publishing company, more than a hundred batch interfaces existed, most of them undocumented and run manually by the operators of the data center. If you have a similar situation, you

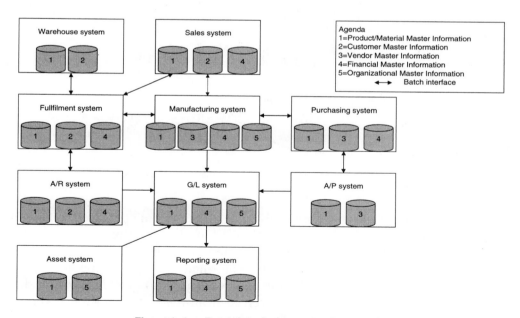

Figure 1–1: Batch interfaces connecting multiple systems

are not alone. Many companies have, over the years, developed a tangle of old systems. Worse, the company depends upon a series of undocumented interfaces to gather a picture of the business as a whole.

1.2 One Database/One System

SAP developed its systems to solve just this problem. The SAP software was developed from the perspective of a corporation as whole rather than any one of its business departments. This is a major improvement. This view automatically suggests that the entire corporation works as one team instead of separate teams coming from different departments. Figure 1–2 illustrates the integrated nature of R/3.

Figure 1–2:   The Integrated nature of SAP R/3

All information is kept only once in the system compared to Figure 1–1 where similar information resided in several different systems. All SAP programs use the same database with little data redundancy. When people from the sales department meet with people from accounting to look at sales information, they will quickly agree on the validity of the reports they received from the system since everybody retrieves the data from the same set of data tables.

Many key concepts implemented in the SAP software were developed either by SAP itself or by other software companies. They include:

- On-line system; no traditional batch interfaces
- One database for all data
- Clear definition of every data item, documented in a data dictionary
- Software functionality configurable to customer's requirements
- Client-oriented data structure
- Definition data within the framework of a document to reflect the relevance for the business

The basic idea behind R/3 was to develop one database for the entire corporation without any data redundancy and with a clear definition of each field. On top of this database, a comprehensive set of software applications was developed, providing all logic necessary to process the data of the corporation. The software was designed to support business processes rather than business functions. It also used documents to reflect the business context of single data items.

To do this the developers of SAP gathered the requirements of different companies within the same industry and combined them with research results from major research institutions. This compilation became the basis for the creation of each application within R/3. In this context, the term *best practices* is used to reflect the success of the implemented standardized business processes.

1.3 Client/Server in R/3 Applications

The SAP R/2 system had been developed to run on costly mainframe computers which were housed in specially air-conditioned data centers and which needed much care from the technical staff. With the advent and quick development of PC technology, the processing power of these desktop units started to outgrow the processing power of data center-hosted mainframes. At the same time, the development of networks emerged rapidly. Thus a natural next step was to link many PC-type computers through networks and distribute the workload of data processing. Instead of loading one program into one expensive mainframe computer, this program would be split into parts which then could be executed on different inexpensive PC-type computers.

R/3 was developed, based on the R/2 experience, as a way to deploy a less expensive hardware environment for the new software. It was correctly envisioned by SAP that the client/server approach to computing would be the next step in the evolution of systems platforms.

Client/server technology is seen by many as the solution to the difficulty of linking together the corporation. It is the outgrowth of the traditional network that hooked a number of terminals onto the mainframe processor. The shortcoming of the mainframe/terminal structure is that it can be magnified only so far before it begins to fail, primarily because of competition for time on the network. Many companies have switched to the client/server approach, which allows the company to connect many sites across the globe. In addition, client/server systems provide improved analysis tools such as drill-down, reporting, consolidation, and *what-if* scenarios.

But, client/server technology is immature; users report that it is expensive to maintain and manage, and that there is a long learning curve. Simply stated, there are many potential points of failure.

Client/server architecture is made up of a number of clients (generally desktop devices) who request services from a number of servers (specialized larger computers). It is a client-centered approach as contrasted with a mainframe-centered approach.

The job of the server is to reply to all the requests made of it—requests for data, for communicating messages, for updating master files. In short, all the work a user needs to accomplish must be managed in terms of signals for either transaction processing or for data to support a decision. Transaction processing (TP) is far more complex to carry out than is decision support; however, TP is a major reason that client/server applications are needed by companies.

The request from the client travels along the network, for example, a local area network (LAN), to the server. The server's job is to determine how best to fill the request made by the client. Because of the system structure, a number of users can look at and even update the same document, file or table. Clients are generally terminals on the desktop operated by end users. They may be other servers. Clients may also be termed the *desktop* or the *presentation layer*.

As one can imagine, the combination of hardware, software, and networks needed to construct a client/server architecture becomes complex. For some applications a two-tier environment (clients and servers—see Figure 1–3) will suffice. For others, a three-tier

Figure 1–3:   **Client/server-basic model**

environment (database server, application server, and desktop) improves overall response time. This approach separates functionality by placing the databases on yet a third level (Figure 1–4). Thus, the functionality of the server in the two-tier structure is divided in order not to overload any individual system. If more users need to be connected to the system, more servers and terminals will be added.

Middleware is considered to be the collection of software needed to provide the connections and process the interactions between the layers (see Figure 1–5). Middleware is installed on each of the two or three tiers of the client/server structure. It includes such functions as the network operating system (NOS), transport stacks, routers, bridges, and gateways. Middleware is the software that runs the process of distributing the system. There is a vast world (primarily designated by acronyms) of specialized functions that must be coordinated to put together an efficient client/server architecture. Companies that decide they must implement this approach to distributed processing will find they have taken on a systems integration role. They need to match and manage the offerings of numerous vendors. Surveys indicate that this undertaking is difficult because of the technology, and because it creates a shift in the availability of information, and for many, power. In addition, companies often have difficulty implementing a client/server approach because they lack the necessary skills (two

DESKTOPS

**APPLICATION
SERVER(S)**

**DATABASE
SERVER**

Figure 1–4:   Three-tier client/server structure

weeks of client/server training won't do it) and because the IT industry simply does not understand this environment very well.

The elements of the three tiers (database server, application server, and presentation or desktop) may be linked by various communication protocols such as TCP/IP or SNA-LU6.2. In addition, the SAP gateway is always required. Populating the protocol are task-oriented agents whose role is that of managing the communications from one server to another—from the applications server to the database server, for

NOS
Transport Stacks
Routers
Bridges
Gateways

CLIENT   **MIDDLEWARE**   **SERVER**

Figure 1–5:   Middleware Structure

DISPATCHER

Communications Agents

Update Agents

Batch Agents

Spool Agents

Figure 1–6:   The Communications Gateway

example (see Figure 1–6). The agents are specialized and report to a dispatcher who sends jobs to the agents. The dispatcher identifies the type of task (update, batch, spool, etc.), and sends the job to a waiting agent, one who specializes in that type of command.

A great deal of the work is done at the application server level; however, the database is the real workhorse of the system. It is accessed and updated constantly. Depending upon the hardware selected, the database may be distributed among multiple machines. The database makes constant use of the data dictionary, a critical portion of the system. The data dictionary sits between the database and the application modules, and provides the logical mappings of data relationships and conditions.

SAP has designed R/3 for a client/server environment. Most R/3 applications are implemented in a three-tier environment, while smaller applications can be implemented in a two-tier environment. The three-tier structure has the following advantages: it is easier to increase throughput by adding servers; I/O-intensive functions can be placed on larger computers; workstations provide desktop computing that does not place a load on the system as a whole; and an integrated system can be made available across multiple locations. Of course, the advantages bring with them the difficulty of managing and maintaining a complex web of systems and protocols.

The application server can contain either third party- or user-developed software, as long as it is written in ABAP/4. By means of Application Program Interface (API), these pieces of software can talk to SAP using the agents. It is possible to query and copy data from the data dictionary, but not to update it, since the system would lose integrity if the normal update procedures were not followed.

To provide integrated systems for the corporation, it is essential to master this technology. Figure 1–7 illustrates the client/server concept.

The user, working at his/her PC, wants to process customer information. Since the user interface has no customer data, nor can it process it, the user interface requests this task to be performed by the program part called *application* and communicates this over the network. The application can process customer information but does not store this data. It requests the data retrieval task be performed by the program part database and communicates this over the network. The database retrieves the customer information and sends it back to the application via the network. The application processes the customer data and sends it to the user interface across the network for display. In this transaction, the user interface acts as a client, the application acts as a client and as a server and the database acts as a server only. This setup allows one to distribute the parts of the SAP system to different small and inexpensive computers rather than running all parts on one expensive mainframe.

1.4 Basis Technology[1]

The System Architecture

The *basis* is defined as the technical premise on which the R/3 system is built—the total system architecture. It includes the client/server structure, the network, and the hardware platform. It also includes issues of scalability, the database engine, and performance management. R/3 is hardware vendor neutral, and will run in a wide variety of environments, from a small Windows NT application up to massively parallel systems.

The system manager will find several online help documents to aid in the development of an optimally functioning system. All of these documents are available in CD/ROM format, primarily Windows-based, although some are available for the Macintosh. Currently, SAP is developing what they term *SAP Knowledgeware*, a multimedia CD/ROM form of system administration information. It was made

---

[1] Much of the information in this segment was condensed from the SAP online help documentation ©1994 SAP AG. The reader who needs a deeper treatment of this material should contact his or her sales representative.

Figure 1–7: A three-tier client/server interaction

ready for general availability in the first quarter of 1996, and integrated online into the system by the third quarter of 1996.

The central system configuration consists of an application server, a message server, a gateway server, and the database system. These three servers are generally combined at the server layer, and addressed by the desktop or presentation layer. (See Figure 1–4.) The system manager will need to decide, based upon projections of throughput and response time, how to distribute the system. The purpose is to divide up the most time-intensive uses of the system to balance the load. Background processing, for example, might be moved to its own server.

The system manager will plan and monitor the distributed system to maximize performance and availability. The database server will prove to be the bottleneck for throughput. It should be loaded with the database, shared files, the update server, the message server, and the lock server. Other functions that can be offloaded should be.

A variety of SAP communications interfaces are available. The Common Programming Interface-Communications (CPI-C) is a standard call interface to make possible the exchange of data between programs.

The SAP R/3 architecture also consists of these three main software layers:

- SAP GUI (presentation layer)
- SAP application
- SAP database

The SAP GUI program runs on the client PCs in the user departments. It is responsible for presenting all data of the system to the user. It takes care of creating buttons, windows, scroll bars, and so forth, on the screen and takes on all user input. It communicates with the SAP application across the network and passes on all user requests. No manipulation of the data in a business sense occurs here.

The SAP application contains the entire processing logic for the business data. This is where the program code of all of the SAP modules like FI (financials), SD (sales and distribution), and others are executed and the data manipulated. In all subsequent chapters we will refer to this segment as the SAP software, since it alone is configurable to meet the company's needs.

The SAP database is a program which interfaces (retrieves and stores data) with a third-party *database management system* (DBMS) like Oracle or Informix. The DBMS itself stores the data on disks. No manipulation of the data in a business sense occurs here.

Figure 1–8 provides an overview of this architecture:

As described previously, the three program parts—SAP GUI, SAP application and SAP Database—can be distributed to physically separate computers which are then connected through a network in order to make the SAP software function as a whole.

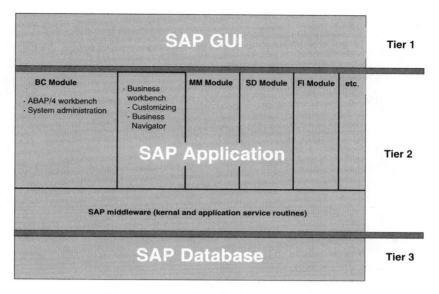

BC Module		MM Module	SD Module	FI Module	etc.
· ABAP/4 workbench · System administration	· Business workbench - Customizing - Business Navigator				

Figure 1–8: The SAP software architecture

Systems Administration

The smallest R/3 application may run on a single server, and support a modest number of terminals. The database may run on a separate machine, or again, in the simplest circumstance, the server and the database machine may physically be the same equipment. Within that machine, the database and the applications server will logically be different entities.

Stopping the central SAP System assumes that all processes have ended normally. When there are several instances, each must be stopped individually. An instance is a specific application of R/3, complete with its set of servers, which share a common profile. During the process of implementing R/3, project teams will generally establish up to three instances to separate test systems from actual production systems.

Stopping an instance does not automatically shut down the database system. Processes are shut down in parallel rather than sequentially. It may be necessary to stop the system during an upgrade or for a full backup, but not always. For example, in some cases it is possible to block access to a certain database to do a backup. When the backup is complete, the system manager can initiate a roll forward, applying any transactions that occurred during the back up to the actual database. SAP is working to make the system available 24×7 (24 hours a day, seven days a week).

Starting up the R/3 System requires that you start the database and the application servers, including the gateway server, the system logging process, and the spool system transfer process. The gateway server opens connections between the application and the communications protocol. The logging process maintains records of system errors and is essential for debugging problems. The spool system transfer process will pass files for printing, faxing, or output to the correct host spooler. The host spooler, in turn, knows which device (specific printer, for instance) is to be activated.

Starting up the system may be accomplished for the entire system or for a single host system. The start-up profile can be accessed from any application server, and can be used to indicate exactly what is being started up.

You will need to identify which system you wish to start up since you will likely have several instances. You will want to install at least three instances—for development (configuration), testing, and production. Each must be kept separate, and its integrity must be maintained.

System security is always a concern for the systems administrator, who must maintain records (located in the user master records file) of approved users having various levels of security. You may add additional password checks to increase security. Additions of this nature are maintained whole even when new releases are implemented. Individual users will have differing access privileges. For example, one user may be allowed to only read information about a particular customer, while another may be allowed to add or change information for that customer. It is possible to separate privileges so that one person may enter the access information, but is not able to activate it, while another may activate, but not edit, the information.

The systems manager will need to activate a system of tracing access to programs. Trace files are written by the individual host system processes. The data are used only in the event of problems in the system that require the manager to know exactly which transactions were executed and which were not.

1.5 R/3 System Features

The Data Repository

A data dictionary is a central source of information about a company's data.

In modern data management systems, data dictionaries constitute the information base both for users and for various software elements. They enable a fast response to the following questions:

- *What data is contained in the corporate database?*
- *What are attributes of this data (name, length, format and so on)?*
- *What relationships exist between the different data objects?[2]*

The R/3 Repository (data dictionary) serves primarily as a tool to enter, manage, and evaluate information about your company's data. It is an active data repository, embedded within the Development Workbench. Thus the information is always up-to-date and available to authorized users at all times. One needs only to identify a data element to be displayed on a screen, and its related information is automatically available.

The Data Repository provides current information to language interpreters, report functions, and screen generators, as well as to certain help tests. The rules for structuring this information are consistent with the concepts of the relational data model: the use of tables, domains, and fields. A *table* is a matrix that describes a relationship between sets of data. A *domain* describes the value range for a certain field. (A discount schedule is an example of a value range.) A *field* is a subset of a table. Each entry in a table (a customer, for example) contains a set of fields (name, address, type of customer, etc.). The type of customer might be coded to indicate the appropriate value in the discount schedule. The field itself may be made up of one or more data elements.

---

[2] Quoted from the SAP online help documentation, sub-section entitled "What is a Data Dictionary?"

Tables

The data repository is built on the table structure (see Figure 1–9). Tables are the feature mentioned most often by those who have implemented the system. They are defined differently by different people. Tables contain various types of information and can both manage data and carry out control functions.

There are three major types of tables: system configuration tables, control tables, and application data tables. All are defined in the data repository. System configuration tables are maintained primarily by SAP, or in some cases by the IS department. These are the tables that define the structure of the system. The programming for the data repository in ABAP/4, for example, is contained in a system configuration table. A table exists to define table types, and another exists to define objects used for transport. Customers do not change these tables. Other system configuration tables identify peripherals such as printers. These are set up and maintained by the IS department.

To customize the system, the project team will use both control tables and application data tables. Control tables define functions that guide the user in his or her activities. For example, a control table might be set up to require that a customer service representative enter

Figure 1–9:   R/3 table structure overview

a line item to reference the material master data before a purchase order is accepted. Control tables contain the structure of the company, including such data as company codes, which plants are related to which companies within the corporate structure, which sales organizations relate to which products, and which storage locations hold certain products. This is the central repository of the company hierarchy, which must be determined prior to installation and configuration.

Application data tables are divided into two main types—transaction and master data files. Both are updated using the appropriate R/3 applications. Transaction tables are the largest, since they contain the daily operations data, such as orders, payments received, invoices, and shipments. Master data files describe sets of basic business entities such as customers, vendors, products, materials, and the like. There are also master data files that contain static data such as zip codes.

Application data tables follow the logic of the subject matter. They are relational in that keys in each may point to different views of other tables. A customer master table, for example, will be surrounded by a layer of tables, each of which represents an attribute of the customer: pricing schedule, discounts, location of warehouses that supply the customer, and so forth. The subtables can be thought of as fields in a record. The value of a table structure is that similar tables, such as types of customer (government, key accounts, retail customers) will apply to all customers, and thus are identified only once and referenced via elements in the file for each customer.

A material master table may contain descriptive text, the title of the material and engineering data, for example. It has a layer of tables that apply to a plant defining the procurement data, minimum order quantities, and persons authorized to order. Another layer related to the materials master table will provide the warehousing information. The user may obtain different views of these related tables for sales, inventory, or accounting purposes.

Business Workflow

The Business Workflow feature allows the project team to provide procedural automation of the steps in a business process. It can provide suggestions to the end users regarding tasks that must be done, and can track work that has been accomplished. Sales managers, for example, can easily track numbers of orders and the status of individual orders. Orders will (presumably) flow through the system faster because of the prompts the system provides to individuals.

Managers can assign tasks based on capacity, competency, and skills, and can reassign work if necessary due to illness or special assignments. The Business Workflow feature is linked to the organization structure, and tasks are tied to position descriptions and responsibilities.

No one interviewed for this book spoke of using this feature, which new in Release 3.0.

Correction and Transport System

The Correction and Transport System (CTS) manages changes to the system, and provides the capability of moving these changes from one system to another. Any change to an object receives a correction number. SAP defines objects as groups of data like screens, help text, dynamic programs, and ABAP programs. CTS propagates these changes from one instance to another, or when the system receives an upgrade (see Figure 1–10).

Figure 1–10: Correction and transport system

One SAP basis guru reports that fully 70 percent of hotline calls are ultimately traced to misuse of the CTS. He states that customers sometimes turn off the CTS because they do not wish to see the correction numbers appear on the screen. In one case, an SAP customer went six months with the CTS turned off, and then was dismayed to find that changes the project team had made to the system did not appear when the development instance was moved into a production instance.

The ABAP/4 Development Workbench helps to solve this problem. When this application is used, it collects the changes even if CTS is turned off; thus they are saved. However, most table entries are accomplished outside of the Workbench, since that is the normal way customers will configure the system to meet their needs.

ABAP/4 Development Workbench

The ABAP/4 Development Workbench is the development environment for customer-specific applications. It includes a repository, editor, and dictionary, as well as tools for testing, tuning, debugging, and optimizing performance. The Workbench is considered to be part of the R/3 middleware, the software and engines that link the servers to their clients. (Refer to the prior section on client/server technology.) It is a 4GL (fourth-generation language) application development tool.

A key feature is the ABAP/4 Query feature, which allows users to define their own reports without learning ABAP/4. End users can use this function to select and sort data, develop statistics, and create ranked lists of customers in any desired configuration, such as by dollar sales volume.

Reports can be programmed to suit the needs of the users. Almost every company implementing R/3 surveyed indicated that they had found it necessary to develop their own reports. This is a function generally reserved for the IS department members. It requires a knowledge of ABAP/4 and can be executed only within the ABAP/4 environment. A report is defined as a series of processing rules. Running the report invokes the ABAP/4 processor, which controls access to the appropriate database.

In addition, the Workbench can be used to develop customized application modules. This will aid the implementation team if they discover some needed functionality that is not contained in R/3. They can write their own procedure and incorporate it within the R/3 structure.

The ABAP/4 Development Workbench encapsulates these changes and places them in the transport system. It is then up to the systems administrator to ensure that the changes meet quality control standards before they are released into a new system—whether a new instance or an upgrade. The changes are not brought over automatically.

1.6 Overview of Modules

The modules within R/3 are described in SAP documents as being organized in a variety of ways. The organization we will use contains four elements—financial accounting, human resources, manufacturing and logistics, and sales and distribution.

As is the case with any major release in a software system, increased functionality and integration across all the modules is provided with Release 3.0. The system now provides Application Link Enabling (ALE), which allows a company to implement separate R/3 systems and still maintain their interaction. This makes possible distributed enterprise applications.

We will describe the four elements in terms of functionality. The descriptions are by no means complete, and are intended only to convey the variety and completeness of available modules. Modules are designed to follow current best practices, and are updated twice a year. Updates are designed based upon changes in business practices, technological advances, and the changing requirements of the customer base.

Financial Accounting

The accounting segment of R/3 is generally defined as including three major categories of functionality needed to run the financial accounts for a company—financials (FI), controlling (CO), and asset management (AM). FI includes accounts payable, accounts receivable, general ledger, and capital investments. Also included in the FI category are the procedures to post accounts, close the books for the month and year, prepare financial statements, including the balance sheet, and planning functions. Naturally, the system provides the capability to document processes, prepare reports, archive certain data, and make additions and changes to the financial data as necessary.

As with all the modules in the R/3 system, the user will find all information current and integrated. Thus, an individual manufacturing plant or sales organization will be able to run a profit and loss report at any time during the month and be shown the most up-to-date information. This, of course, depends upon having set up the company hierarchy in such a way that the plant or sales group is designated as a profit and loss center.

The controlling category includes costing, cost center, profit center, and enterprise accounting and planning, internal orders, open item management, posting and allocations, profitability analysis, and a variety of reporting functions. It also includes a project system to track activity and costs related to major corporate projects, such as the implementation of an R/3 system. This is not the same thing as a project management system, which can be found in the manufacturing modules.

Release 3.0 includes a module to add activity-based costing (ABC) to other types of costing approaches. ABC is recognized as an effective approach to model the flow of costs between cost objects. Activity costs can then be allocated to business processes. Research studies of new products and new markets are examples of activities that have generally been associated with a certain cost center, but haven't always been passed on to the process of engineering or identifying sales prospects.

The asset management category includes the ability to manage all types of corporate assets including fixed assets, leased assets, and real estate. It also includes the capital investment management module (new in Release 3.0), which provides the ability to manage, measure, and oversee capital investment programs. Treasury capabilities are offered, including the ability to manage cash and funds belonging to the corporation.

Human Resources

R/3 contains the full set of capabilities needed to manage, schedule, pay, and hire the people who make the company run. It includes payroll, benefits administration, applicant data administration, personnel development planning, work-force planning, schedule and shift planning, time management, and travel expense accounting.

Since the structure of most companies shifts frequently, one of the functions in the human resources category provides the ability to represent organizational charts and organigrams, including organizational units, jobs, positions, workplaces, and tasks. Thus, you can represent and plan matrix organizations, split responsibilities, and form temporary project groups.

Capturing data from the human resource module, the SAP Business Workflow system (new in 3.0) provides management with the ability to define and manage the flow of work required in a cross-functional business process. Process owners will find this module useful for monitoring activities and deadlines either by individual or by position.

Manufacturing and Logistics

This is the largest and most complex of the module categories. It can be divided into five major components. They are: materials management, plant maintenance, quality management, production planning and control, and a project management system. Each is divided into a number of subcomponents. Materials management covers all tasks within the supply chain, including consumption-based planning, purchasing, vendor evaluation, and invoice verification. It also includes inventory and warehouse management to manage stock until usage dictates the cycle should begin again. Electronic Kanban/Just-in-Time delivery is supported.

Plant maintenance supports the activities associated with planning and performing repairs and preventative maintenance. Completion and cost reports are available. Maintenance activities can be managed and measured.

The quality management capability plans and implements procedures for inspection and quality assurance. It is built on the ISO 9001 standard for quality management. It is integrated with the procurement and production processes so that the user can identify inspection points both for incoming materials and for products during the manufacturing process.

Production planning and control supports both discrete and process manufacturing processes. Repetitive and configure-to-order approaches are provided. This set of modules supports all phases of manufacturing, providing capacity leveling and requirements planning, materials requirements planning, product costing, bills of material explosions and implosions, CAD dialog interface, and engineering change management. The system allows users to link rework orders to production schedules. Release 3.0 allows one to generate orders from sales orders, managing the availability-to-promise interface.

The project management system provides the user the capability to set up, manage, and evaluate large, complex projects. While the financial costing project system focuses on costs, the manufacturing project system is used for planning and monitoring dates and resources. The system walks the user through the typical project steps—concept, rough-cut planning, detailed planning, approval, execution, and closing. It manages a sequence of activities, each with its interrelationships to the others. *Activities* are defined as tasks which take time, are processed without interruption, require resources, and incur costs. *Projects* are measured based on projected and actual dates and results. The system supports budgeting, capacity and cost planning, time scheduling, and the management of availability and project status.

Sales and Distribution

This set of modules provides prospect and customer management, sales order management, configuration management, distribution, export controls, shipping, and transportation management, as well as billing, invoicing, and rebate processing. Since this, like the other modules, can be implemented on a global basis, you can manage the sales process globally. For example, an order may be received in Hong Kong. If the products are not available locally, they may be internally procured from warehouses in other parts of the world and shipped to arrive together at the Hong Kong customer's site. With the addition of ALE in Release 3.0, this can occur even if you have implemented separate systems in the Americas, Europe, and the Pacific Rim.

In sales and distribution (SD), products or services are sold to customers. In implementing the SD module (as in other modules) the company structure must be represented in the system so that, for example, R/3 knows where and when to recognize revenue. It is possible to represent the structure of your company from the point of view of accounting, materials management, or sales and distribution. And you can combine these structures. The correct (for you) and inherently logical structure is necessary for the system to function properly. For example, the relationship between the plants and the sales organizations must be defined to determine the distribution channel.

When a sales order is entered, it automatically includes the correct information on pricing, promotions, availability, and shipping options. Batch order processing is available for the food, pharmaceutical, or chemical industries. Configuration management is enhanced with Release 3.0. It allows users to reserve inventory for specific customers, request production of subassemblies, or enter orders that are assemble-to-order, build-to-order, or engineer-to-order as well as special customized orders.

The modules included within the R/3 system are built on best practices, the most efficient and effective ways to complete any process or subprocess. These can be discovered by research and study of different companies. Many of the consulting companies keep track of this information. However, best practices change over time. Companies continue to discover improved ways of carrying out their business. Part of the job of the SAP R&D department is to bring out system upgrades that reflect the newest best practices. You may find that they slightly lag your industry simply because of the nature of system redesign. If the process is a major one, it is likely to be changed rapidly, and if minor, the change will take longer.

CHAPTER 2

Basics for Configuring the R/3 System, Training, and the Users' Group

2.1 R/3 Basics: The Window   38
2.2 Online Help with Configuring the System   40
2.3 Training   48
2.4 The Users' Group   51

This chapter will provide a brief tutorial of the R/3 system. The purpose is to acquaint the reader with what he or she will see when first logging into R/3. The chapter will also describe the three online help modules that can be used to assist the project team through the complex process of configuring the system to meet the company's unique needs.

2.1 R/3 Basics: The Window

The basic R/3 screen is shown in Figure 2–1. The title bar will display the title of the current application or task. It also contains buttons for changing the size of the window and for moving it around on the computer screen. It is possible to open more than one application at once and to view them simultaneously.

Figure 2–1:   The basic R/3 screen

The application menu bar contains various menus for the application. There may be several menus available at once, and the user will choose among them. The application menu bar will change, depending upon the application. Each entry is a pull-down menu with choices appropriate to the application.

The toolbar contains a number of buttons to accomplish the task set out by the application. It generally will include an *enter* button which is activated by the user when he or she has completed the task—for example, entering new customer information. When all the data are entered on the screen, the user will position the cursor on the enter button and click to enter the data into the customer master table. The toolbar also has a command space, where the user will enter individual commands that, for example, will allow movement from one function to another. There is a *save* button, so that the user can save work in the midst of a process. He or she may, for example, need to obtain additional data to complete the screen and will want to be sure the work completed to that point is saved. Note, however, that the save button does not transfer the information to the master table as does the enter button.

The user can use the *back* button to return to a higher level of detail. This is useful when the user must drill down to obtain detailed information, for example, regarding an order a customer placed in February 1994. After obtaining this data, the user can back out of that level of detail and return to the higher level, where he or she can resume the original task.

A button having an upward arrow indicates the *exit* feature. Pressing this button will exit the user from the current application and resume the prior application or activate the system menu. A button having an *X* cancels the current task returning the user to the prior location. A *possible entries* button gives the user information about the entries possible in a specific field. This may, for example, include a range of prices for a certain volume of orders. The *?* button provides online help for the application task at hand. *Scroll* buttons allow the user to navigate within a list or document.

Each screen has improved (over prior system versions) GUI functions, such as *pull-down*, *pop-up*, *radio*, and *option* buttons. By using transaction codes, the user can navigate to the correct screen. For the user familiar with the codes and the system peculiarities, this will provide a fast way to move around. For the naive user, the codes may be confusing. A typical command field entry might be */nfd01* for example, followed by clicking on the entry button.

Users were asked by SAP if these transaction codes should be eliminated. Some were adamant that the codes should be retained. Since only a few codes are used by any user group, they are easily learned. The codes provide rapid access to the required screen.

After logging on to the R/3 system, you must first select the application and the task desired. You may use either the transaction code as described above or a menu supplied by the system. In addition you may create a *user menu* specific to your duties. Release 3.0 provides a *session manager*, a way to define a hierarchical menu structure unique to the company. The session manager puts together remote function calls that become a self-defined user menu.

Once the project team members are conversant with the basics of the R/3 system, they will turn to the task of configuring it to meet their unique needs. For this, they will make use of the online configuration tools.

2.2 Online Help with Configuring the System

There are three major tools to help the project team members configure the system to fit their company requirements. These tools are not for general use by end users, and access to them can be blocked at final implementation. The tools are the Procedure Model, the Reference Model and the Implementation Management Guide. They were built in reverse order, starting with the most detailed, the Implementation Management Guide. The help functions are linked to the modules purchased by the R/3 customer; thus you will be provided only with the applicable documentation. It is expected that the complete documentation will be provided via documentation servers in the future. None of the three tools is accessed by its name.

One of the first screens encountered by a project team member is the *main menu* screen. It is also called the *dynamic menu*. It has a list of the several tools used to configure the system, such as the ABAP/4 Development Workbench, Business Workflow, Communications, and Hypertext. The two tools that provide access to the online help modules are Customizing and the Business Navigator.

Clicking on Customizing will provide access to the Procedure Model. The Procedure Model is a project methodology—an overview at the highest level of activities that are required (and optional). Within the Procedure Model are the various steps that must be taken by a project team to implement the system. Each step, when displayed, has four buttons—*text*, *action*, *status*, and *documentation*. The text and action buttons will provide specific procedural information about each individual step. Clicking on the status or documentation buttons will allow the implementation team member to enter or view information about his or her specific project.

The Business Navigator provides either a business application view or a process flow view of the structure of R/3 which is termed the *Reference Model*. The Business Navigator is newly integrated into R/3 in Version 3.0. It contains the entire reference model. The Reference Model is a collection of predefined business processes along with a description of the functionality of each. The project team is able to select and modify these event-driven process chains to fit the business.

The next section describes the online help functions, starting with the Reference Model. The project team members will need to begin the implementation process with an understanding of the structure of the processes within R/3. Following sections will discuss the Procedure Model and the Implementation Management Guide(IMG). The Procedure Model and the IMG provide specific assistance in the process of customizing the R/3 system to fit the company's needs.

The Reference Model

The Reference Model is the atlas to R/3. It contains the maps of all processes contained within the R/3 system. It is the document the project team will use to identify exactly what R/3 will do in any particular module. The Reference Model can be used to understand the differences between how the company works or will work, and how R/3 operates—a gap analysis. It provides graphical descriptions of the business processes. These are generally more useful than textual descriptions alone.

See SAP for a description of The Reference Model found in an SAP booklet called the *R/3 Analyzer.* In brief, the Reference Model is made up of tasks or functions, organizational units, and data or information objects. They answer the three essential questions: "What needs to be done? Who should do it? What information do they need?" To these three, we add a fourth, asking what the relationship or interactions between them are. The question of how best to define and use these elements has resulted in a certain amount of IT confusion.

The event-driven process chain (EPC) adds another element that actually helps to sort out the confusion. The *event*, that is, an action that initiates the sequence of steps, answers the question, "When should something be done?" The EPC replaces the flow chart as a way to describe a sequence of actions. Each EPC must begin and end with an event. To use the EPC, the modeler must avoid the temptation to illustrate information flows. Information is subordinate to events. Once the events and functions are illustrated, the modeler can return to the diagram to identify the essential information required and produced in the process. Complex interactions can be illustrated by logical operators, a descriptor of the relationships among events and functions. The resulting diagrams can be analyzed to determine weak points in the chain.

The modeling capability inherent in the Reference Model was constructed using the Aris Toolset from IDS. It is also called the *Analyzer*, as is the small booklet noted above. The Reference Model was, in the past, available only to companies who also purchased the Aris Toolset. In Release 3.0, all the models are available in R/3; however, if you wish to do more than view the models (that is, to develop your own models), you will still need to purchase the Aris Toolset.

The Reference Model follows event process chains from top to bottom. It uses simple nomenclature. The project team can use this tool to view an entire business process rather than stepping through function after function. It will illustrate, for example, the process stretching from a requisition, to a purchase order, to goods received, and finally to an invoice, or from procurement through production and inventory management.

The Reference Model starts with a trigger event (a requisition for stock material) and follows what has to be done as a result (Figure 2–2). It may branch numerous times. In the requisition example, it may follow a manual requisition, an automatic one, and the case where the requisition makes reference to another document. Each of the chains is linked to one another.

The Reference Model is divided into Enterprise Areas. Should the project team require vendor invoice processing (not all companies will), it can walk down through the major functions of a business to arrive at the process in question. The team members may elect to view the process in a diagram or flowchart. Figure 2–3 is an overview of the Vendor Invoice Process produced by R/3. Figure 2–4 enlarges a portion of that process. Any process view or portion thereof can be shown to enhance readability. Process views are made up of events (something has occurred), functions (something you have to do), external processes (to that view), and decision points.

The Reference Model can be used to access the SAP R/3 data model. This provides definitions of all data elements. The Reference Model can be used to identify and define the business scenarios that will be needed by the project team. Once defined, the extent of customization can be determined.

In addition, with Release 3.0, R/3 provides a preconfigured sample company including all modules. It is fully documented with scripts

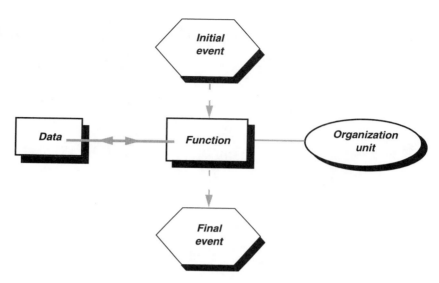

Figure 2–2:   Overview of event-driven process chain structure

following the IDES (International Demo and Education System) standards.

The Procedure Model

The Procedure Model is a framework methodology for implementing R/3. It diagrams the implementation in four steps, and describes each step. (See Figure 2–5.) The four steps are: organization and conceptual design, detailed design and implementation, preparations for production, and productive operation. Running parallel and concurrent with these four steps are the functions of project administration, project control, system maintenance, and release upgrade.

Organization and conceptual design (step 1) suggests that the users must analyze their requirements, organize the project, set up the test environment, and train the project team. A transition between the first and the second of the major steps is a quality check of the target concept. In step 2, detailed design and implementation, the project team will define the functions and processes to be implemented, and design the interfaces and enhancements.

In step 2, the team is urged to establish global settings, the company structure, and the master data. It will also establish (and finalize) the functions and processes. Next, it will implement the interfaces and

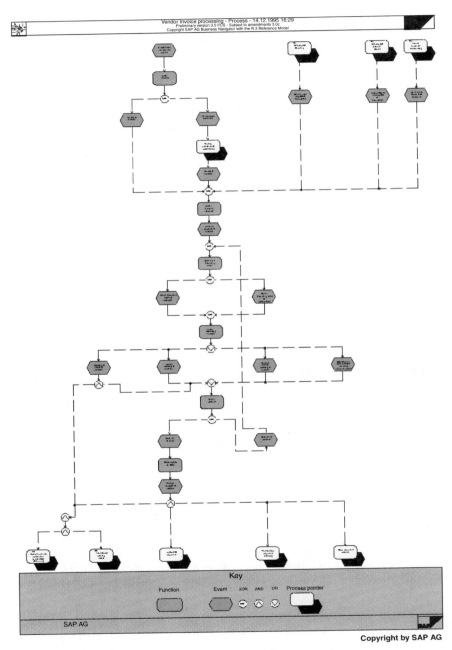

Copyright by SAP AG

Figure 2–3: Overview of vender invoice processing

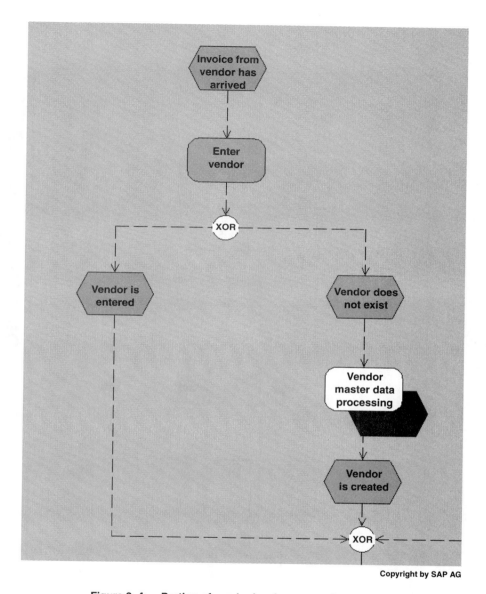

Copyright by SAP AG

Figure 2–4: Portion of vendor invoice processing

Figure 2–5: Procedure model

enhancements that were previously defined. It will establish the reporting, archive management, and authorization management, and perform the final test of the system. This step concludes with another transition and quality check of the application system.

In preparations for production (step 3), the team will prepare the production start, create the user documentation, and actually set up the productive environment. It will train the users, establish system administration, and transfer the data into the production system. Again, a final quality check is made of the production system.

This leaves step 4, that of establishing an ongoing production operation (productive operation). This responsibility generally falls to the IS department that will support the production operation and optimize the system's use. This involves ensuring that the technical configuration is adequate to the load created on the system by the users.

During the process of implementation, the project team can refer to the implementation framework to ensure they have completed each step adequately. The Procedure Model is heavy on the technical issues, and light on the change management issues.

Steps 1–4 comprise the recommended list of tasks that must be completed by the project team. The description of each of the tasks is contained in the Implementation Management Guide (also called the *Implementation Guide*).

The Implementation Management Guide (IMG)

The IMG is an online documentation tool that steps the project team through the implementation process. It is created in hypertext, with links to the individual functions. It guides the project team in determining the business requirements, the documents, and the individual fields.

For example, if the team's task is to create the warehouse system, IMG will define the important characteristics of good receipts and how to issue goods. If the task is to set up appropriate user accounts for the purchasing system, it will guide the team members to consider whether the user can view prices, enter purchase orders, change purchase orders, or order materials for a plant or set of facilities.

From the Procedure Model, the IMG is accessed via either the text or the action button. The text button will provide a detailed description of the step selected. For example, the step *Establish Company Structure* is displayed in Figure 2–6. The description will provide an overview of the step, the trigger needed to begin it, the information required as its input, a listing of the substeps that must be taken, any recommendations that apply, a summary of its output, and the result that will occur from correct completion of the step.

The action button in the Procedure Model will present the specific steps needed to create the required table settings. Again, continuing the example of *Establish Company Structure*, the project team member can open up the complete IMG and drill down into each area required. Figure 2–7 shows the R/3 company structure process.

The project team will find it necessary to examine the Reference Model and compare the R/3 business processes to its own processes prior to beginning customization of the R/3 system. Once the team has identified which processes will be used as provided and which will be customized, it can turn to the IMG for detailed instructions regarding the table settings.

Customizing is the function that actually allows the project team to establish its own ways of using R/3. As was stated earlier, this function is accessed from the main menu. It can also be accessed from within the IMG. As the project team understands the details of R/3 and compares them with its redesign preferences, it can set up tables to accomplish the required tasks.

The IMG allows R/3 customers to create their own documentation by taking the selections made along with the rationale and dropping them into a Word for Windows document. When more mature, this capability is expected to replace the need to create scripts to fully document the system.

2.3 Training

The three online tools described above will allow the project team to develop excellent online documentation. Such documentation must be sufficient to provide the end user with the information needed to understand each function and field. Although instructions can be put into a text document and printed, the most efficient use of them as a training tool is to make them available at the desktop.

Training individuals in class sessions is extremely costly and time consuming. In addition, much of the information conveyed in that environment is lost, especially if the employees do not immediately

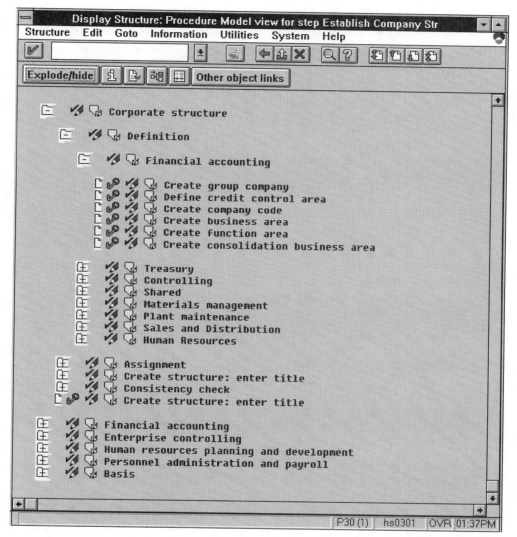

Figure 2–6: Establish company structure

begin to use the knowledge in their jobs. Training departments are becoming more sophisticated in developing alternative methods.

Historically, online help has been disregarded because it has not been particularly useful or accurate. However the concept remains a viable one. When an individual is sitting at a terminal entering a

Establish Company Structure

Every application of the R/3 System uses one or several system organizational units for the representation of their functions and processes.

These are related hierarchically or within a network.

Examples of system organizational units are:
- Accounting
  - company codes
  - controlling areas
- Logistics
  - plants
  - purchasing organizations
- Human Resources
  - personnel areas

Trigger
- The conceptual design has been released.

Input Information
- Requirements for the configuration.
- Project guideline.
- System defaults in client 001.
- Company structure.

Contents of the Work Package

In this work package
- check the occurrence of the organizational units of the standard system.
- adapt the organizational units of the system, if required represent your company structure as organizational units of the SAP System.
- document the adjustments.

Recommendation
- This work package should be processed by all project teams in unison. A cross-team reconciliation is necessary.
- Only a few team members should be allowed to make these adjustments.

Output Information
- Configurations for company structure.

Result
- The system organizational units have been set, documented and compared.

Figure 2–7:   Establish company structure

customer order and comes across an order type or a shipping problem he or she has never before encountered, an online answer to a question is the most effective way to assist him or her, assuming the online help actually answers the specific question. The improved design of the software and the help processes is the way to solve the problems encountered in early versions of the online help. The ultimate goal is to design the interface in such a way that a person who has never received any training can figure out the answer to his or her question.

The challenge in the documentation/training field is to revolutionize the ways in which knowledge is transferred. The approach today is to enable the user to use the system to learn how to use the system. Online help is changing into an electronic performance support system (EPSS).

Steelcase, a major manufacturer of office furniture, is working to define their business model and to link it to the SAP documentation, to set the stage for the next generation of training methodologies. The goal, after providing an orientation to the system and its functions, will be to teach people how to use the tools. In other words, to teach people how to learn. To do that, Steelcase believes it needs to differentiate the various types of information. These can then be attached in a hierarchical fashion at the appropriate places so that users can explore increasing levels of detail about a subject and stop whenever they have learned enough to accomplish the task at hand.

Carl Moushon, documentation and training manager at Steelcase, describes three major access points to the documentation. The first is the SAP system itself. If an individual needs specific information, the system is sufficiently context sensitive to provide the appropriate level of documentation. The second access point is from the developing business model. One will be able to start with the required process and from there move into the SAP functions available to complete the process. The final access point is a document management and query system that will assist the user in finding the information that is needed.

2.4 The Users' Group

SAP has a large and active users group called ASUG (American SAP Users' Group). For many involved in the implementation and maintenance of R/3, it is an extremely valuable source of information. At a recent meeting, seven sessions were held. Four were presented by SAP users, while the rest were updates on SAP developments presented by

SAP employees. Topics included managing change: the soft issues; document management systems (EDMS): considerations for SAP implementation; the right help at the right time: performance support systems for R/3; and business event driven education: the new SAP project team training. It is highly recommended that you join this group.

Any company that is implementing R/3 will find that the process of customization is complex. With Release 3.0, the number of tables (including those pertaining to the technical requirements) that must be set up and maintained has risen to 8,000. SAP has improved the capabilities of its online help for project team members to better walk them through the sea of options available.

CHAPTER 3

The R/3 Basis Technology

3.1 SAP R/3 System in Depth   54
3.2 System Administration   56
3.3 ABAP/4 Workbench   66

3.1 SAP R/3 System in Depth

Technical Architecture

Modern software architectures are built-in structures where every part has a defined function. The definition of the building blocks and the functionality they each contain determines their position in the blueprint. The SAP software architecture can be seen as being constructed of four building blocks:

- *Business application* These are all the functional modules which are used by the business. They were summarized earlier in Chapter 1.6. They contain all the business processes and their functions for finance, manufacturing, sales, and distribution. Details of these modules can be found in the SAP documentation. To discuss them more fully would be beyond the parameters of this book.

- *System administration* This block includes the computer center management, user authorization, database administration, and so forth. System administration is used by the technical staff to install or upgrade the unconfigured software on the servers and to provide connectivity and security within the SAP's networked work environment. While we provided an overview in Chapter 1.4, we will more fully describe the elements of system administration below.

- *ABAP/4 Workbench* The R/3 software package comes with a complete set of software development tools including an active data dictionary and SAP's proprietary programming language called ABAP/4. This language has evolved since the 1970s when SAP started its development. All tools and data models are part of the ABAP/4 workbench which will be described below.

- *SAP Implementation Guide (IMG) and Business Navigator* As stated in Chapter 2, these tools are accessed through the Business Workbench (also called the Business Engineering Workbench). They are tools which the implementation project team uses to configure the SAP package according to the business requirements. All documentation and data can be stored here, allowing the project team to stay on top of the masses of information it generates. The Business Navigator gives the project a graphical overview over processes and the data model. The process of configuration using these tools is discussed in Chapter 4.

All components above reside on top of a software kernel which is a collection of service routines supporting the Business Applications and

Administration/Configuration functions. SAP calls it the middleware of the R/3 System.[1] It is the interface between the third-party database system in which SAP stores its data and the SAP applications.

System administration, the ABAP/4 Workbench, and the SAP Business Engineering Workbench comprise the SAP basis technology. Before these building blocks can be explained in more detail, we need to discuss the concept of *objects* and the ABAP/4 Repository within the SAP system.

Objects and the ABAP/4 Repository

SAP has adopted objects as one of its key implementation concepts. The use of objects is an emerging software architectural concept with a big impact on the way end users work with their system.

The object-oriented approach is characterized by the depiction of objects from the real world in program-internal software objects.[2] (See Figure 3–1.) This means that any real or abstract object and its behavior can be re-created using data and a program to manipulate it.

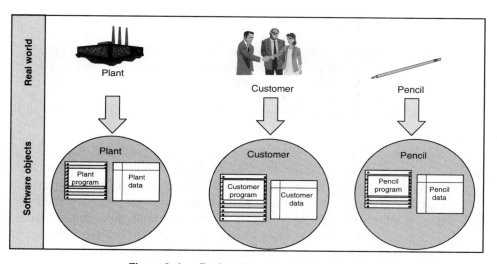

Figure 3–1:   Real-world and software objects

[1] Buck-Emden, R. and J. Galimow, *The Client/Server Technology of the SAP R/3 System*, Addison-Wesley, Harlow, Essex, Eng., 1996.
[2] Ibid.

An SAP object is a collection of data and programs to process this data. An object can be a table field, a business object (e.g., a purchase order), a function module, a change request, an authorization for a user, a project, and so forth. The description of SAP objects is stored in the ABAP/4 Repository which is an area within the Basis system. Objects in the ABAP/4 Repository are created by the people who program, configure, and document the R/3 system. This includes the project teams at SAP AG and the project teams of all of SAP's customers. Everybody who makes any changes to the R/3 system is automatically working with the objects in the ABAP/4 Repository. This ensures consistency of how data and programs are being used in the R/3 system. The use and function of the ABAP/4 Repository is explained later in this chapter.

3.2 System Administration

To physically install and maintain the overall R/3 system, special functions for system administrators are provided by SAP. These functions are:

- Computer center management system and system services
- Correction and transport system
- User maintenance (authorization)
- Application data archiving
- Database administration

When SAP started the development of the R/3 package, client/server technology was in its infancy. The installation and management of software where one part is running on one computer and another part on another computer was unknown and no standardized tools were available for the UNIX environment on which R/3 development began. In the mainframe environment of that time, these administration tools were typically offered by the manufacturer of the operating system or by third-party vendors. They are absolutely necessary to run business application software in production mode. Since SAP's customers were running a mainframe environment, they expected these administration tools as a prerequisite to purchasing the R/3 system. Due to their unavailability, SAP had to develop its own set of tools and provide them to its customers to increase R/3's acceptance.

Computer Center Management System (CCMS)

This function is provided to manage the entire SAP R/3 environment. It includes tools to start and stop the R/3 system, monitor server and network and alert the administrator in case of critical conditions, balance loads between servers for optimal resource usage, and schedule and execute batch job (background processing).

The system also comes with an application programming interface (API) to allow for system accounting in order to provide reports of resource usage by user process.

The CCMS controls two system processes which are the key to a good performance of the overall R/3 installation: the dispatcher and the update process.

The Dispatcher

The dispatcher is responsible for balancing the loads of the servers. This means that it controls which process runs on which server. There are two principle kinds of processes, dialog (online) and batch. A dialog process is used to interact with the user at the screen. This can be any transaction such as order entry. In contrast, batch processes do not have user interaction; instead all input is submitted from a file.

The role of the dispatcher is to decide where to execute the different processes based upon the parameters set by the system administrator. Server resources are also assigned depending on the time of day. During the day, more resources are typically allocated for dialog processes (to support the business users) than for batch processes. This is changed at night, when long report programs are executed.

Application servers are grouped by the administrator into classes depending on the applications they run. One class might, for example, run the financial modules while others might run the sales and distribution modules (see Figure 3–2). The figure also illustrates the way in which those servers are further connected to the SAP database server.

In general, the more homogeneous the application mix on a server, the better its resource usage. The reason is that every application uses different sizes of buffers, has a different access pattern to the database, and creates files of different sizes. By specializing the servers, they can be better tuned for performance.

Figure 3–2: Application servers running separate modules

The Update Process

The update process, based on a concept which SAP implemented earlier in its R/2 system, is a very effective way to accommodate hundreds or even thousands of users on a single database server and still provide satisfactory response times.

The traditional approach of building a dialog system with an SQL database is to have the user wait at the screen for the database to commit updates. This is called synchronous update. For a user this means that, after pressing the enter key, he or she has to wait for the system to reopen the on-screen data fields for input. This waiting time is called response time. Ideally the response time is less than a second to allow a continuous workflow for the user. An insufficient system response time has a very negative effect on work efficiency.

If numerous users work with the same database, the response time might be longer than a second, depending on the size of the hardware and the parameters set in the collaborating software parts, such as the operating system, database system, application software, and so on. The problem lies in the nature of concurrent access of many users to the same database. One solution might be to sequence the database updates in a way that no concurrent accesses of the database would occur. See Figure 3–3.

Figure 3–3:   The update process

SAP addressed this in its software by decoupling the user's interaction with the system from the process of updating the database. All data coming from dialog transactions are stored in an intermediate file and prioritized for storage in the database. On the other side, a continuous update task runs on the application server scanning the intermediate file for new records to be processed. The update task then takes the records from the intermediate file, sequences them, and stores them independent of any user interaction in the appropriate database tables. If many users enter data at the same time, the update process taking records out of the intermediate file might be slower than the stream of incoming records. In order to prevent overflow, the system switches to synchronous update mode. The user then has to wait until all records of the intermediate file have been processed, including the one he or she has just queued. Then the system switches back to asynchronous update mode.

Correction and Transport System (CTS)

The Correction and Transport System (CTS) is a tool to organize the ABAP/4 program development and to migrate programs and data from the development environments to the integration or production system. It is used by system administrators and developers. CTS has two parts: the Workbench Organizer to develop and change ABAP/4 and DYNPRO source code and the Transport System to move code and data to the target system. Both tools are tightly linked and work together in the development process.

Workbench Organizer

With the workbench organizer (one part of the ABAP/4 Workbench), members of a development team are coordinated in the creation of programs, data, documentation, and configuration objects. When a developer works on a program, a table, or any other object, it is critical that no other team member be able to modify or delete the object during this process. The workbench organizer protects the development object in use by one developer from being concurrently modified by another.

When a development team member creates or modifies any program or table, the workbench organizer creates a change request and reserves the object for exclusive use by this team member. No one else can then accidentally modify or delete the object until the person working on it releases it. In this way the work of individual team members is protected. Starting in Release 3.0 of the R/3 system, the workbench organizer can track versions of each object. With this capability, team members can go back to previous versions of a particular object. This is useful when a complex change does not fulfill its intended purpose but the team member does not want to create the object from scratch.

During a development project, a team works together creating programs and data which comprise the application. In Figure 3–4, the development team creates a set of sales reports. For such a project a *development class* within the ABAP/4 Repository is created. A

Figure 3–4:   Several team members update different portions of their system

development class is a categorization of the development projects in order to keep all development objects together which belong together. For example, programs and tables which belong to the order entry application in the SD module are grouped in the development class *VA* (*Vertrieb Auftrag*) which stands for *sales order*.

In the following example, the programs report A and B as well as tables, screens, and other elements which were created for the use with these reports are grouped in the development class "sales reports."

The Transport System

The transport system is the mechanism which copies objects from the development system to the integration system and/or the production system. The system administrator defines how transports take place. He or she defines in the system how an object is routed during the transport. An object could be transported from the development system directly to the production system. In Figure 3–4 the objects are routed from the development system to the production system via the integration system.

In Figure 3–4, two team members work on different objects—report A and report B—within the development class sales reports. The workbench organizer has reserved these objects on the development system for their exclusive use. In general, any project team should work only on the development system. The integration system and the production system have other purposes, and all objects inside are protected against any changes from the project team.

Once report B is completed and tested by the developer, the system administrator queues it for transport to the integration system. Here, the object is tested in a production-like environment, meaning that data and programs, operating system, and database configuration are similar or the same as on the production system. This is the final check before the object is queued to be transported to the production system. An integration system is generally recommended for this type of testing since the development system often has a very different configuration than the production system, and test results do not necessarily resemble results under production conditions. Testing of objects on the integration system should not be conducted by the developers but instead by those users from the business departments who will use the programs once they are transported to the production system. Figure 3–5 illustrates the complete development cycle.

The developer reserves an object with a change request in the workbench organizer. Once the object is developed and tested, the programmer releases it and the administrator queues it for transport

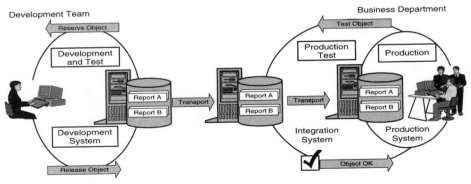

Figure 3–5:   The complete development cycle

to the integration system. On the integration system the business department tests and finally accepts the object. Then, the administrator queues the object for transport to the production system where it is ready for use by the business department.

User Maintenance

The SAP R/3 system provides the ability to create, change, delete, and authorize users. This user maintenance function has two parts: protected objects (what is protected) and organization of authorization (who can authorize).

A user is represented in the R/3 system with a user master record, as depicted in Figure 3–6, which stores the name of the person, the user ID and the links to the assigned authorization profiles. The *authorization profile* is a record which contains a number of different authorizations. More than one user can be linked to a specific authorization profile. This allows the system administrator to specify groups of people who share the very same authorization. For the business, it means that people with same or similar job functions can use the same authorization profile.

Each authorization is linked to a specific object in the ABAP/4 Repository. The authorization record describes what fields within the object are protected (what are the allowed values or ranges of values), which user group has access to the object, and what actions this user group is allowed to do (create, change, delete, display). Because of the high complexity of the R/3 system and the great number of objects, SAP comes with a set of standard authorization profiles, which in turn are linked to authorizations and objects. This means that a company does not have to start from scratch defining all the authorizations in

Figure 3–6:   The authorization definition

the system. In fact, for a small company, the standard defined authorization profile might be sufficient. For large corporations, R/3 provides the flexibility to define authorizations in great detail. Figure 3–6 shows how authorizations are defined.

Here, user John Doe, an employee in the accounts payable department, is assigned to two authorization profiles. The first profile AUTH_PROF1 contains authorizations for check data and calendar information.

Companies can organize in great detail how authorizations should work. There is a simple approach for small companies and a complex solution for large and distributed corporations.

The system administrator for all authorizations is called the *superuser*. This person has the ultimate responsibility for all user authorizations within the SAP system. The superuser can create user master records, authorization profiles, and authorizations. For a small and centralized company, few user master records and authorization profiles need to be created. In a large and distributed corporation, many people come and go without the superuser being able to track everybody. For this reason, the superuser can delegate authorization functions. To achieve highest security, the superuser can delegate different parts of the authorization process to people adopting three different roles: one person to create and maintain user master records, a second to create and maintain authorizations and authorization profiles, and a third to activate/deactivate authorizations.

Since responsibility for the authorization process is now shared, it is very unlikely that authorizations will be misused, because none of the three people involved, acting alone, can effectively empower a user. In addition, the superuser can delegate the authorization responsibility to distant departments or subsidiaries.

Application Data Archiving

Housekeeping is a very important administrative task which is often not given the priority it deserves. This is structured in R/3 in two steps:

1 Read all records from the SAP database which should be archived and store them in the archive (e.g., tape, optical disk, etc.).

2 Delete all archived records from the SAP database and reindex tables.

These two steps are executed independently in order to prevent data from being deleted from the SAP database too early since the archiving step might fail due to a technical error.

Archiving in SAP is done by module (application) and within the module by document. This means that data which logically belongs together is archived. A *document* is a collection of business objects such as a purchase order. A purchase order contains a header, line items, text, and so forth, and each of the elements is stored in different tables in the SAP database. SAP maintains all the relationships between the tables involved, but in order to archive a document, a special sequence has to be coded in the system and followed. Since documents are also in relationship with each other, a certain sequence of archiving documents also has to be followed. Due to the tight integration of SAP, relationships between documents of different modules also have to be taken into consideration when archiving is required.

SAP has laid out the dependencies and sequences of archiving documents from the database in a network diagram. From this diagram, the administrator can easily identify the appropriate sequence of archiving.

The periodic housekeeping ensures that the system does not have to process data, which is not used anyway. Archiving improves the online response time, because the data load of the database is reduced and indexes are optimized. System resources are utilized better when unneeded data is removed from the system.

Archiving also includes the issue of retention. Data must be retained for some period of time, based on the type of document. For example, the retention period for many financial documents is set by law. For other data, like sales statistics, the organization must define how long it wants to track this information. These decisions have a direct impact on hardware layout since the longer the retention period, the larger the archive needs to be.

Database Administration

SAP itself does not provide the DBMS needed to create and maintain the data-filled tables. Popular DBMS solutions for SAP software are Oracle, Informix, and SQL Server. The database administration is a task which uses the tools of both the DBMS and the SAP software. SAP provides the functionality to start, stop, and back up the entire database. This eases the task for the administrator, because SAP makes sure through its procedures that all SAP-relevant information is maintained.

3.3 ABAP/4 Workbench

The SAP software comes with its own set of tools for software development called the ABAP/4 Workbench. These tools are extensive and give users the ability to create software for a complete life cycle. Tools include:

- ABAP/4 Repository
- Application hierarchy
- Object browser
- Data modeler
- ABAP/4 dictionary
- ABAP/4 programming language and editor
- Screen painter
- Menu painter
- Data browser
- Program test aids
- Workbench organizer
- Correction and transport system

The developer is supported through graphical data and process models which allow a much better overview than just textual information. This type of support is also absolutely necessary because, otherwise, a developer will be lost in the amount of information and complexity. The graphic charts of the data and process models cover entire walls and are the road map to the overall SAP system. Most of these tools allow project team members and technical support people to list and navigate development objects. Depending on the data, the tool that manipulates this data is always part of the information contained in the ABAP/4 Repository.

ABAP/4 Repository

The Repository is a catalog of all information within the ABAP/4 Workbench and supports the navigation of the developer through code and data. All information about data and process models, programs, tables, fields, projects, change requests, and so forth, including their location, is kept here. It ensures that no development object can get lost in the depth of the system.

Data stored in the Repository is an abstraction of the real world, and every piece of data needed by a business is represented. Since this level of abstraction is very technical and difficult to understand for people without a programmer's background, a higher-level view exists in the SAP system. Access to this view on data is given by the SAP Business Navigator. This is a function in the R/3 system which is outside the ABAP/4 Workbench, giving business people access to this representation of a real business world.

Figure 3–7 shows how the ABAP/4 Repository and Business Navigator relate to the real world.

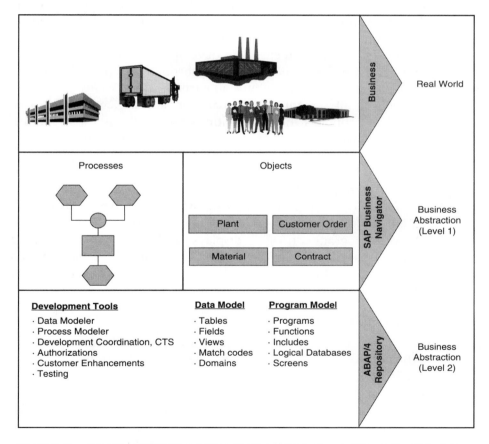

Figure 3–7:   How the ABAP/4 Repository, Business Navigator, and the real world relate

67

While business people work with the Business Navigator and the Implementation Guide, ABAP/4 developers work with the Repository to transform requirements for additional functionality into ABAP/4 programs and data tables.

Application Hierarchy

The application hierarchy is another navigation tool. It allows the developer to use the SAP application (e.g., the Materials Management module) as an entry point to find and manipulate a specific program, screen, or data structure belonging to a certain transaction. When entering the application hierarchy from the ABAP/4 Workbench, the developer decides whether to navigate the standard SAP system or the custom-developed extensions every SAP customer typically creates (reports, for example). From here, the developer can drill down to a list of program objects. Each program object can be exploded into its parts, such as program modules or functions, including structures, tables, fields, and screens. The developer reaches the same information level as if he or she were going through the ABAP/4 repository.

A program object contains all parts of ABAP/4 and DYNPRO code as well as all screens which make up a complete SAP transaction. DYNPRO controls the interaction between the user's screen and the system. This interface can be a very simple program with only one module or a very complex online transaction such as the R/3 order entry program containing hundreds of data structures, code modules, screens, and subroutines. By using the application hierarchy, the developer reaches the transaction with which the object can be manipulated. If the object is a code module, then the system brings up the ABAP/4 program editor and displays the ABAP/4 program code. If the object is a table, then the system brings up the table maintenance transaction and displays the table structure. In every transaction, the developer has the option to edit this object.

The Object Browser

The object browser is yet another entry point to navigate through the ABAP/4 development objects. While the application hierarchy starts navigation at the application level, the object browser gives the developer faster access to the lower levels of the development objects.

Figure 3–8 gives an example of how a developer can navigate to find the components of the order entry program of SAP R/3 which is called *SAPMV45A*. If the developer only knows the application area (accounting, sales, etc.) the program is in, then he or she can drill down to the sales order. From here, R/3 takes him or her into the object browser and immediately displays the top-level structure there. While tables and data structures can be found under the dictionary objects, the order entry program can be found under the programs menu. There, the developer will find the order entry program SAPMV45A. From here, he or she can drill down to the components of the program and find the screens and processing logic.

Since drilling down from the application hierarchy takes several steps, it is faster to start with the object browser if the developer knows what to look for. The screen of the object browser requires the developer to enter either a development class or a program name. A development class is a collection of development objects by application area. If the developer enters the VA menu, the object browser displays all development objects (programs, data structures, etc.) in this area. From here, the developer will find the SAPMV45A program under the programs menu.

If the developer knows the program name, then he or she enters it directly into the object browser screen which takes him or her quickly to the lowest level of detail, displaying all components of the SAPMV45A program.

...bject browser

The Data Modeler

The data of SAP R/3 reside in about 8,000 tables contained in a relational database or relational data model.

Based upon this modeling approach, SAP created the entire data structure underlying the R/3 system. In order to get an overview and navigate through this data model, SAP provides the data modeler. (See Appendix A for more information about this approach.) With this tool a developer can start at the highest structure level (e.g., accounting, logistics, etc.) and drill down to the details of the data model. The data modeler allows its user to view the entire SAP data model at once and to display it as a graphic (if your application server and your PC have sufficient hardware resources). It appears as a gigantic blueprint showing all object types and their relationships. The developer can zoom into the graphic display and get to each entity type and each relationship. Of course it is also possible to start the navigation at a lower level. The data modeler displays only the respective section of the overall data model. From the graphic display a developer can branch into different views for each entity type. With a mouse click the developer can display the data dictionary definition, browse the data within the entity type, get a list of all attributes and their definitions, or get a list of all processes in which the entity type is used.

This tool also allows customers to build their own data model which then can be linked to the SAP data model. This is particularly useful when designing large-scale, custom enhancements to the standard system. To build a data model, the developer will find it useful to create the model first as a sketch on a piece of paper before starting to enter anything into the R/3 system. Building a data model is a creative act wherein the resulting model depends completely on the person or team designing it. One person or team is likely to come up with a different model than another person or team when modeling the same part of the real world. The reason is that everyone sees his or her world differently based upon education and experience. The example model, in Appendix A, describing pencils, prices, and color can also be modeled in a totally different way depending on the view the designer takes. The data model as a whole defines its potential and its limits for its use by a program accessing the data within this data model.

ABAP/4 Data Dictionary

The ABAP/4 Data Dictionary is a tool to maintain important information about the content and the structure of the SAP database. This includes information about:

- Tables
- Data elements
- Domains
- Views
- Locks
- Match codes

See Appendix B for an explanation of each of these elements.

The ABAP/4 Dictionary is the place where all these items are referenced and described. The purpose of the ABAP/4 Dictionary is to ensure data integrity. This means that no data element can be used more than once, regardless of whether it is used as a field in a table or as a variable in a data structure. All data elements are defined by a name, characteristics like field length, whether its content may be numeric or alpha numeric, the domain of values allowed to be used with the data element, and a textual description of the meaning of the data element. It also provides a function through which a developer can list all tables and programs where a data element is used. This cross reference is a great help in finding all programs where a data element is manipulated.

ABAP/4 Programming Language and Editor

SAP provides the following tools to develop software within the R/3 package: ABAP/4 programming language and editor, screen painter, menu painter, data browser, and test aids. See Appendix C for a deeper discussion of the language and the processing logic for screen interactivity, and of DYNPRO, an essential element in understanding how to program changes or interfaces to R/3.

The ABAP/4 editor itself is very flexible and allows for immediate syntax check of the program code without leaving the editor. This is very convenient for the developer since this enhances the productivity. This is possible since no immediate translation of the ABAP/4 code into machine language takes place during the syntax check. The translation into machine language is performed by the R/3 run-time system when the program is executed.

The ABAP/4 editor also allows for easy run-time testing of the code. A developer can set break points right within the code to stop and investigate the program and its variables during execution. Online help is available for all ABAP/4 commands.

The SAP database with its massive data structure could easily become a data graveyard if it took a major effort to produce reports. In order to simplify the development of reports as much as possible, SAP created a tool called ABAP/4 query. This is a menu-driven report generator which can prepare basic lists (sorted and unsorted) and statistics on the fly. With this tool, developers and even end users can produce reports in a fast manner by retrieving data from the SAP database. Report execution can be restricted by the SAP authorization mechanisms.

The Screen Painter

For the design of any R/3 screen two tools are necessary: the screen painter and the menu painter. SAP divided the user screen into two areas: all data fields displayed on the screen, and all menus, buttons, and function keys

The layout of a screen with fields, their position and appearance, and the link of the fields to the data dictionary is determined by the developer using the screen painter. In general a screen has four components: flow logic (DYNPRO), screen attributes (screen number, program to which the screen belongs, etc.), fields (as defined in the ABAP/4 Dictionary), and screen layout (position of fields on the screen).

The screen painter allows the developer to create all attributes a screen might have. All screen parameters are stored in the database, together with the DYNPRO, which is also developed with an editor in the screen painter. The design of the DYNPRO determines the sequence of ABAP/4 modules to be processed before and after user input to the screen. Fields to be displayed on the screen are pulled from the ABAP/4 Dictionary or an existing program. In this way the system makes sure that no undefined field is used.

The Menu Painter

The other parts of the user interface are the menu bar, menu function, function keys, the standard tool bar, and an application tool bar. The menu bar is the row of menu entry which is always visible on the top of the screen. The menu function are the entries which become visible in drop-down lists once the user clicks on a menu bar entry. The standard tool bar and the application tool bar are the two rows of push buttons under the menu bar.

All these items are defined with the help of the menu painter. The specific setting of menus, function keys, and tool bars for a particular program is called GUI status. A GUI status has to be developed for every screen. At the very least, the menu and help systems are always generated automatically.

The Data Browser

One of the fast and simple tools within the ABAP/4 Workbench is the data browser. This function allows a developer to enter a table name and get the table content displayed. The data browser lists the rows contained in the table. A selection screen allows the user to define which table rows should be retrieved if the table is large. This tool is useful as a quick lookup function during ABAP/4 program development.

Program Test Aids

After developing a program in ABAP/4, the developer has to test his or her creation. SAP supports this with a full suite of test aids. A developer can analyze program behavior during runtime, optimize database access, and simulate data input and processing of large data volumes. The tools provided make sure that a developer can prepare the program in an optimal fashion for its use.

SAP developed the ABAP/4 Workbench to deliver a complete framework of development tools as an integral part of its software package. In contrast, for home-grown legacy systems it is very common to use a mixed bag of proprietary tools from third parties for administration, software development, and testing. This patchwork of tools often inflates administration and development costs since it might be very difficult to integrate them into the legacy environment. In such an environment, source code is typically scattered throughout the development department, not stored in a central database. Versions of program source code are hard to track, and loss of program sources contributes to the maintenance challenge of custom legacy software.

With the ABAP/4 Workbench, companies can replace most of those tools and clean up their development environment when the SAP R/3 software becomes the core business system. Even though the ABAP/4 programming language has some elements which take time to get used to (like the DYNPRO commands) it is very effective when creating custom transactions as bolt-ons to the standard software. Maintenance is also simplified because versions of program source code are tracked and cannot get lost anymore. All of this contributes to a more efficient IT department.

CHAPTER 4

Configuring SAP R/3

4.1 Configuration Concepts   76
4.2 The Client Data Structure   76
4.3 Architecture of SAP Applications   79
4.4 Tables and Data Types   81
4.5 Configurable Elements   85
4.6 Configuring an SAP Document   93
4.7 Working with Master Data   100
4.8 Working with Documents   104
4.9 Working with Reports   109

4.1 Configuration Concepts

The SAP system is a standard business software package based on a data model. The SAP data model is implemented in relational database systems such as Oracle or Informix. SAP training does not typically include an explanation of the concepts underlying configuration since it is not its intent to train course attendees in relational database concepts. While this is reasonable, it still is very helpful to understand the basic ideas behind the configuration of the SAP system in order to assess the consequences of parameter settings. We have included this discussion of these basis configuration concepts used in the SAP software in Appendix D because, in our experience, the question, "What does configuration mean?" is central to team members' ability to complete the task of configuration.

Understanding the meaning and effect each configuration table and parameter has in a particular SAP application takes a lot of experience due to the complexity. On the other hand the software can be configured quickly if experienced support staff is available and all business requirements have been defined and can be met by the software.

Before we can turn to the architecture of the SAP application, we need to explain the concept of a client-oriented data structure.

4.2 The Client Data Structure

A client is an independent legal entity maintaining its own organization and data (e.g., a company). Companies traditionally have built their own proprietary systems responding to the unique business requirements of their user community. These requirements vary from company to company in all areas except one: finance. The accounting departments in U.S. companies are bound by the law to apply standardized accounting rules to maintain the financial data of the company and to report it to the Internal Revenue Service. This means that financial systems have to be built the same way for every company, making this department a prime candidate to be supported by a standard software package.

Accounting firms maintain the financial data of many large client companies. Since the data of the different companies are structured the same way it is useful to maintain this information within the same system rather than having to create a different system for each.

However, the data for one company must be maintained independently of the data of any other client. This triggered the development of client-oriented systems.

A client-oriented system is a software package which has the ability to maintain and protect data of different clients within the same database using the same program code. This works only if the data structures of all clients are identical.

SAP implemented the concept of a client-oriented system with a different purpose. During the implementation of the SAP system, several sets of the data are needed. A project team has the requirement to set up the SAP environment for different uses. The most typical ones are for development of the production system, training of users, and the playground to try configurations without disturbing fellow project members (the sandbox).

These environments can be set up within the same physical SAP system, eliminating the need to purchase hardware and software for each of them individually. The SAP system itself comes with the two clients. Client 000, in which a standard company has been configured, and client 001, which is an empty client shell.

Technically, a client-oriented system is implemented by defining a client key field for all data tables which should be client dependent, meaning where data should be separated by client. Figure 4–1 shows

Figure 4–1: Several clients in R/3

an R/3 system divided to accommodate the development, training and sandbox clients.

In Figure 4–2, two materials (steel beams and sheet metal) have been configured in the development client 010 (the numbering of clients can be chosen by the project team). The other clients also contain configurations of material. A user who logs into SAP using the client key 010 in the initial screen can access only data that has the client key 010. All other data is hidden from this user during this session and cannot be accessed. The SAP programs which access client-dependent tables automatically use the client key provided during the logon procedure by the user to retrieve the data. The user has no way to manipulate this access since it is coded in the program logic of the application. As a result, different users can access the data of different clients which are physically stored in the same table but are still kept separately. During the SAP project, while the production system is being developed in client 010, training can be conducted with the same system in client 011 without disturbing the work on client 010. The same is true for the sandbox client in this example and all other clients which might have been set up for other purposes.

In SAP the client concept is implemented for most of the data tables. One important exception is the ABAP/4 programming environment, which is called the *workbench*. ABAP/4 programs are stored in client-independent tables, which means that all clients have to share the same programs. A user cannot develop a program within client

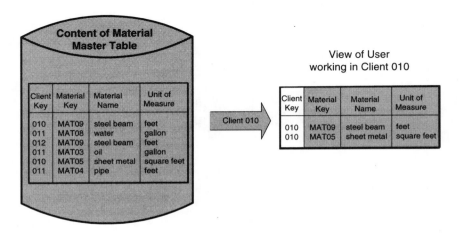

Figure 4–2: Configuring in the development client

010 and develop a variant of this program with the same name for client 011.

There are standard tools available to support the client structure of the system, to install, copy, transport, reset, delete, and compare different clients on the same installation. These tools are ABAP/4 programs (e.g., RSCLI001, to copy a client) and can be retrieved from the system through the directory or via menu paths. Details about those tools are described in the documentation of the SAP R/3 system. There are authorization checks within the tools to provide this functionality to system administrators only. This of course assumes that authorization profiles are set up accordingly.

4.3 Architecture of SAP Applications

While the functionality for the end user, the data, and the business processes are different in every SAP R/3 application, there is a common architecture all applications share. Understanding this architecture in one SAP R/3 application means that learning and understanding the configuration and use of other applications will be easier. We call these common elements *architectural elements*. Together with the configuration concepts explained above, these architectural elements are the foundation for the configuration and use of the SAP system. They are:

- Central and client-independent functions
- Organizational elements
- Control elements
- Master data
- Documents/operations
- Reports

Figure 4–3 shows how architectural elements fit into the SAP environment.

Client-independent functions, central functions, organizational elements, and control elements are software functions within the SAP system used to configure and program it to a company's specific requirements. The functions are used by the SAP project team, the system administrator, and the ABAP/4 developers. They can be found under Tools in the SAP main menu after logging on to the SAP system.

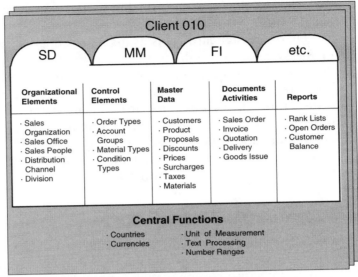

Figure 4–3: The SAP system

The most important ones are the ABAP/4 Workbench, Business Engineering (which includes customizing), the Business Navigator and Business Workflow. All functions to run the system can be found under the Administration menu. They are used by the system administrators.

The architectural elements—master data, documents/operations, and reports—are the SAP functions used by the end user who is working with the system on a daily basis. They are the vast majority of software functions SAP has. All SAP application menus in the system fall under this category.

During the SAP project, the configuration team works with the Business Engineering function, manipulating the configuration tables, as we will describe in the next sections. Configuration tables and data tables exist for every SAP application, as shown in Figure 4–4. The project team works with a tool called *Implementation Management Guide* (IMG), which is found under the Business Engineering menu, to configure each application by selecting parameters and assigning the tables. The team can store the parameter setting in the project documentation with the project history. The ABAP/4 Developers work with

Figure 4–4:   The SAP software architecture

the ABAP/4 Workbench to create reports and new custom applications.

To test the configuration, the project team also creates master data and documents. Once the customization process is complete and the R/3 system goes live, the business users work only with the functions provided by the SAP applications. When the business requirements change, the configuration of the SAP system will also have to be changed. For this reason, it is important to document the configuration in detail in order to allow better maintenance of the system.

4.4 Tables and Data Types

The SAP system uses tables and data in various ways. Depending on the purpose of the data, the tables and their contents can be categorized in the following way (see Table 4–1):

Table 4–1: Types of tables in R/3

Major table category	Table sub-category
Application data table	Master data
	Transaction data
Configuration tables	Organizational elements data
	Control elements data
	Data validation
	System control

Application Data

Application data tables contain either master data or transaction data. The difference between the two is the duration the information is active and in use. While transaction data is used only once, master data is used multiple times after it has been created. The majority of transaction data is derived from master data at the time of transaction. This composition results in a transaction and is called a document by SAP. A document ties together all data of the transaction. A transaction is unique and gets a unique document number assigned by the SAP system.

Since these terms are abstract, we want to explain them with a simple example: A grocery store carries items like milk, butter, and cheese. These are master items of a grocery store since these items will be sold as long as the store exists. We would find this general information in the master file of the grocery store. If you go to the store and buy a particular container of milk, you take a container from the shelf and walk to the cashier. At the register, you conduct a transaction by receiving the milk in exchange for your money. You also receive a receipt which is the document of your transaction. You conduct this transaction only once, since you pay for this particular container of milk only once. The data on the transaction document (your receipt) is frozen since no one can change the information on this piece of paper. It is the evidence that the transaction occurred. The receipt carries transaction data which was derived from master data and additional input by the cashier. Master data, such as the item description (milk), the store name and address, and perhaps a text, "Thank you—come again," is copied from the store's master file.

Additional input may come from the scale if you have bought fruit. Your credit card number is additional input and not from the master data of the grocery store. A document number may or may not appear on the receipt; however, it will exist in the store's information system identifying your transaction.

Of course the same principles are true for a corporate environment. A purchase order consists of header and line item information. All pieces of information like the vendor name and address, product, price information, and so forth, are stored in master data tables and are referenced at the time the purchase order is created by the buyer in the SAP system. Certain pieces of information like the document number, the date, and the purchase total are generated by the system at this time, and others, like quantities, are entered by the buyer. Once the buyer completes the purchase order document by storing it in the SAP database, this document is frozen.

Figure 4–5 shows a purchase order with master data and transaction data. The document number is the purchase order number which makes the transaction on this document unique.

Configuration Data

The adaptation of the SAP R/3 system to your business requirements is a key process in the SAP project. The following is a list of examples of typical adaptations which can be achieved via setting parameters in the specific configuration table:

- Create the companies' organizational structure (e.g., your organization has five independent companies and two different currencies)

- Change table entries for validation (e.g., valid order reasons used by your company)

- Change a business process in its flow (e.g., delivery notes can be created without being forced to reference a preceding order)

- Change the characteristics of a business transaction or business function (e.g., how pricing is carried out)

- Change report selections, displays, summation levels (e.g., you want additional predefined fields on a report)

- Change screens (e.g., you want to have the ZIP code on the customer master file as mandatory entry and not display the "TITLE" field at all)

The degree to which this adaptation can be performed through configuration depends on the flexibility of the specific application and

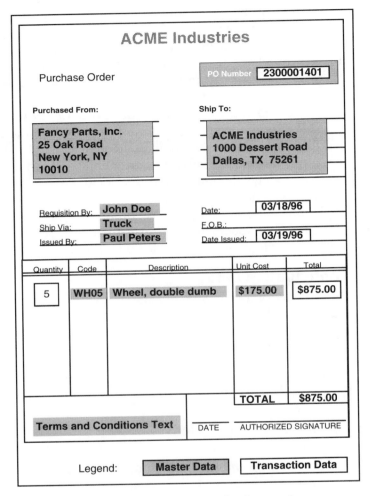

Figure 4–5: A purchase order document

the type of request from the business since the configurability has its limits.

In the next section we explain, based upon the principles presented in the architecture of SAP R/3 applications, what the different kinds of configurable elements mean and what their parameters influence in the SAP system.

4.5 *Configurable Elements*

As stated earlier, the SAP R/3 software contains elements which can be configured. The configurable elements, which are accessed through the IMG, are central functions, organizational elements, control elements, data validation, and system control. We will discuss each in turn.

Central Functions

When a project team starts to configure the SAP system, it first describes its current environment. Any company is set up in a specific environment where it deals with vendors, customers, taxes, the law, currencies, time, measures, and so on (see Figure 4–6).

The corporate environment has to be described, and its description entered into the SAP global settings configuration. This description includes such information as:

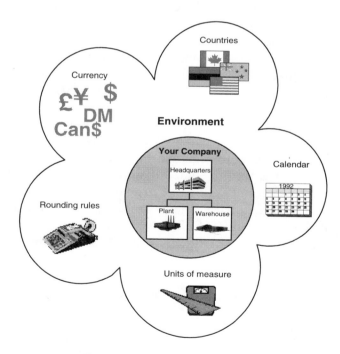

Figure 4–6: A company environment

- The country in which the company is legally registered
- The currency used and the exchange rates with other countries
- Which units of measure are being used for products and services
- Which rounding rules are applied when dealing with currency
- What calendar is used

Once you start to collect the current information, you will find that it is not always readily available or not available in the format the SAP system requires. This is the beginning of a process called *mapping* which the SAP project team has to go through in order to implement the system. Mapping means to match the existing data fields of your legacy systems with the data fields available in the SAP system. This is a very important process since you will be laying the foundation for moving your existing data into the SAP system.

Organizational Elements

The organization of the company has to be configured after you have entered the environment information into the configuration tables using the IMG. A company can be described by its organizational elements, that is, the entire company, a department, a division, a plant, or a subsidiary. It is the skeleton of your corporate information structure which reflects how your company is organized. Later, all company master and transaction data will be linked to these organizational elements. Due to this fact, it is imperative to finalize and decide on the future corporate structure before any other configuration work is done or even before master and transaction data are created. For this reason, it is recommended that you conduct a workshop in the early project stages to define this structure for your company.

Organizational elements are defined in the corporate structure of the enterprise IMG. SAP uses its own language to name things. Teams have to learn and understand SAP's meaning of *controlling area*, *functional area*, *plants*, *sales organization*, and so forth. These elements are part of the description of the company which is then configured by entering the respective data of your company into the appropriate tables. All these elements exist today in your company but they have to be identified and named in order to get them into the SAP configuration. SAP describes the organizational elements in their documentation CD-ROM and gives a brief overview by application.

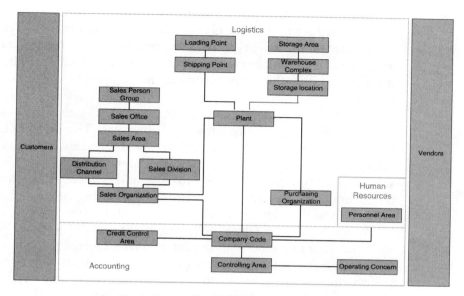

Figure 4–7: SAP's organizational elements

Figure 4–7 shows how SAP's main organizational elements can be overlaid onto the functional structure of an organization.

Figure 4–7 also shows the integration between the organizational elements depicted by the main relationships between them. SAP implemented each of these organizational elements as a table or a combination of tables for each element. With the IMG, the project team is shielded from the physical table by using the appropriate configuration screens.

SAP provides definitions of every organizational element in its data model. High-level terms like *plant* are defined in a way that the explanation fits many definitions:

> *A PLANT is an organizational unit within the Logistics that subdivides the ENTERPRISE from the viewpoint of production, inventory management, material requirements planning and plant maintenance.*[1]

Since every company has its own interpretation of the term plant, SAP defines it generically. The explanation does not give much help

---

[1] Plant Entity Description, SAP Data Model, SAP R/3 Version 3.0D

with what data are expected when establishing a plant within the SAP system. In order to provide greater clarity, the data entry screen within the enterprise IMG is helpful. The information required is a name and an address, which means that a plant is a physical location. The project team must know this when mapping the company's data into the R/3 system.

Other elements are not so obvious because the element's only purpose is to define your organizational structure. The division is such a case where only the name is defined and then is associated with the sales organization and the distribution channel into the sales area. The sales area allows the SAP system to store and retrieve sales information based upon the aspects of the three contributing organizational elements: division, sales channel and sales organization

When looking at Figure 4–7, you might wonder whether you have to define and implement all organizational elements provided by SAP. Some organizational elements are mandatory, such as the company code which defines the company as a legal entity and separates the general ledger accounts from accounts of other companies you might want to set up. Every company is automatically a legal entity in order to conduct business. For this reason you must define a company code. If you are selling products or services you must define a sales organization, a division, and a distribution channel in order to process orders within SAP. Once you are productive with SAP and you want to enter an order, the system will ask you in the initial order processing screen to submit the names of these elements before you can continue.

After you have defined the organizational elements, you will enter the information into the configuration screens guided by the IMG. Once you have entered all elements, you will have to complete the assignments. That is, you have to tell the system how the organizational elements (tables) which you defined (your company codes, plants, distribution channels, etc.) relate to each other. In the SAP system you do this by using the assignment functions of the IMG. Assigning elements is accomplished by entering the appropriate key of one element into a connecting field with the same name which is part of the other element. Figure 4–8 provides an example.

This example illustrates the two organizational elements and their respective physical tables in the SAP database. We have created the company Battco Inc. as an organizational element company code. The fields of this table include MANDT (client), BUKRS (company code), BUTXT (name of company), ORT1 (city), LAND1 (country), WAERS

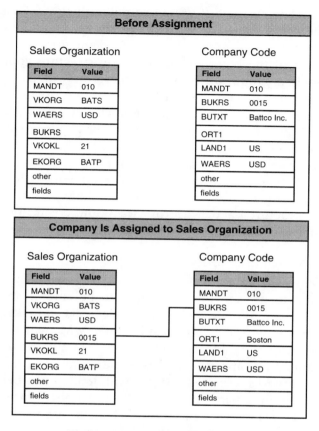

Figure 4–8: **Assigning elements**

(currency), and so on. The words in capital letters are German abbreviations. SAP contains a number of German words and phrases. It will be useful for certain team members to learn their meanings.

The company code we chose is 0015. As a sales organization, we created BATS which is in the field VKORG. In this table the field BUKRS is empty. This means that the sales organization BATS is unassigned. In order to record business transactions in the general ledger, we have to assign the sales organization BATS to the appropriate company code. We do this by entering the company code 0015 into the field BUKRS of the sales organization. Now the relationship between sales organization BATS and the company 0015 is established, and the SAP system can record sales transactions in the general ledger.

The entire SAP system works in this way. First, an element has to be created (a table record is physically created) and then the assignment takes place (the key of one element is entered in the connecting field of the other element). If you structure your company into five sales organizations, for example, you will have to go through the assignment screen of SAP for these two organizational elements five times. Depending on the complexity of your structure you might end up with a lot of work just to enter all organizational elements and assignments.

The definition of the organizational elements for your company and their relationships is what is known as the SAP hierarchy. The project team determines in this step how your company's organization is structured and, with this definition, creates or limits the flexibility of the overall system for your company.

Control Elements

The next configuration tables are the ones which define and control documents and the way data can be entered into these documents. They are referred to as control elements and take various appearances depending on the application (SD, MM, which stands for Materials Management, FI, etc.). The project team defines structures during the configuration which influence the behavior of the SAP system when a user works with it. The team will define what fields are visible on the screen for a particular user or what number ranges can be entered by a user. Dealing with the control elements is probably the most challenging part of configuring the SAP system.

As we have said, in R/3 a document is a transaction which is composed of master data and additional input. The composition is assigned a unique number by the SAP system at the time of creation to identify it throughout the existence of the SAP installation. The sales order contains customer information, item information, and shipping information, as well as the date and summarized data (totals).

In order for the system to assign a document number, display the right fields of the document for data entry, walk through the right sequence of screens, post the data into interrelated tables depending on the documents configuration, and so forth, many decisions have to be made and the appropriate selections done in the configuration settings. The programs and configuration tables used to configure documents or operations are called control elements. Let's take a look at the documents used in the sales and distribution area.

With Version 3.0 of R/3, SAP supports about forty different sales document types, such as, customer inquiry, quotation, cash sale, and standard order. Each document type can have line item categories. Line items are the products/services to which a price is assigned. The project team must choose among 70 line item categories. Each line item category can have schedule line categories. SAP delivers about forty schedule line categories with R/3. Schedule lines are used, for example, for delivery information of one line item (see Figure 4-9).

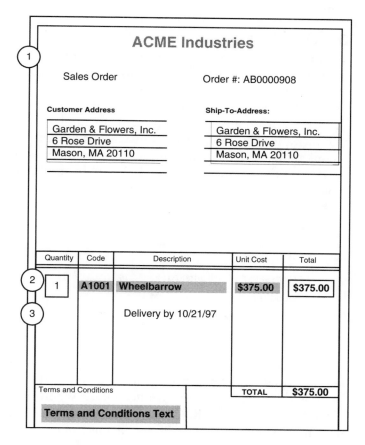

Control Elements:
1 Sales document type (e.g. quotation, standard order, returns)
2 Line item category (e.g. quotation item)
3 Schedule line category (e.g. goods issued from inventory)

Figure 4–9:   Control elements of line items

For each sales document type more than fifty parameters have to be set. In addition, the person who does the configuration has to choose from two to thirteen standard values depending on the parameter. For each line item category there are about thirty-three parameters and for each schedule line category there are about ten parameters to set. This illustrates the flexibility and the concurrent complexity of SAP R/3. It also explains why significant experience is necessary to configure the system rapidly without doing much research. All parameters need to be understood in order to assess their impact on the configuration.

Data Validation

Tables used for data validation are simple configuration tables used to maintain text information that appears as straight output only. This means that no calculations or any other manipulation of the information in these tables is performed in order to display the information on the screen or on a printed document. Examples of information stored in data validation tables are order reasons, billing block, and terms of payment. These tables only contain a key and an associated text which appears in the document. Table 4–2 is an example of a data validation table.

Table 4–2: Text validation table

Key	Text
01	Newspaper advertisements
02	Good service
03	Customer recommendation

The R/3 system uses the key in order to determine the text. The key is stored as a reference in other tables that the order relates to, such as the sales document header table. When the document is displayed or printed, the R/3 system uses the key to find the appropriate text in the validation table. Project teams can easily extend these tables to satisfy their requirements.

System Control

System control tables are used to configure the Basis System of R/3. This includes the ABAP/4 development environment, user authorizations, printer setup, and others. These tables are maintained by the system administrator.

4.6 Configuring an SAP Document

When configuring a document type there are often information items which are automatically generated on creation of a document. For example, the price which appears on a sales order during order processing is typically generated based upon the product/service item and certain pricing rules (e.g., applicable discounts by customer).

When a user creates a sales document in the SAP system he or she has to enter the following information into the SAP screen:

- Document type (e.g., sales order, quotation)
- Customer (sold-to party)
- Sales area (sales organization, sales channel, division)

From this data, the system determines all information (sales price, tax, material, etc.) which has been configured and is now generated during data entry. There are six types of information on a sales document which can be generated automatically:

- Price
- Tax
- Material
- Business partners
- Output
- Text

Price and tax information will be taken directly from tables. The material is determined at the line item level of the sales document. The system has to determine exactly which material has been sold. Material might be the original product or a substitute (like a custom version). Depending on the business situation (season, promotion, etc.) products might be sold in different configurations and for various prices. The configuration of SAP allows it to accommodate these cases.

The *business partner* is information about the parties involved in the transaction. These are typically the customer with the sold-to and ship-to information, the sales representative who took the order, or a prospective customer (in inquiry documents). The business partner is a special generic business object in SAP since it allows the configuration team to define a specific meaning for it.

Output information determines which forms to use when the document is printed, where to print the document, and so forth.

Text information contains all standard texts on the document like "Thank you for your business" on an invoice. Various ways of determining the right text for the document are possible.

In the IMG, SAP provides the necessary configuration tools to set the parameters. The parameter setting determines whether or not the system pulls out the correct information when a user creates or changes a sales document. In many cases the R/3 system has to go through many steps pulling data together from various tables and performing calculations in each step. All steps to determine the data appearing on the screen (e.g., the price) within a document during its creation or change are called a *determination procedure* in the IMG. The price determination procedure is one of the most complex within the SAP system, but also one of the most important ones. That is why we will explain the configuration concept of it here in greater detail.

In any business, the sales price is determined using a set of calculation steps based upon various factors. Figure 4–10 gives a simple example for the calculation of a sales price as it may appear on a sales order.

A company is selling a wheelbarrow to its customer Garden & Flowers, represented in our system by the customer number 4655. The wheelbarrow's list price is $375. The customer will receive a discount of 20 percent on the list price bringing the price to $300. In

Price Calculation			
Item	Description	Base Price	Total
Material	Wheelbarrow	$375	$375 +
Discounts	Customer	% Discount	
Customer Discount	Garden & Flowers, Inc.	20%	$ 75 -
Sales Price			$300

Figure 4–10: Sales price calculation

the SAP system the list price, the discount, and the customer are master data and are maintained by the business.

When the user wants to enter a material or a price, the system accesses the configured procedure to determine the data for the field on the screen.

When the user reaches the price field on the screen, the system executes the assigned price determination procedure and fills the field with the correct price considering the material, the customer and all the configuration parameters. The price determination procedure is assigned using the IMG at the time of configuration and is stored in the configuration tables. Once all information has been entered in the sales document, it is stored in the tables containing the sales transaction data (see Figure 4–11).

The determination procedure will select the correct price. When the project team creates the price determination procedure during the configuration, it assigns it a name, for example, ZVA004.

Figure 4–11: Storage of sales document information

The price determination procedure is a set of tables which the SAP system processes sequentially to generate the value for the price in the sales document. For the sake of explanation we call these tables PPTable (for price procedure), CTTable (for condition type), and ASTable (for access sequence) as shown in Figure 4–12.

The price determination procedure is assigned to the sales area, the sales document type, and the customer type during the configuration of the system. The project team will configure many price determination procedures since the way your business calculates the price for a material might vary depending on the customer, the sales organization, the distribution channel, and so forth.

In the price determination procedure the PPTable contains one or more rows called levels. The system processes all levels of the price procedure sequentially, going from the lowest to the highest number (level 10, then level 20, etc.). Levels are used to enable the system to calculate subtotals. During configuration, the project team can determine from

Determine the Price for a Line Item

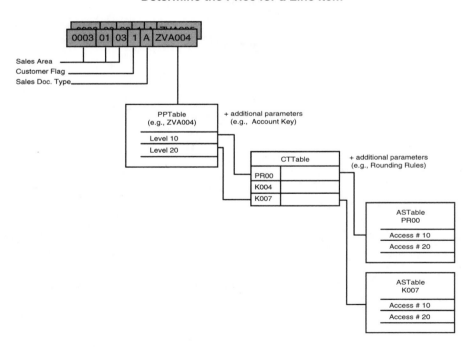

Figure 4–12: Price determination procedure

which level to which level price components shall be totaled before other price components (e.g., taxes, discounts) are calculated.

On each level several parameters can be set (for example, the account key for G/L posting). The condition type is assigned here to link the subsequent CTTable for processing. Once assigned, the system processes the condition type record in the CTTable first before moving on to the next level.

For each level within the price determination procedure an account key for G/L posting can be assigned. This account key is used by an account determination procedure to find the correct G/L account for the value. The account key can point to a revenue account or a rebate account, for example, depending on the condition type. SAP is delivered with over a hundred standard condition types which customers may use as templates. Examples of condition types are shown in Table 4–3.

Table 4–3:   **Examples of condition types**

Condition type	Master data	Calculation	Account determination
PR00	Price		Revenue
K007	Customer	%	Discount/surcharge
K004	Material	$/Qty.	Discount

Figure 4–13 shows how the SAP tables relate to our business example from above.

For every line in our pricing procedure SAP defines a level together with the condition type. The condition types are stored in the CTTable and maintained with a different function in the IMG. A condition type can be a price, a discount, a surcharge, or combinations of those and has direct impact on the determination of the G/L account to which the generated value is posted. The SAP system executes different calculations depending on the condition type. The project team can also configure its own condition types. To configure this table about thirty parameters have to be set. Also, the access sequence is assigned here (recall Table 4–3). The system processes the parameters of the condition type which are assigned to a particular level in the

Price Calculation				Price Determination Procedure ZVA004	
				PPTable (Pricing Procedure)	CTTable (Condition Types)
Item	Description	Base Price	Total		
Material	Wheelbarrow	$375	$375 +	Level 10 + parameters	PR00 + parameters
Discounts	Customer	%Discount			
Customer Discount	Garden&Flowers, Inc.	20%	$ 75 -	Level 20 + parameters	PR00 + parameters
Sales Price			$300		

Figure 4–13:   Relationship of tables

PPTable. Before the system jumps back to process the next level in the PPTable, the records of the access sequence are processed first.

The access sequence is a set of rows within the ASTable which is assigned to a particular condition type. Each condition type can have a different access sequence. Each row in the access sequence has a unique number because the SAP system processes these rows sequentially, going from the lowest number to the highest. Each row contains a set of field names which actually are fields displayed in the sales document during data entry. This is shown in Figure 4–14 as (1). In this example we use the fields VKORG (sales organization), VTWEG (distribution channel), KUNNR (customer number), and PMATN (material number). When a user creates or changes a sales document (e.g., a sales order) he or she has to enter information into mandatory fields, such as, the sales organization and the distribution channel. This means that by the time the system runs through the price determination procedure, the user already has entered these values into the fields. If not, the system returns with a procedure error.

The combination of values from those fields is used by the price determination procedure at that time to find the key for the correct condition record in the condition table (2). From here, the price determination procedure takes the condition record key and looks up the price or discount in the condition record table (3). The condition record is master data which is maintained by the user department using the appropriate SD application function. It contains a price in currency or a discount in percent, for example, depending on the material or service. See Figure 4–14.

Figure 4–14:   Pricing a sales order

The system runs through all rows within an access sequence until it finds a value in the condition record table. If it does not find any values, the system continues with the next level row in the PPTable. In this way it runs cascading through all levels downward into the condition types and access sequences in order to determine the value for the price field. If the price procedure does not find any valid values in the condition record table throughout the procedure, it returns to the user with the message that this combination of customer, sales organization, and material is not maintained, and, for this reason, the price cannot be determined.

The cascading nature of the price determination procedure also has impact on the performance of the system. The more levels and access sequences in the price determination procedure that are defined, the longer it will take the system to find and calculate the value for the sales document. While the system is generating the information, the online user has to wait. It is a good idea to keep the pricing procedure as simple as possible to avoid time delays for the user.

The SAP system comes with about thirty standard price determination procedures. It is highly recommended you use those as a template only and not change any of the parameters in those procedures. For customization a project team should select the procedure which closest matches the requirements and copy it using a name that starts with a Z. This letter is reserved by SAP for its customers for customization. If the project team gets stuck in the customization process it can easily create another copy from the template rather than having to copy the entire client 000 into the development client. This also means that a project team should never customize the client 000 since this is the general client template SAP delivers.

4.7 Working with Master Data

Users may have to maintain master data in the course of their daily work. The creation of master data is not part of the configuration process and should not be confused with it. As it was explained earlier, master data changes from time to time. Responsibility for the maintenance of master data is assigned to departments by defining the appropriate authorizations. Since master data is the primary source for transaction data, it has to be dealt with carefully. For example the purchase price for a material is master data. This price might be used for various purposes and is typically maintained by the purchasing department when the material is bought from a vendor. A change of the purchase price of the material in the master data file has significant impact throughout the business and might directly influence the sales price of a final product which has been derived from it. Another example is the creation of a new G/L account. When a new G/L account is created, the name, the account number and other important information is stored as master data in the system. Table 4–4 has examples for master data by area within a company.

Dealing with master data can become complex depending on the aspects of its use. Employees of different departments often have a different perspective on the same data. For example, the master data for a vendor consists of information which may be maintained by the purchasing department and the accounts payable department. The

Table 4–4: Examples of master data

Area	Master Data
Accounting	G/L accounts
Asset management	Asset
Controlling	Cost elements, cost centers
Materials management	Materials
Sales	Customer
Purchasing	Vendor
Human resources	Employee
Production	Work center, routings
Plant maintenance	Plant
Warehouse	Storage bins
Projects	Work breakdown structure (WBS)

responsibility to maintain the relevant vendor master data may also be split between these departments.

In the following example, we use vendor master data to explain the shared responsibility of departments to maintain it. Table 4–5 shows data items of the vendor master along with which department typically is responsible for the data maintenance.

Table 4–5: Data maintenance responsibility

Responsibility	Master data of vendor
Purchasing	Address, price per material, units, salesperson, minimum order quantity, purchasing group
Account payable	Reconciliation account in G/L, banks, payment method

SAP calls this a *view of the master data*, which depends on the department and the user who maintains that part of the master data. Accounting-related master data is referred to as the *central view* when maintaining vendor data through the purchasing function in the MM application. Responsibility for data maintenance can be shared or can be strictly separated depending on the authorizations given to the users in the different departments, as shown in Figure 4–15.

Figure 4–15:   Separation of data maintenance

The same principle applies for the sales side. A user who works with the SD application can take the central view and maintain the same information as he or she could through the accounts receivable application.

The most complex master data structure in the SAP system is the material master. When creating a material entry, the user has to step through several levels which determine what fields will be visible on the screen for data entry. This determination is derived from the material type (finished product, trading goods, raw material, service, etc.), the industry sector (pharmaceutical, mechanical engineering, etc.), and other characteristics.

The correct selection of material type is particularly important when creating an entry in the material master table. The type determines what you can and cannot do with the material. Raw materials, for example, have the material type ROH. Materials of this type cannot be sold by definition and for that reason the SAP system does not allow companies to maintain sales-related data (a sales view) for such material.

Table 4–6 is a list of views a user can take when maintaining material information. Every view has different data items depending on how the data item is used

Table 4–6: Views on materials

Views on material master	Dependencies	Sample information in view
Basic data		Material description, weight, volume, UPC
Purchasing	Plant, purchasing org.	Foreign trade, export licenses
MRP I	Plant, storage location, MRP profile	Material planning, lot size, scheduling
MRP II	Plant, storage location, MRP profile	Requirements planning, BOM requirements, repetitive manufacturing
Forecasting	Plant, forecast profile	Forecast model, periods, factors
Storage	Plant, storage location	Container, label, shelf life
Warehouse management	Plant, warehouse, storage type	Hazardous material, palletization, storage strategy
Quality management	Plant	Inspection, documentation, authorization
Sales	Plant, sales organization, distribution channel	Commissions, rebates, cash discount, minimum delivery, shipping data, packaging material
Accounting	Plant, valuation type	Valuation class, division, prices
Classification	Class type	Class
Work scheduling	Plant	Work tolerance, setup time, processing time, production scheduler
Costing	Plant	Standard cost estimate, planned prices, current price

The number of data items in the material master file is very large. It is the heart of the SAP system and should be configured through the integration group in the project team. Once it is set up correctly, the various user groups can easily use it.

4.8 Working with Documents

The term *working with documents* means to execute a business transaction within the SAP system. A document contains header and item information. The *header* contains the document number and context information for the transaction while the *line items* specify why the transaction takes place. A purchase order header contains the document number and vendor information specific to that purchase order, such as, the current vendor address, payment terms for this purchase, and the date of purchase. The line items specify the articles bought from the vendor. In a general ledger document (journal entry), the header consists of the document number, date, company code, currency, and the fiscal year; whereas, the line items are the account number and the posting amount. In the controlling application, the cost for operations is entered in line items under the controlling document header.

In areas which are production-related, SAP uses the term *operation* instead of line item. In production planning, an operation is a processing step within the context of a production plan for a specific product. In the plant maintenance application, for example, the equipment is maintained through operations which are performed by a service technician. An operation might be to change oil or replace the door lock.

The main source for transaction data within a document is the master data. The master data is retrieved from the master tables and manipulated by the SAP programs before it appears on the screen. The user has the ability to further change some of the data items (manual override) before he or she stores the set of data items as a document.

Depending on the configuration, either the SAP system assigns a unique document number or the document number is manually assigned by the user. Some organizations do not want to give up their numbering schemes since often they contain meaning to the people who are using them. Numbering schemes are often segmented so that each segment has its own number range.

Let's look at a simple example of this. Figure 4–16 shows an intelligent article number. The number is segmented into three parts which describe the article, the warehouse where the article is stored, and the production date. This type of numbering is often found in legacy systems since it combines the access key of the system to the article information along with the ability to identify the product on a report or screen.

Figure 4–16: Intelligent article number

Number ranges which contain meaning often cause problems, however, when parts of the number hit the range limit. In the above example the manufacturer of the article can have only ten warehouses since only one digit represents the warehouse identification. Perhaps when the system was created, no one imagined that the company could grow to the point where it would have more than ten warehouses. It is typically both expensive and difficult to change the system in order to expand the number range.

This is the same type of issue which is now causing the famous year 2000 problem where most companies and governments in the world have to expand their systems' capabilities to process four digits instead of two to indicate the year. SAP advertises its software as being year 2000 compliant, meaning that the software uses four digits for the year throughout all programs.

Relying on the idea that the structure of the number and its inherent meaning will never change proves fatal sooner or later. For these reasons SAP uses straight sequential numbering for documents. Document numbers can have up to twelve digits allowing for 10^{11} documents when using only numeric numbering. Customers may continue to use legacy manual numbering but will face growing problems as they outgrow their proprietary number ranges.

In contrast to legacy systems where one screen of data comprised one transaction, in R/3 transactions the user has to fill more than one screen of data. The number of screens a user has to go through and fill can be configured within limits. Once all data have been entered into all required screens, the user has to save the document in order to complete the transaction. The number is assigned at the time the user saves the document in the database in order to establish the access key.

Documents are linked in the SAP system and build processing chains. One type of document is used for a specific business event.

When a customer calls to obtain a quote, the sale representative uses the quotation document. The quotation can be used by the sales representative as the basis for creating the order document. The data for the order document can be copied by the SAP system from the quotation document if the user provides the quotation document number as a reference. In this case, very little additional information has to be entered. This saves much time and prevents errors during data entry. The amount of data carried forward into the next document in the chain can be configured by the project team, within limits. The limits are set by the SAP system itself.

In order to create a document, the user has to enter values into key fields. These are fields which have to be filled since they contain information vital for later finding data related to the document. Without them the document cannot be created. The keys then establish the assignment of the document to other objects in the system. In the case of a sales order, the user has to fill in the key values: sales organization, distribution channel, division, sold-to-party, and document type in order to create the header information

The user can store the document together with a raw material for each line item. When this is accomplished, he or she then receives a document number which is generated by the system. Figure 4–17 illustrates the derivation of the document number.

Document #		3000000456			
Key Values:	TA	0023	01	01	3776
Key Fields:	Document Type	Sales Organization	Distribution Channel	Division	Sold-To Party (Customer)

Figure 4–17: Derivation of the SAP document number

While the values for sales organization, distribution channel, and so forth establish the assignments to these objects in the system, the document number uniquely identifies the document as a whole. The key values allow the system to find related data which are not part of the document.

Before accessing a document, the user has to enter key information into the initial screen of that transaction in order to enable the R/3 system to find an entry. Fortunately a user does not have to remember all valid existing keys for the documents with which he or she is working. SAP provides a lookup function for keys which always works the same way across the entire R/3 system.

Since it is tedious to remember long codes, SAP allows the user to search for a document using match codes. Match codes are combinations of key values which a user can specify in order to find a specific document. The key fields which make up a match code are defined in the ABAP/4 data dictionary as match code objects. The number of key fields specified in a match code object determine all possible search paths to a particular document. Figure 4–18 illustrates the match code objects for sales documents consisting of thirty-six key fields, thus giving a large amount of flexibility when searching for a sales document.

Since it is not often practical to present all key fields to the user for input during a search, SAP defined match code IDs. These are subsets of a particular match code as shown above. The match code ID selects

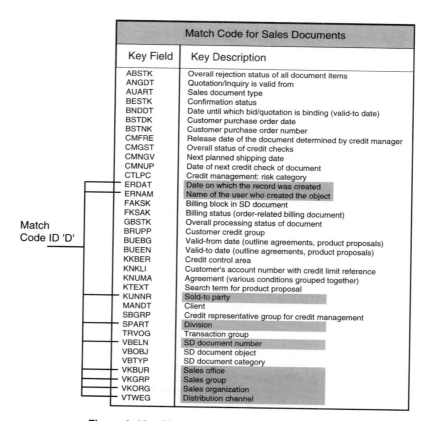

Figure 4–18:   Match code for sales documents

a certain combination of key fields and presents them in a screen to the user.

When a user wants to display a sales document and does not know the sales document number, he or she can put the cursor in the document number field and hit F4 on the keyboard. The user will be presented with a screen showing the match code ID key fields. Here the user can enter search criteria like customer name, sales organization, and so forth, in order to narrow the number of potential documents to be displayed. See, for example, Figure 4–19.

The match code screen allows the user to enter key values and other information related to the document the user is looking for. If the match code ID does not contain a key field which the user needs to narrow down the search, then he/she can select a different match code ID.

This gives the user many choices for the search. The search criteria can be further restricted by using logical expression like *greater than*,

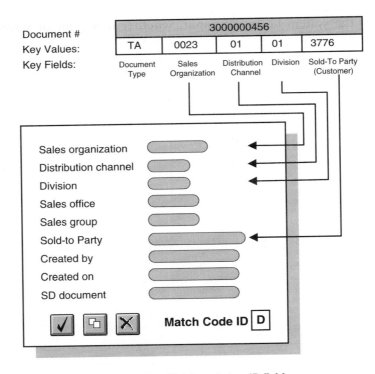

Figure 4–19:   Match code key ID fields

less than, or *equal to*. The SAP system produces from the match code search a short list of documents which fall into the search criteria. From this list the user can pick the right document for further processing.

SAP uses match codes throughout its entire system. Once a user becomes familiar with this tool, he or she can use it in any application. It is very powerful and flexible. Programmers can build custom match codes where users have special search requirements.

4.9 *Working with Reports*

Users will enter far more information into R/3 than they did into their legacy system. Legacy systems do not have a database with as many tables and fields to fill, and data entry for many fields is not typically enforced or validated. A third difference is that data in legacy systems is produced and stored with different levels of detail, limiting potential drill-down capabilities during reporting.

The user of the legacy system may feel it is very flexible because the system takes any input, whether it is right or wrong, and allows the user to enter less data. A user might find the R/3 system too rigid at the beginning because it rejects invalid data. In reality this protects the overall system and guarantees the integrity of data. This also makes the output very reliable and reconciliation of data unnecessary.

Within every application, SAP gives the user the capability to select from the menu standard reports which display information about a certain subject. These reports can be distinguished by the way they are produced.

Online reports are executed and produce results on the screen while the user waits for them. Batch reports are like online reports except their execution is scheduled for a later time. They are placed into a queue to wait for their execution. Whether the user should execute the report online or in batch depends on the runtime of the report itself. The runtime depends on the complexity of the report and the amount of data that has to be processed. Depending on your company's policy you should run the report either online or schedule it as a batch run at night. Running the report in batch at night defers processing to a time after office hours and reduces the workload for the online system.

The simplest report is a straight list which can be displayed on screen, printed, and/or sent via email to another user. Once the list is displayed, the user can read through it and print and/or send it with no further processing options. It's the type of list most users know about from their legacy system. In the A/R and A/P applications, R/3 supplies a great number of standard reports for the user to select under the Periodic processing | Information system menu. When using these reports, the user has to provide input parameters to narrow the resulting set of information. The list can also be downloaded to a PC for further data manipulation.

A more sophisticated approach is the type of report where the layout is configured by the project team. The user may select from different report display variants. A report display variant is a preconfigured layout where a different set of fields is displayed for each variant. It is like a view a user wants to take of an object of interest. In these types of reports the user can also restrict the selection of items he or she wants to appear in the list. A typical example for these reports is the general analyses under the reporting menu for purchase orders in the SAP R/3 system. The user can select the appropriate report display variant—whether he or she wants the report to list data by vendor or by material—and can determine the scope. The scope is the configured set of fields which should appear on the list.

Another feature is that a user can double-click on, for example, the purchase order number in the report, displaying the underlying purchase order document with all the details such as delivery schedules and conditions. From there, the user can explore further into related activities like purchase order maintenance. This branching from a list into related information screens makes the SAP report very powerful and allows the user to understand the source of the data displayed on the screen. In addition, data can be summarized directly on the report.

The interactive reports give even more flexibility to the user. These reports give users direct control over how the data appears on the screen. Users can directly change the sort sequence or the displayed columns, and generate graphics from the data, or branch into transactions related to the data on the screen. An example for this type of report can be found in the service management application under the contracts menu.

When displaying the list of contracts of plant maintenance objects, the user will get a report which has very little in common with a report from a legacy system (see Figure 4–20). The user can configure the report layout by choosing the columns in the report on the fly.

Columns can be hidden or additional columns can be displayed as part of the report. The report can be resorted, printed, or sent via email to a colleague. From the fields in the report, the user can directly branch into the maintenance transactions for the displayed data. When returning from the maintenance, the user can refresh the report and see the changed data immediately. A Gantt chart to visualize the run time of a contract on a timeline can be generated with a click of a button. The user can download the report data into an MS Excel spreadsheet or into a PC database for further individual processing. In this specific report the user can also branch into a multilevel list which allows the display of all the equipment parts within a functional location under a specific contract.

A report like the one described is very powerful. The report is a list of SAP objects which can be manipulated directly by double-clicking on a specific data element. When selecting a sales document number, the user branches into the maintenance transaction of the contract. When selecting the equipment number, the user branches into the maintenance transaction of the equipment. When selecting a customer, the user branches into the customer maintenance transaction. By branching into a related transaction when selecting an object on the report, SAP allows users the ability to circumvent the menus and step directly into the underlying function. This is very convenient

Contract List for Plant Maintenance Objects

Sales Document	Item	Sold-to Party	Sales Doc. Type	Contract End	Net Value	Equipment
31000044	000010	1164	AV	31 Jan2002	2,850	10000175
31000044	000010	1164	AV	31 Jan2002	2,850	10000176
32000002	000010	1152	WV	19 May2001	70,667	10000000
32000003	000010	1152	WV	29 May2001	78,710	
32000004	000010	1158	WV	03 Jun2001	16,695	10000001
32000005	000010	1158	WV	10 Jun1996	11,622	
32000006	000010	1158	WV	05 Jun1997	10,924	10000006
32000007	000010	1163	ZC	06 Jun2001	22,183	
32000008	000010	1163	ZC	10 Jun2001	17,565	10000006
32000009	000010	1158	ZC	11 Jun2001	14,128	10000003

Figure 4–20:   Creating an interactive report

111

for the user since he or she can return directly to the report from the maintenance transaction without stepping through menus and sub-menus.

Since SAP always stores data with the highest amount of detail, it produces a tremendous data store which can then be sliced and rolled up in any imaginable fashion. This is one of the big benefits of the SAP system—correct data at every level of detail with the ability for management to gain information about the status of the business instantly. As we have seen, SAP provides a number of tools to do exactly this.

Within this chapter we explained the basics of data modeling and configuration and how they impact the way the end user works with the SAP R/3 software. Understanding basic IT concepts becomes more and more important for business people since some roles are shifting from the IT department into the business departments. For example, a classic function of IT development departments was the development of custom reports. With the SAP R/3 software this function will be taken over by the business departments which develop reports on their own based on specific information needs without having to compete with other departments for resources within IT. Configuration of SAP is very complex due to the flexibility the package provides. Functions or processes which are relatively easy to configure can be also be maintained by key users in the business departments.

The greater challenge the business departments have is to develop and maintain the organizational integration of their business processes. Traditionally, IT's role was to coordinate the integration of software functions and, with this, the integration of business processes. As this role of IT starts to diminish, responsibility for coordination and proper hand-offs also shifts into the business departments. Thus, line business users must understand how their software tools work in order to apply them most effectively.

CHAPTER 5

Plan for Reengineering

5.1 What Is Reengineering?   114
5.2 The Many Faces of Reengineering   115
5.3 Reengineering Process   119
5.4 The Case of Hill's Pet Nutrition   120
5.5 The Role of Information Technology in Reengineering   122
5.6 Reengineering Is Organizational Change   128

We seem to have run out of words in the English language. Each new buzz word that appears is current for about a year before taking on ever broader meanings, until it is all things to all people. At that point, there is no word to describe the original concept. Reengineering falls into this category. A receptionist recently reported that "they" had reengineered the front lobby where she works. She now has new furniture, drapes, and artwork. This example takes the meaning of the word to new depths, but illustrates the way common usage overuses new words until they become meaningless. For this reason, we will start by defining our terms.

5.1 What Is Reengineering?

The term *reengineering* originally described significant changes to basic business processes that yield 50–100 percent rates of improvement. That is, it creates step function changes in such major corporate metrics as sales per employee, cost to produce goods, cost to administer the company, cycle times, inventory turns, and the like.

A *business process* is the group of activities required to produce something for a customer. The product development process, for example, may be thought of as starting with an idea and ultimately producing a working model to meet a customer need. Manufacturing is the process of taking raw materials and combining them to produce a product which is then shipped to the customer. In order management, a company takes in a customer order and ultimately receives money for the delivered product. When looked at from this perspective, any company, no matter how large, will be comprised of approximately eight to twelve core business processes. Each process is subdivided into smaller and smaller processes á la Frederick Taylor, the king of task decomposition. Due to the complex nature and interdependency of these processes, companies often define a portion of a process as their target for reengineering, simply because taking on the whole is an immensely difficult undertaking.

A few years ago, a computer manufacturing company decided to reengineer its customer liaison function. This process was carried out by a group of individuals located in the manufacturing facility, with the object of ensuring that orders were correctly configured and shipped to customers. While the redesign project team developed some useful recommendations to enhance the effectiveness of the process, it became clear it was such a small cog in a large wheel that effective change had to occur several levels above. At one point, the consultant asked the team how it could be more effective if it were located outside of the facility. The team immediately assigned, in theory, the bulk of its duties to others either in manufacturing or in the product line administration group. One man, realizing what he had just said, spoke for the group, "Oh look, I've just given away my whole job!" In fact, he had suggested the elimination of his organization and a reassignment of the essential duties to accomplish the function. This realization, of course, stopped the group cold. In this case, the team attempted to appeal to management to raise the scope of the project, but to no avail. When properly scaled, attention to a business process can pay rich rewards; however, the company has to be aware of the implications prior to defining a project. When the scale of the effort is too small, little can be accomplished beyond incremental improvements.

Business process activities are generally accomplished in a sequential manner. An extremely useful exercise in understanding a process is to follow its *paper trail*, even if segments of the process are no longer actually paper-based. At IBM Credit, senior management did this by asking the first person in the process to describe how an application for financing was processed. They proceeded from desk to desk, and observed each person performing his or her job regarding the financing request. This process is what Symmetrix, a management consulting and reengineering firm, calls *chasing the rabbit*. Symmetrix uses this phrase because the paper often goes down unexpected holes.

5.2 The Many Faces of Reengineering

The term *reengineering* was originally applied to such sweeping changes as a new sales and delivery mechanism that increased sales by 60 percent, reducing the cycle time to process an order from 10 days to 10 minutes; or a new manufacturing facility that delivered 10 percent more products in 25 percent of the space using 50 percent of traditional employees. Hammer and Champy in *Reengineering the Corporation* describe it as fundamental, radical, dramatic business process change. Davenport used the term *innovation* in *Process Innovation* to distinguish it from incremental improvements.

Symmetrix, one of the pioneers in business process redesign, believes strongly in reinventing only the critical business process. To make this 80/20 cut, it focuses on a deep understanding of the economic implications of the proposed changes. By so doing, it concentrates its efforts on the changes that will substantially improve the business.

The word *reengineering* today often implies changes from the most mundane to the most significant. The term most commonly used is *BPR* (business process redesign).

Not all companies wish to make massive changes to their business processes. The changes companies require are on a continuum from *streamlining* to *reinvention* (Figure 5–1). Streamlining a business process implies making incremental changes to the current process to increase quality, decrease cycle time, or reduce cost. Reinventing a business process means scrapping the current one and creating a process that truly meets the needs of the company. This usually requires a fresh look at the purpose of the business and the core competencies needed to serve that purpose.

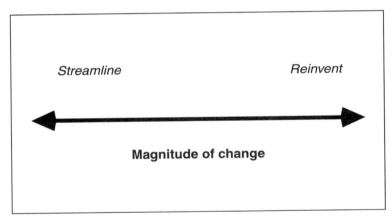

Figure 5–1:   Change continuum—streamline to reinvent

Projects are often identified at points along this continuum. While some companies engage in massive full-scale reengineering, many are content to solve major business problems that plague them today while setting the stage for future efforts. Thus many reengineering efforts, especially those that are combined with the implementation of R/3, are grouped somewhere in the middle of the streamline-to-reinvent continuum. As such, the effort may be a combination of solving old problems and creative redesign of selected processes.

Many companies identify changes that are meant to streamline their business processes and find that to implement change successfully, the project team will need to reinvent the corporate approach, and that change will have major implications for individuals, jobs, and structures. One organization made up of several divisions decided to centralize its accounts payable. On the face of it, management reasoned, centralization was not a change in the way the process operated, only a change in location. When the business owners considered the change, they realized its value, but identified numerous changes they would have to make in their operations to extract accounts payable. The organizational impact of the change pushed it in the direction of reinvention on this continuum.

R/3 is well suited to efforts anywhere on this continuum, although a company should develop a high-level design prior to the implementation of any project at the far right (reinvent) of this line.

There is another dimension worth noting—the scale of the change effort involved (see Figure 5–2). Projects at any point on the

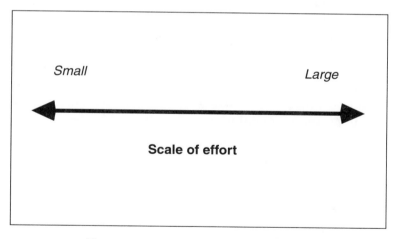

Figure 5–2:   Scale continuum—small to large

streamline-to-reinvent continuum can involve small to large portions of the business. The more departments and people involved in the change, the greater the scale and therefore complexity of the effort.

A company can decide to start a BPR project with a small element of the business for any number of good reasons such as:

- The project may be a pilot to test the changes prior to involving the entire corporation.

- The purpose may be to test a hardware or software product, or to gain the skills needed in the long term.

Though small, a project can have high leverage. SAIC (Scientific Applications International Corp.), a corporation made up of a number of companies, began its R/3 implementation in its commercial sector, using this as a pilot case for the rest of the company. It implemented financial accounting, a project system (basic data, planning, and forecasting), controlling, materials management, and human resources for a group of 100 users. Lessons that were learned were passed on to the next project, which had an enterprisewide scope.

Projects that include major sections of the company will be undertaken by those who feel they are ready for a larger scale project, or who feel the larger scale is essential.

We can align these two dimensions in a matrix (Figure 5–3) that will give us a sense of the size—and thus difficulty—of the undertaking. The indications of possible projects within each quadrant are examples to illustrate the concepts.

In the lower left quadrant, a company may decide to automate the cash application process, increasing the speed and quality of this relatively minor process. In the upper left quadrant, a company may implement a process to standardize the human resource services. In this example, the change will streamline the collection and delivery of information to employees across the entire corporation.

Moving to the lower right quadrant, a company may decide that its highest-leverage move is to completely reinvent the lead management process, a minor segment of the business.

And finally, the effort with the greatest amount of change across the largest portion of the company may be to implement a new business model across all the strategic business units, which might entail changing the order management, the sales and distribution, and the supporting financial processes.

Identifying the correct quadrant helps the project team and the executive sponsor choose the appropriate project process and appreciate the amount of change required. This knowledge will positively influence their success rate. This is a critical point that will be emphasized throughout this book. The larger the scale and the closer to *reinvent* the project is, the more attention must be paid to the critical

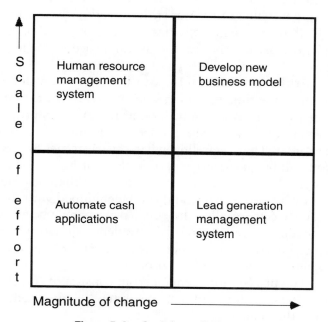

Figure 5–3:   Scale/magnitude matrix

success factors and the change management issues. Nothing will cause a project to fail more spectacularly than less-than-full attention to these matters.

5.3 Reengineering Process

How does one go about reengineering a business? The process will depend upon your goals.

If you wish to streamline a process, you will engage in detailed analysis of the current approach, seeking to understand, for example, the gaps in time between each value-added action. An order may enter the company and go to one department to be checked for availability; to another group to check that all the pieces of equipment being ordered actually work together; to sales, in the case of a custom order, to apply the correct price and relevant discounts; over to the accounts receivable department for a credit check; back to the order desk to identify the funding source; and so forth. Many companies have discovered numerous handoffs in their process and inevitably the customer order, in this case, waits for the next person to be ready to add their value to the paper. Eliminating those gaps when no value is added, by grouping activities together or by automating some or all of the process, will shorten the overall process time and usually lower the cost.

At the other end of the continuum, to reinvent a process you may spend some time to understand the nature of the current process, but you will quickly move to look at the business problem. It is useful to start, in the case of a sales order, with the end of the cycle—a satisfied customer. Understanding what the customer wants and needs from you will begin the process of looking at how your company processes orders. In this case, you may discover the customer is very familiar with your product line and can be equipped with the ability to send in orders electronically. The entire process may be automated with a few individuals available to solve problems, should they occur. The system should detect these exceptions early rather than waiting until the customer takes receipt of the product.

The process for reengineering consists of four basic steps: choose a process, understand it to the extent needed, redesign it, and implement the change.

Nothing about this simply stated process is easy. The entire process must be identified by executive management as essential to the company's success or survival; else why do it at all? Each step will take considerable deliberation, and will be broken into several components. Along the way, the ultimate recipients of the changes must be kept involved and informed. The process requires a combination of attention to detail, and creative out-of-the-box thinking, which is scarce.

For more information about the details, there are numerous books written about this process. All major and most smaller consulting firms have their own approaches and methodologies. A cursory examination will show most of their approaches to be well thought-out. The challenge inevitably comes in managing the process of change.

5.4 The Case of Hill's Pet Nutrition

Hill's Pet Nutrition is currently in the process of implementing nearly the entire suite of R/3 modules. Hill's develops, manufactures, and distributes nutritional products for companion animals. The company has been in the forefront of progressive change for many years. Their story is illustrative of the approach taken by many. It falls roughly in the middle of the scale/magnitude matrix shown in Figure 5–3.

In early 1994, Hill's convened a task force charged with identifying the information system needed for future growth. The executive team realized that the company's recent substantial growth meant it had outgrown the infrastructure that had supported it in the past. In particular, it was hampered by a lack of useful and up-to-date information. The company had originally used a mix of third-party and direct sales and delivery mechanisms. The requirements of the business shifted, and today Hill's deals more directly with its customers—veterinarians, pet store owners, and large scale retail outlets. The development of the products is, of course, focused on the pets and their owners; however, the distribution channel is through experts in pet care who recommend the product.

Because Hill's systems had been built to support the earlier structure, it realized its information system was a barrier to future growth. The company found it difficult to evaluate the effectiveness of marketing campaigns; the financials had to be pieced together; and its reporting systems didn't easily line up with its parent company.

The company has multiple manufacturing and distribution facilities. In the past, each functional area had been encouraged to utilize the systems that best supported its various needs—a best of breed approach. The multiple systems, however, were inefficient in their ability to talk to one another, and the company could not wait for that problem to be fixed by the various vendors. Instances of employees taking information from one system and hand keying it into another were discovered.

Hill's chose SAP for the robust, integrated nature of the system. Early on, the project team developed a mission statement and a set of guiding principles. It also identified four key enablers. This early focus proved to be extremely useful during the course of the project. The project team divided into several functionally based subteams to assess the current environment. These teams evaluated the processes in place and generated ideas that would provide significant improvements in the bottom line. They were rigorous in reporting back to the business areas that would be affected (most of the company). For example, they developed a communication grid to identify key business individuals and groups, along with team members responsible for sharing information and progress reports. They tracked who was to keep whom updated and when was the latest contact. (This tool helps the team to organize its one-on-one communications.)

With the results of the assessment and external information regarding best practices in hand, the team entered the design phase. It divided this process into two parts: first, divergent thinking, wherein it collected as many ideas as possible; and second, convergent thinking, wherein it collected the ideas that survived scrutiny and organized them into possible process tracks for the company. The teams developed event-driven flowcharts of the major business flows, and again they returned to the business owners for feedback. Using SAP experts, they mapped their ideas to R/3 to ensure there was a match and began to construct the pictures (literally covering the walls) of how the new business processes would look.

When asked if he would consider this true reengineering in the radical, dramatic sense of the word, Steve Whitney, Hill's Pet Nutrition's director of change management answered, "It's a matter of perspective. We're probably in the middle ground, but many of the changes seem radical to some of the business owners."

5.5 The Role of Information Technology in Reengineering

In the past several years, information technology has been recognized as a major force in reengineering. It is typically identified as an enabler of the changes required. That is, reengineers develop a conceptual approach to changing the business processes expecting that IT will make it possible. For example, reengineering the sales order process means providing a wide range of product, scheduling, customer, and financial information online to the order entry people. This is not possible without an integrated networked information system.

R/3 has changed the nature of the reengineering process in two ways: First, it provides a system that is integrated and based on best practices. It makes available, as a matter of course, many of the improvements that companies identify in the process of reengineering. In this respect, it serves as the technology *enabler* identified by most reengineers and writers on the subject.

Second, and more importantly, R/3 is a driver, not merely an enabler of substantive change. R/3 forces the implementation team to specify how it wants to organize and run the business in an integrated way at a detailed level. Many companies have not done this and continue to operate with mixed, and often conflicting organizational structures, processes, and standards. This lack of clarity and integration is often based on history or on culture. The successful implementation of R/3 requires you to define these elements.

R/3 will not actually conduct the reengineering for you, but will trigger you to do it for yourself. With this force in hand, even companies who simply wanted to replace their 20-year-old legacy systems that cannot communicate with one another, will do some level of reengineering *because of the structure of R/3 itself,* and probably more than they imagined was needed.

With the advent of R/3, information systems have, more than ever, become a major force in creating efficient and effective business processes. This change in status, from support function to key driver of change, carries with it several significant implications:

> - You must decide when to reengineer your business.
> - IS and user roles change—dramatically.
> - The IS implementation process changes—dramatically.
> - Implementation skill becomes a new, distinct competency.

When to Reengineer—Before, during, or after R/3?

When companies have chosen R/3, the question arises, "When should I do reengineering?" The approach you take will, of course, depend upon your business situation and thus your motivation for choosing R/3. To provide some structure for answering this question, let us return to the scale/magnitude matrix and add to it an indication within each quadrant of the type of approach that is most successful. (See Figure 5–4.)

In the lower left quadrant, the project team can successfully undertake reengineering during their implementation. The system will require identification of the structure, procedures, relationships, and standards, and will provide the latest in best practices for the modules selected.

In the upper left quadrant, the project team should engage in a BPR process to identify the problems and issues caused by their current processes (streamlining). It should define a high-level design for those changes, but move onto the system as quickly as possible to

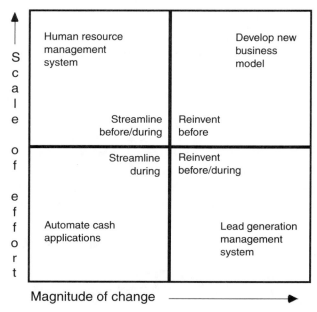

Figure 5–4: Scale/magnitude matrix, with indication of reengineering timeline

identify the details of the changes. Thus it will do reengineering both before and during the R/3 implementation.

In the lower right quadrant, the project team is tasked with reinventing one of its business processes. It should begin by designing in some detail the changes the company wishes to implement. As Hill's Pet Nutrition did, team members should assure themselves they have not strayed too far from what R/3 will provide; however, the focus of the effort will be to change completely the process in question.

Many customers report that having followed this approach, they were pleasantly surprised at how much of what they needed was supplied by R/3. In some cases, the system did not provide some functionality, and they were faced with the decision as to whether to eliminate it from their design or to provide a systems work-around that they would have to maintain in the future. The outcomes of these decisions depended upon the criticality of the missing feature. Many companies have accepted a somewhat less-than-perfect solution to save themselves the time and expense a "fix" would entail. A senior partner at CSC stated, "Yes, you will modify the business to fit the system." He goes on to say that this is usually only in minor cases, and the alternatives are generally not worth the trouble.

The upper right quadrant identifies efforts that are focused on reinventing significant portions of the business. These change projects will take significant time and effort, and are usually accomplished with the help of a consulting firm having expertise and experience in managing major changes. A successful effort here will focus on the dramatic, radical changes that are essential to long-term survival and growth. Major reengineering projects should be undertaken prior to implementing R/3. As in the lower right quadrant, some relatively minor decisions may be impacted when R/3 is implemented.

This matrix provides some indication of what type of process redesign to attempt under various circumstances. In any case, it will be counterproductive to delve too far into the details of the new business environment without understanding something about R/3. Several project teams reported they had to back up, in one case losing three months of work, because they had defined the new environment too tightly, and the work had to be redone when the R/3 implementation started.

What about reengineering *after* the implementation? Some companies assume they will implement R/3 without going to the trouble of a BPR project and address any needed changes after the fact. In cases where the corporate structure and processes fit well with R/3, this approach is possible, though not recommended. In cases where R/3 requires greater or different structure than the company possesses, the project teams will find themselves making decisions that will affect the company for years to come. Thus they may reengineer their company without the benefit of a structured process for doing so. We strongly advise against this approach, although one potentially successful example will be presented in Chapter 15.

NEC Technologies has implemented R/3 and is beginning a reengineering effort based upon the assumption that the system will provide the capacity to change whatever might need to be changed. It is too soon to tell whether this approach will provide the freedom to consider radical corporate changes.

Companies that have implemented R/3 in several different projects may find their staff has become very experienced with certain modules. There is so much richness inherent in R/3 that it takes considerable experience to even begin to understand what it will do. A representative of one manufacturing company stated that they were starting to use the system to suggest improvements they might make in the future. This approach is a creative use of reengineering after implementation.

IS and User Role Changes

We will address this topic in greater depth in Chapter 12; however, it is useful to note here that the change in status of IS that results from R/3 will mandate a change in the skills and attitudes of IS individuals. IS will become increasingly considered by line management as belonging to the business.

The difference in the words and concepts used by business people and IS has already changed dramatically with the introduction of R/3. Business people talk offhandedly about line speeds, data feeds, response times and good or bad GUIs. R/3 project teams are typically made up of more business people than IS people. A business person is the best choice to carry out the detailed customization, to make entries in the tables, and to define how the system should collect and report the data.

Correspondingly, IS people, more than ever, speak of the business process flow, and creatively introduce ideas to reduce costs or improve cycle times. The IS department is responsible for ensuring that the technical architecture is appropriate to the business needs and that it can expand as those needs grow. It must track interfaces, revisions, and system performance. The IS department will provide the individuals who will write the ABAPs. These are the customized reports and interfaces between R/3 and other systems, and must be written in ABAP, SAP's proprietary language.

IS Implementation Process

In the old days (five years ago or so), system users applied to their IS department when they wanted a new system or a fix to an old one. The business analysts and programmers assigned would confer with the business owners as to their requirements. They then began a long, involved process of analysis, design, coding, testing, and, finally, implementation. Assuming the business needs stayed the same during this process, the system was developed with little involvement by users. Usually those needs changed, delaying implementation and causing universal frustration. Eventually, the system would be unveiled, to cries of delight, amazement, or possibly consternation.

This process has generated an increasing level of frustration by business managers and executives who generally know little about the technical issues and who only want the pain to stop.

Enter SAP stage left.

R/3 demands a new process, one that takes far more resources from the user community than ever before. This book will describe that process in detail. It is typically user driven, is based on reengineering approaches, and will usually drive greater change than any system developed the traditional way. It also costs a great deal and may be delayed if insufficient attention is paid to the political and organizational shifts occasioned by the magnitude of change. The ability to successfully implement R/3 becomes a critical skill. The traditional IS systems implementation process must be augmented to reflect the broader focus and skill set demanded by an enterprisewide integrated information system such as R/3.

Implementation Skill Becomes a New, Distinct Competency

If everyone were to implement R/3, where would there be an IS competitive advantage? Companies have astonishingly varying degrees of success with implementation. The difference is in their abilities to address each of the critical success factors that we will discuss in the next chapter.

A company's ability to select a project it can support and manage, to appoint the right people to the various positions, and to walk the line between energizing people and calming their fears is no small task. More than ever, the ability to manage change must become the job of everyone involved, not just that of a consultant or the project leader.

Thus, successfully and skillfully managing change is the distinctive competency that emerges from the integration of reengineering and information technology. This skill has been required in the past, but has been ignored or given lip service. It is needed even more today and is still given less attention than required. Companies that recognize this factor will be more successful than those that do not. The issue is not the technology. Technology, as ever, is neutral. The issue is the ability to make creative use of that technology and to manage the massive change the system produces. Managing the change process with the same degree of discipline and rigor as the technology will begin to happen more regularly when organizations see this as a core competency and start to manage it as a competitive advantage.

5.6 Reengineering Is Organizational Change

Reengineering (and implementing R/3 is a form of reengineering) must be seen as a mechanism for organizational change. Teams that approach the implementation of R/3 with this mind-set are more successful than those that do not. With R/3 implementation comes the need to help employees cope with massive changes in their jobs, their organizational positioning, their decision-making processes, even their pay.

This is true at all levels of the company. It includes the order entry clerk who is now asked to make decisions that commit the company to a course of action, and the operations manager who discovers that his or her empire has grown or shrunk by 50 percent, and that he or she is required to manage in a vastly different way.

Pay attention to helping people see the potential in the redesign for themselves and for their company.

CHAPTER 6

Implementation Guidelines for R/3

6.1 The Case of Battco   130
6.2 Nine Critical Success Factors   133
6.3 Unique Aspects of R/3 Project Management   140
6.4 Implementation Time Frame   144
6.5 Implementation Approach Choices   145
6.6 Communicate to the User Organization   146

6.1 The Case of Battco

The director of Battco, the battery division of a major manufacturing company, was frustrated by an antique order processing system that constrained company growth. (*Battco* is a composite company.) It took two weeks on average to enter, process, and fill orders. Order entry people did not have rapid access to product information and delayed the customer on the phone while answering inquiries. This was reflected in the customer satisfaction surveys, and more seriously, resulted in lost orders.

The process was complex, sequential, and slow. For example, each order was first routed to the Finance Department to ensure the customer's credit rating was satisfactory. There had been occasions when the product was shipped to a customer, that in the meantime, had been identified as a cash-only customer because of its slow payment for prior orders.

The customer base was comprised mainly of large corporations who used the various energy sources in a number of often changing applications. To ensure the customers had ordered the right battery for their product, the Battco sales force had to be up to date on their customers' business needs. While they were attentive to this portion of their jobs, the information was carried in their heads, and hardly ever reached the order entry people. Thus, there were many instances when the Battco sales person advised his or her customer on the appropriate battery, but by the time the order was placed, that information was lost or inaccurate. The Battco order entry people relied on knowledge of prior ordering patterns and product lists and were unable to advise customers correctly.

The solution to these problems seemed to be an update of the order processing system and an interface into both the product and the accounts receivable databases. Jean, the Battco director, and Jim, her CIO, reviewed several software packages and selected SAP as their vendor. They anticipated some difficulties, realizing that the implementation would force them to rethink how they did business, but they felt the changes would be good for them in the long run. They presented their findings to the management team and the BOD, who concurred with the need for change.

While the software selection was a good choice, the management team underestimated the difficulties. What seemed simple on the surface became a difficult problem in managing change in a relatively stable organization.

The first challenge to be addressed was how the duties between the sales force and the order entry clerks should be reallocated. Battco decided it would serve its purposes to maintain a sales force who spent time with its customers and learned their business. They could be on hand when ordering decisions were made so as to advise and influence the customer to go with Battco products. In addition, the information they gained could go back into the product specification and packaging departments. The next question then arose—how to handle orders? Should the sales people enter them online using portables? If so, then the order entry job remained a relatively unskilled one of a clerical nature. This would not solve the problem of customers calling in with inaccurate product information which the order entry people could not correct.

The management team decided that it would be better to put the product, customer, and A/R information online, and train the order entry people to manage the orders. Some on the executive team argued that ultimately they could put the customer online and eliminate the sales force. For the majority, however, that was too radical a shift.

It was not until they were well into the implementation process that they realized they were faced with four more challenges, only one of which was a technical one. None of these problems was impossible; the difficulty was that no one had realized the extent of the changes in work flow and employee reskilling they would have to absorb.

First, they realized they had to convince the sales people to structure and report the information they had received about their customers' changing requirements. This went against the grain for the sales people who gained prestige by being the sole source of esoteric information regarding the newest directions their customers might take.

The second problem was in educating the order entry people. Battco had chosen to reduce expenses by hiring low-level clerical support for this function. Many of these people would not be able to make the transition the management team envisioned for them.

The third concern was on the part of the finance manager. She felt that the information for which she was responsible should not be made available to people who did not understand it or its security requirements. She was also concerned that a portion of her job, that of deciding upon the conditions of credit to be extended, would be out of her control.

Finally, Jim, the CIO, was faced with a major change in his technical architecture for which he was unprepared. He had been running on mainframes using a network that extended across the company, including several geographical locations. He had a hodge-podge of PCs and applications in the user community, and had only begun the process of training his people to understand the client/server environment.

Battco structured their project teams to include all points of view (Figure 6–1). They added the manufacturing VP because of the need for product information, because Jean felt it would strengthen the relationship between manufacturing and sales, and because, depending upon the success of this project, Battco planned to add several of the project management and materials management modules in the future. The project leader was a member of the steering committee and managed the progress of each of the four teams. Because of the changing interface between the sales force and the order entry people, two sub-teams were formed to ensure an equal representation.

This case serves to point out a number of elements that must be addressed completely and successfully—critical success factors for managing technological change.

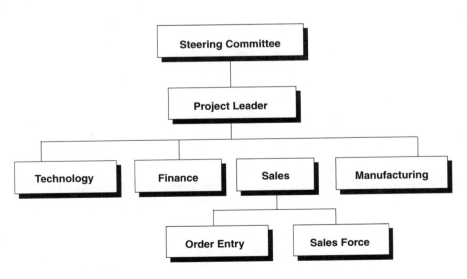

Figure 6–1:   Battco project team structure

6.2 Nine Critical Success Factors

Nine success factors emerge as critical to success in any major complex implementation. You will notice they are classics, and none is specific to SAP. However, in the current systems environment, and specifically in implementing SAP R/3, each takes on a greater level of significance than previously recognized.

Because the corporate stakes are so high in an enterprisewide implementation, there is very little margin for error. Each success factor requires a great deal of skill and a degree of support hitherto unnecessary. In the past, project leaders could do a good job on most of the factors, and eventually repair any lapses. Their project would be implemented, albeit with some difficulty. In today's changing corporations, failure to adhere to these nine rules of implementation will mean increased cost, a delay in bringing the system on line, or even outright failure.

Each of the nine success factors will be discussed in greater depth throughout this book. They are:

1. Understand your corporate culture in terms of readiness and capability for change.
2. Begin business process changes prior to implementation. Make the hard decisions early and stick to them.
3. Communicate continuously with all levels of new users in business, not technical, terms. Set reasonable expectations. Then communicate again.
4. Provide superior executive championship for the project.
5. Ensure the project manager is capable of negotiating equally between the technical, business, and change management requirements.
6. Choose a balanced (IS and business) team, and provide it with clear role definitions. Expect to shift to nontraditional roles.
7. Select a good project methodology with measurements.
8. Train users and provide support for job changes. Don't forget to train the project team.
9. Expect problems to arise: commit to the change.

Understand Your Corporate Culture

Both readiness for change and the capability to make that change must be present for success in choosing the right technical/business solution and implementing it. At Battco, the management team was ready; however, the employees in several departments were not.

There is a difference between seeing the need for a change and being willing to leap right into it. Time and increased understanding, particularly of the opportunity to change and the cost of not changing, will help increase readiness. The order entry people and some of James' IS people may not be capable of making the change, regardless of how ready they might be.

James Dallas suggests we ought to "identify potential disconnects by seeing if a project involves new people, new processes, and new technology."[1]

The more change involved, the greater the potential implementation challenge will be. Excellent project leaders prepare for a change effort by understanding the degree of difficulty they face. The Battco executive team did not realize until it was well into the project that it needed to address the four departmental issues that stemmed from a lack of readiness (sales force and finance) and capability (order entry and IS).

Place this understanding within the context of your company's risk profile to define your project approach. Be sure not to underestimate the complexity of the initiative.

Begin Process Changes First

Battco intends to use the R/3 implementation process to identify the changes in business processes and in skills and attitudes that must be made. While the company is willing to do this, it does not have a complete understanding of the implications of the changes it is adopting. It will be useful for Battco to engage in a brief business process redesign effort prior to engaging in implementation. In that effort, however, it will have to keep in mind the structure of R/3 so as not to identify some new requirement that is incompatible with the system. Most companies have discovered the advantages of understanding the packaged software and completing process changes in that context.

---

[1] James Dallas, "Maintaining Proper Communication, Focus Key to Information System Implementation," *Pulp & Paper*, Feb. 1995.

On this point, David Rittenhouse, director of strategic planning and information technology for the Polymers Divisions of Bayer Corporation, states, "Since one of the reasons we will extensively reengineer is that SAP R/3 will give us capabilities that we do not now have, it does not seem feasible to implement the reengineered organization prior to implementation of the SAP R/3 system. Our current IS simply could not support the reengineered organization while we waited for SAP R/3 to come on line. My concept is that we should design our reengineered organization concurrently with the design of the SAP R/3 system."

Others prefer to carry out a redesign project prior to implementation. In discussing the successful general ledger implementation, Steelcase project manager Diane Schwarz says, "We did the financial business process changes first, and they were significant. Then we used what SAP had to help firm up the design. Completing the conceptual level first was extremely helpful in our process."

Contrary to the indications of some writers, most managers we interviewed indicated they had completed some level of business process reevaluation or redesign in conjunction with the implementation of R/3. Many had set up specific decision-making processes, knowing that the choices would affect the company, sometimes significantly.

> *The broader issue is that enterprisewide applications require IT managers to nail down their business processes before they pick a package. Because software... is so tightly integrated, making modifications to core capabilities difficult, and oftentimes, extremely costly.*[2]

The cost and difficulty of changing the way a packaged system is configured after implementation is far greater than that of making the most informed decisions early.

Communicate

Rotman, Spinner, and Williams state that obtaining support from executives was a key criterion for their success. "This successful

---

[2] Robert Scheier and Wendy Pickering, "When Business Suites Don't Fit, Tailoring Can be Costly," *PC Week*, May 15, 1995, pp. 1, 112.

communication to upper management addressed their concerns, and provided a forum for their input and direction."[3]

Employees at all levels who are affected by the new system need to be informed by a rigorous communications program. The key to success in this effort is repetition and accurate setting of expectations.

People need to be told several times about a change. The old saw applies: Tell them what you are going to tell them, then tell them, then tell them what you told them. Expectations must be managed. If they are set too high, people are bound to be upset, frustrated, and disappointed by the results. Set too low, employees will be surprised by the extent of change and will find it difficult to adapt. Either case will slow their ability to accept and fully use the system.

Provide Superior Championship

No successful (or unsuccessful) project manager will fail to appreciate this success factor. However, numerous executives can be supportive of a project, yet fail to provide real hands-on leadership and commitment. The difference between informal support and active leadership can be the difference between success and failure. Chuck Norlander, director of human resources for Monsanto, says, "You have to develop a steering team. You have to teach them change management and the process of redesign and integration. Once they have been through a project, they accept the need to learn these about these topics."

In the case of Battco, the management team is prepared to be personally engaged in the process. It has been convinced by its early analysis of the situation that the company must change, and that the change will be difficult. Its goal is to shorten the order processing time to two days at most, and to provide superior customer service. Those two goals alone will significantly increase Battco's profitability.

Ensure the Project Manager Is Capable

Managing complex large-scale change is best done by blending the organizational and technical solutions in a process of integrated change.[4] One approach to this blend is inherent in the skills of the project manager and subsequently the entire team. The successful

---

[3] Laurie Rotman, Margaret Spinner and Julie Williams, "The Draper Laboratory: A Team Approach to Building a Virtual Library," *Online,* March/April 1995, p. 23.

[4] Nancy H. Bancroft, *New Partnerships for Managing Technological Change,* John Wiley & Sons, New York, 1992.

project manager integrates concerns that would otherwise fall between the cracks, and communicates with all those involved. These apolitical issues require a sensitivity to the three perspectives—technical, business, and change management.

Integrated change means that these three aspects are viewed as a whole, wherein a change in one affects each of the others. In the past, technological change, business change, and organizational and individual change were viewed as disparate elements. Each could (and usually would) trigger a change in each of the others. These changes have historically been carried out sequentially. With the advent of enterprise-wide integrated information systems (R/3 being the market leader), integrated change is not only available, but required.

The result of integration in managing change means that projects are far more complex than ever before. Thus, the project and its leader must deal effectively with new technology, new business processes, and changes in organizational structures, standards, and procedures which affect the jobs of individual employees—all at the same time. Unless the project leader is sensitive to the impact of each of these elements on the project as a whole, he or she is likely to get caught by the sometimes conflicting requirements.

Choose a Balanced Team

The systems environment of today is complex. The hardware/software package is increasingly seen as a utility, similar to the network. Customizing the software to fit the requirements of a particular function of the business will become the responsibility of the user. No longer are reams of paper produced when an inquiry function will suffice. One user manager noted, "There is a shift in user responsibilities to include the former IS responsibilities. The doer of the job is the expert in the process."

The majority of project teams in the companies studied were comprised primarily of individuals from the business departments to be affected. They configure the systems, using the tables and functions available, to run their business in the new way. After implementation, they take on the responsibility of maintaining the systems should changes occur. Thus, if new products, pricing schedules, or even sales organizations appear, they will modify the appropriate tables.

At Battco, the team (as we saw) included members of the IS, order processing, manufacturing, sales, and finance departments. In addition, the company hired an outside consulting firm to provide project leadership support (they will maintain control) and experts in the selected modules of R/3 and in ABAP/4. The IS members of the team were selected from among the best Battco has available, to ensure they can learn the system and the new language as quickly as possible. They were the first employees to be sent to R/3 training.

Select a Good Methodology

You may not follow every step in the process you choose, but it is extremely helpful to have a road map. Project leaders must set out clear, measurable objectives at the beginning of the process, and review the progress at intervals. Realize that client/server projects are systems integration projects. This means that they are complicated and require attention to the implications of the slightest change. In R/3, with 70 interacting modules, you never know if a table setting is disrupted when changing another unless you document all the interfaces.

Train Everyone

A new system inevitably means new ways of operating. In Battco, the requirements of the client/server SAP R/3 environment have initiated a project to reengineer the business process. Users must be informed as to the business needs for such change as well as "which keys to press when." Battco intends to begin the communications effort early and to repeat the essential messages often. It also believes that it will need to involve the human resources manager in the process, since the jobs will change so radically. He has already started an analysis of the current skills in sales and order entry so that he will have a baseline. He will develop a template for the new skills as they are identified. With those two documents he will begin to analyze the gaps and identify change processes to close them. These will not just be training, as important as that effort is. He realizes that changing the nature of a job means he will have to provide supporting management practices such as good job definitions, rewards and recognition, and a reevaluation of the pay schedules.

Of course, the project team also needs to be trained in the technology, the business, and such change management issues as basic communication skills, decision making, and the stages of team development.

Commit to the Change

Experienced project leaders say they succeed because of their ability to persevere. John Morrison, Director of Global Systems at Steelcase, cautions new implementers that they need consistency and determination. "You must stay the course," he says, "This is how we expect to support the business for the next 20 years."

Sinneck reports that one should expect problems. He says that nearly 75 percent of his respondents had to change their organizational structure to respond to issues.[5]

In a project of the scale and complexity generally found with R/3, it is natural that problems will arise. The technical architecture may not be adequate, the system may not have been configured to accomplish some set of tasks, the requirements or scope may change, the users may revolt. It takes management persistence and consistency to maintain focus on the project goals and to overcome all obstacles.

And you never know what might happen. When IBM's Storage System Division implemented R/3, it did so to provide online pricing, ordering, shipping, and repairs on a global basis. The project manager, Judy Johnson, reported that shortly after the system was linked to IBM's Asian offices, she received a phone call in the middle of the night. The caller was quite upset because the communications cable had been "eaten by a shark." Underseas cables line the ocean floor and are sometimes torn up by trawlers, as was the case in this instance. Luckily for IBM, there was a duplicate cable, since repairs were estimated to take six weeks. But the story did not end there: in the middle of the repair cycle, Judy received another panic call—"A shark has eaten the other cable." In fact, the duplicate cable received the same treatment as its cousin. Now cut off completely from the Pacific Rim, IBM had to resort to satellite communications to provide the 24-hour service they required.

The special character, complexity, and requirements of SAP require diligence for all the critical success factors; there is little tolerance for mediocre performance. The success rate for implementing R/3 will increase dramatically when all these factors are taken seriously.

---

[5] Michael Sinneck, "It's All in the Implementation," *Information Week*, Dec. 12, 1994, p. 87.

6.3 Unique Aspects of R/3 Project Management

From our research, we also identified several guidelines, unique to the implementation of R/3, that must be followed:

> 1. R/3 is not a silver bullet.
> 2. R/3 does not support loose boundaries or gray areas.
> 3. Customize, don't modify R/3.
> 4. Be sure your business fits within the limits of R/3's flexible tables.
> 5. When you've completed the R/3 training, you are only at the beginning.
> 6. The project team must be both visionary and detail focused.

R/3 Is Not a Silver Bullet

It is costly and time consuming to become proficient. Some tips have been identified by prior implementers. Train your own people and allow them the time to learn by experimentation. In this environment, it is better to set up a "sandbox" and allow people to explore the ramifications of setting various parameters in the tables. They must understand what will and will not happen to certain elements. If you set up a system one way, you may not be able to access some data in the way you want. There are hundreds of choices to be made, each one having complex implications.

Training plus experimentation will give your people what they need to set up the system to accommodate your needs. Don't forget that it is not just IS people you need to educate. The project team members will include a large number of end users, preferably at the managerial and supervisory levels. They need to understand in elaborate detail exactly what the system is designed to do.

R/3 Does Not Support Loose Boundaries

You will need to define—or redefine—your business prior to implementation, and it may be difficult to make all the correct decisions at once. It will be necessary to spend time either prior to beginning the R/3 implementation process or in the first few phases to understand the structural and policy decisions that must be made. In the case of a relatively simple company (Battco, for example), those decisions will be obvious when you have identified in detail the way you want your business to operate. When dealing with an international company having multiple divisions, products, and cultures, it may take some time to get the necessary approvals.

Business process scenarios are the most efficient way to test your hypotheses prior to implementation. Unless you have the expertise in-house, it is likely to prove useful to hire a consultant who can assist you to develop the business flow to fit your vision and the R/3 structure.

Customize, Don't Modify

You will change your business to fit within the R/3 framework. This is not as dangerous as it might sound. R/3 provides the ability to accomplish at least 80 percent of what you want according to the companies we surveyed. There are thousands of choices to make. It may take some experimentation to develop a way to achieve your business process objectives, and therein lies the art of R/3 configuration. Complexity equals power.

Experienced implementers say they think of R/3 as a utility that they must customize to ensure it meets their business requirements. Many companies choose SAP because they want to avoid expensive application development for their basic business processes. The successful implementer will find a way to accomplish what is needed within the structure of R/3. Only in special cases will unique software need to be written.

Team members at SAIC, for example, found that the R/3 tax tables did not meet their stringent requirements. After some investigation, they discovered a third party vendor (AVP) who is able to provide the required software already written in ABAP/4. This module will become an integral portion of the system.

Autodesk is in the process of working with SAP to produce a product distribution module that will meet its special needs. It uses a process called *random box shipping*. Their product (CAD/CAM software packages) is built, tested, and placed in a warehouse. Rather than being assigned to a customer up front, it waits for assignment at the end of the sales order process. The product is placed on a conveyer belt. Warehouse people sweep the bar code with a wand, and the system assigns the box to a customer. The shipping label is printed and immediately placed on the product. R/3 does not at this time support that process.

Autodesk has written its own software to take care of the limitation for the time being, but wishes to replace that coding when a version of R/3 contains the required change.

Except for these two approaches (finding an SAP-approved vendor or working with SAP to develop the software you need), it is strongly suggested you make limited or no changes to the R/3 software. The term suicide has been mentioned in connection with making a substantial change. It may work in your current version, but you have set yourself up for a major maintenance problem with each new revision of the system.

Be Sure You Fit within R/3

R/3 may not support the business structure or information architecture you need. It is a centralized, top-down, structured approach. It will work well if you are able to operate within these limits.

One of the major airplane manufacturers is concerned about the system because it does not track serial numbers on parts within its product—it does so only on the product itself. The FAA requires documentation of every part within every assembly. Another company considering R/3 may decide against it because it does not provide the flexibility of distribution of its products to locations within locations, and cannot run a true 24×7. R/3, like most systems, needs to be down for regular preventive maintenance (PM) and upgrades, although SAP has made significant progress in this area. In this company's business, the third-shift hours (when systems normally receive this attention) are frequently the busiest. And several companies decided against R/3 because the structure did not fit theirs. They felt they would have to give up too much of their competitive advantage should they implement it.

Of course, many companies argue that no one provides everything, and an 80 percent fit is better than what they will get elsewhere. Plus the advantage of a single, integrated vendor is not to be overlooked.

Companies who have successfully implemented R/3 are not surprised by areas of misfit. They have studied the system in detail and matched it against their business needs. Being aware of any potential problems, they adequately plan to solve them.

Training Is Only the Beginning

Even though you will send your people to R/3 school, they will not understand everything about everything. In fact, even SAP acknowledges that no one can be an expert in all modules; the system is that complex.

Depending upon the modules you choose to implement, the basic class time will range from four to six weeks for each person on the project team. To gain a base level of understanding of the production planning module, the team will need six weeks; for the sales and distribution module the total time will be around four to five weeks. The technical people who will be required to program in ABAP/4 will need additional training. A consulting partner at one of the major consulting partners to SAP, a veteran of over twenty implementation efforts, states that it takes a year to fully train a person in how to configure a major module. That total includes the from four to six weeks of training plus active participation in one full project cycle.

The best way to make use of this training time is to install the system when the team starts its training. As team members complete portions of the training, they can then log onto their home system and explore using the concepts they have learned. This approach allows team members to experiment before moving on to the next set of concepts. Adult learning theory shows us that without a way to practice, the vast majority of learning will be lost in a very short time. The ability to experiment will lock in the learning, and allow the trainers to build on that knowledge in the next training session.

Even with the best training approach, team members will need to continue to experiment in their own environments to fully appreciate what the system will and will not do. There are multiple ways to achieve the same result. Each one, however, will close off certain other possibilities. Thus, the team members must try multiple options before deciding on the configuration that works best for them.

R/3 is like a vastly interesting logic game. If you choose to enter the house on the ground floor you have cut off your ability to explore the grounds (because the door has slammed shut and is locked from the outside). If you enter the elevator, you can only go up or down one flight, while going down the dark staircase (providing you have found the battery to light the lamp), you will find the locked doorway halfway between floors. Assuming you are not killed by the troll while looking for the key, this doorway will lead you into a magnificent cavern that has many corridors to explore. And so it goes. Choosing one option will block the ability to choose others. However, if you are successful (as many have been) in understanding the various combinations and in mapping out the territory, you will find yourself in that magnificent cavern and begin to appreciate the beauty of the complexity.

Visionary and Detail Focused

Ideally, you should choose project team members who are in management or supervisory positions. They must understand the details of the business segment (accounts receivable or order processing and the like), and also must be able to take the longer and broader view that will enable them to contribute to the definition of how the business might be. Especially if you are combining BPR with the customization of R/3, they will need to *zero-base* the organizational structure and processes-reinvent them in the context of R/3.

At the same time, these individuals must roll up their shirt sleeves and experiment with the system parameters to develop the screens and table entries that will best meet the new business requirements. Some customers of SAP have asked their consultants to take on this task; however, this approach is not generally successful. The consultants cannot possibly understand their client's business and culture in sufficient detail to provide exactly what is required. You will save time and money by letting your project team members know that they will be involved at the table and script level from the very beginning.

Involving your team members has the added advantage of developing a core of people who will be able to understand in detail how the system uses the configured business entities. They are likely to become the leaders of the new way of doing business. If leaders are not chosen in the beginning, the team members may find themselves searching for a way to fit back into their old organizations.

6.4 Implementation Time Frame

The average implementation for R/3 is nine to twelve months. A few companies have implemented in four to six months. This can only be done if the customer chooses a *vanilla* systems approach, wherein there are no changes to the system structure, and the table and function choices are primarily the standard ones provided by the software. In this case, there would be few interfaces and reports to add.

Computervision, for example, implemented R/3 in 4 1/2 months. This rapid deployment was possible because the project sponsors committed to making all decisions within 48 hours. The project team was empowered to make most decisions immediately; however, some decisions crossed organizational lines or impacted corporate policy and necessarily took longer. SAP was encouraged by the mandate to make decisions quickly, but did not believe it could happen. Computervision, however, took its promise to heart and delivered on it. All decisions, no matter how major they were, were agreed to within the 48-hour time frame.

At the other extreme are the more complex corporations, generally (but not always) international behemoths that have to make far more difficult decisions regarding corporate standards or strategy. Implementation in such cases has taken up to eighteen months. R/3 will serve as the vehicle to force such decisions if you have not already contemplated them.

Implementing R/3 is a complex endeavor. It will, for many companies, take longer than anticipated. Murphy's Law (if something can go wrong, it will) often comes into effect.

6.5 Implementation Approach Choices

The first two choices any company must make upon choosing R/3 are which modules to select, and where to implement them. Most corporations choose either a suite of modules (not the entire system) for a major business segment, or implement all modules for a strategic business unit (SBU). These companies then move onto the next SBU, or add functionality. This phased approach has the advantage of reducing the risk of an incorrect interpretation of the business situation. If accounts payable is implemented incorrectly, vendors can wait a week or two for the system to be corrected. If, on the other hand, your order processing is your most critical corporate process, you will want to proceed more cautiously.

Choosing to implement all modules for the entire company is generally termed the *Big Bang* approach. Avoid this approach unless it is imperative for your company. It is a risky strategy. Regardless of the rigor of the testing at both the unit and integrated levels, inevitably something will go wrong. It took one manufacturing company four attempts to complete the monthly closing process to smooth out their general ledger implementation—and theirs is not an unusual situation. People need time to understand and assimilate change even when they have had the appropriate training and time to experiment with the system prior to actual cutover. Processing a real order or doing an actual monthly closing is vastly different than conducting an experiment.

The disadvantages of the phased approach are the number of interfaces that must be discovered, programmed, and tested. An IS manager at a major retail manufacturing company estimated he could have implemented in half the time or less if he not had to program interfaces to legacy systems at every step. This company is working on implementing an order management system that includes billing. They have decided to implement one SBU at a time. This may seem unusually slow and risk averse, but their order management process is critical because of the number of complex custom orders they receive.

SAIC combined these approaches by choosing one of their smaller companies (100 users) and implementing all the appropriate modules at once. This *Small Bang* or pilot approach gave them the expertise to bite off a bigger piece, and they are currently in the process of implementing purchasing, accounts payable, and asset management across the corporation, a change that will affect over 15,000 people.

6.6 Communicate to the User Organization

Regardless of how many people from the user organization are personally involved in the project, the vast majority of end users will know little about the new system. Invariably, when surveyed, people say they did not know about a change, or they knew something was happening but did not understand it. This is true even in organizations that spend considerable time and money on various communication vehicles. People are busy with their jobs and, if they sense a change, especially one that might affect them, they will typically assume that the change will be detrimental or at least difficult to master, and unconsciously reject most information that is given them.

As we said before, it takes at least three occurrences before people begin to hear the message. Of course, management must be prepared to deal with those who have heard the message and have jumped to a negative assumption regarding the impact upon them personally. In situations where there are substantial changes in the way work is done, employees will have grave concerns about their jobs. Managers and supervisors must be told what messages to give and how to help people make the transition.

Implementing R/3 will often mean such changes in work process. In the case of Battco, the order entry people will do all their work online. They will need to do inquiries of product availability and customer credit worthiness, for example, rather than relying upon reports. They will need to take personal responsibility for each order to ensure it is complete and accurate, rather than simply recording what the customer requested. They will need to question the customer as to the eventual use of the product, to be sure it is right for the job. These are significant changes in work processes and skills required. The communication vehicles and the supervisors must inform people about the changes and the implications of them, but must also provide reassurance that training will be given and that everyone will be helped either to adjust or to find a new job. Of course, you can only say this if it is the truth. There is no point in lying—people can spot it a mile away.

The communications effort generally consists of publications, presentations, and other vehicles. These other vehicles could be online messages, brief blurbs in the company newsletter, a video playing in the lunch room, or sky-writing over the company picnic. Use whatever works.

The communication vehicles should cover the following points:

- Overview and rationale for the project.
- Explanation of the business process changes.
- Explanation of the implications of these changes
- Demos of SAP R/3.
- Demos of applicable modules if possible
- Briefings of change management issues.
- Establishment of individual's contact person.
- Testing of scripts and scenarios as they are made available.
- Periodic updates.

The messages should come from the highest-level project sponsor, as well as the management chain responsible for the individual. When the sponsor is an enthusiastic supporter of the change, the individual understands the company is serious, and is less likely to believe the new system will go away if only he or she can wait it out. Once he or she believes it is truly going to happen, the individual will need to hear from his or her direct supervisor an explanation of how it will impact their work group. A key message to be delivered will be the type and schedule of training available.

People will need to see the system and to play with it as modules become available. These hands-on experiences, along with project updates, will help to make the change real.

The communication program, training, and change management efforts are frequently those which receive the least amount of attention and are the most critical to success. Companies that do a superior job with these programs will set their course for the future with a winning tone.

Steps in the Process: Where Are the Pitfalls?

CHAPTER 7

Phase 1: Focus

7.1 The Steering Committee   152
7.2 Identify R/3 Modules   154
7.3 The Project Leader   156
7.4 Structure the Project Teams   157
7.5 Integrate the Team Findings and Decisions   159
7.6 Set Objectives   161
7.7 Develop Guiding Principles   162
7.8 Develop a Detailed Project Plan   163
7.9 The Case of Agrium, Inc.   164

You may be asking yourself, "How did I get into this?" Or perhaps you are excited by the advantages that will accrue by the implementation of R/3 and are asking, "How can I make this project be as successful as possible?" In either case you have just stepped onto the R/3 roller coaster and you are in for the ride of your life.

R/3 is generally sold at the executive level. Board of Director members and executive management love the advantages. They are willing to allocate the investment to implement R/3 even if they don't understand all the difficulties that their teams may eventually encounter. The benefits are simply too significant to overlook. Implementing R/3 will reduce the cost to maintain 25-year-old legacy systems. Each time these systems need to change, the cost is huge, and since there is an average backlog of two years, the time frame is long. In addition, these elderly systems may still take weeks to provide a good picture of the business situation. There are good reasons to implement an enterprisewide integrated system.

The question is how best to focus on the immediate problem at hand. The phase 1 task list is as follows:

- Form the steering committee.
- Identify the R/3 module.
- Appoint a project leader.
- Structure the project teams.
- Integrate the team findings and decisions.
- Set objectives.
- Develop guiding principles.
- Develop a detailed project plan.

Start by naming a steering committee that will oversee the project. You already have an idea of where you want to implement first; usually it is the area that caused you to call in SAP in the first place.

7.1 The Steering Committee

Steering committee members must have clout in the organization and a stake in solving the business problem. The team must include a high-level executive sponsor who will take a personal interest in the timely and successful implementation of R/3. Other members will be the executives responsible for the divisions or departments that are assumed to be the targets for the eventual implementation. The project leader should be a committee member as well. The membership may change somewhat after the team has decided which modules will be implemented in which companies or divisions.

Some senior executives who have gone through an R/3 implementation feel that the steering committee must receive a certain amount of training if it is to be effective. They believe that steering committees don't always understand the depth of the changes required. Senior executives rarely concern themselves with the details of behavior and skill changes, infrastructure changes, and the implications of integration, for example. They hire others to deal with these details. Difficulty arises, however whenever the executives have certain expectations regarding cost and time to implement and are not able to ask the right questions.

Chuck Norlander, director of human resources for Monsanto, believes a steering committee must understand the issues of change management, the process of redesign, and the outcomes of integration, in addition to the overview of the system. In his experience, those who have been involved with such a change accept this, and those who are uninitiated do not.

The steering committee's first task will be to plan and scope the change appropriately. How large a chunk they bite off will be determined by their knowledge of the corporate culture and its readiness and capability for change. The purpose of this scoping is to establish the boundaries of the project; to determine which entities will be inside or outside the mandate for change. Most companies prefer a phased approach to implementation.

Other companies have another philosophy. NEC Technologies, Inc. implemented nearly the entire suite of modules in eight months. This ambitious project was based on strongly held company principles inherent in concurrent engineering. They identified a small team of empowered high-level users and co-located them in a *war room*. The team took a process orientation and was assigned a strong, active team leader. Team and outcome performance were directly linked to tangible rewards. The project methodology collapsed tasks that are traditionally sequential. The design and implementation of the business process redesign was completed concurrently with the configuration and prototyping of R/3 and with the definition of training, interface, and conversion requirements.

7.2 Identify R/3 Modules

Assuming that the *Big Bang* is not for you, the steering committee will need to decide exactly where the system ought to be introduced, and which modules will be used. They may choose a pilot operation and implement some or all of R/3 as a way to gain the experience needed. Once people have been through one implementation, they will be more efficient in the next implementation. For example, if the order management process is critical to a company's strategic advantage, it might be useful to implement the general ledger first.

When a company begins to implement the sales and distribution system, for example, the steering committee must decide up front whether to include the accounts receivable module or the general ledger. The decision must be made in fine-grained detail. Decide whether to include rebate processing, for example. One of the major differences between R/3 and other systems is that this level of detail must be identified very early in the process. It will not be possible (or will be very costly) to decide well into the process that you want to add or eliminate a module.

A simple way to begin this process is to draw a circle on a white board (as in Figure 7–1) and place every R/3 module inside the circle that you want to implement. Modify this diagram to create different

Figure 7–1: R/3 module selection

scenarios before making a final decision. This effort will help you decide the best and most cost-effective scenario for your company. Note those modules or legacy systems that will be outside the circle. For each one outside, you will have to build an interface. For each one inside, you will have to define precisely how you want the business process to operate. This simple exercise will give you a visual aid to understand the complexity and impact of the initial implementation.

In this simple example, the executive team began with the knowledge that they needed the sales and distribution functionality to be integrated across their company. They also wanted to implement project management to solve an engineering problem. They felt they would like to implement manufacturing and materials management; however, they decided to wait for a second phase of the project; it seemed too large a project scope. In the beginning of this process, they felt they also ought to implement the financials later, since their existing systems seemed to give them no trouble. In the discussion that ensued, however, they realized that to implement the sales and distribution module, they wished to change the structure of the company in some major ways. Since these changes would be incompatible with the existing chart of accounts, it seemed prudent to include the financials inside the circle. On reflection, the project management module was a "nice to have" and would increase the scope beyond their tolerance for change.

The executive team discussed whether there would be changes in the chart of accounts when they came to implement the manufacturing and related modules. They decided to commission a separate team to study and propose a new structure. If accepted, this structure would be integrated into the financials in phase 1. Some felt that they might run into the same incompatibility problem using this approach; however, they finally agreed that keeping the scope smaller was worth the difficulty in developing the necessary interfaces.

Inevitably, there will be pressure during the project to change those boundaries. The steering committee will be the project leader's buffer against *scope-creep*, the dreaded disease that prolongs implementation projects.

Diane Schwarz was the project leader for the general ledger implementation at Steelcase. As of this writing, she is implementing accounts receivable. She states categorically, "You need a strong, stable, decisive, supportive steering committee. My group made decisions on date changes, and they really supported me when others wanted to increase the scope of the project. That was really helpful."

The steering committee must consider the risk, not necessarily of the system but of their ability to absorb the change and all the necessary learning. It was this concern that prompted the company described in the example above to limit the scope of their project. They realized they had some major changes to make to remain competitive, and felt it necessary to learn on a smaller project before attempting to change everything.

Once you have the initial scoping, the team must develop a high-level implementation plan. This plan will contain the expected benefits, the scope, the names (when known) of individuals to be involved in the project, the time frame, and the estimated cost. Except for the first two, each of these elements is subject to change when a detailed project plan is developed. The team should, however, rely upon the project leader to give them times and cost figures that are close to reality.

7.3 The Project Leader

The project leader must be an individual possessing excellent leadership skills—preferably one who has experience with R/3 implementation. For this reason, you are well advised to obtain support from SAP or from one of the consulting partners of SAP. This leader will be critical to your success. If you have an employee who is almost ready to assume the role, make him or her an assistant, or give him or her a small pilot project to manage, and provide coaching from outside. R/3 implementation is complex, requiring a combination of business, technical, and change management skills. The project, however, must belong to you, and your leadership is critical to the success of the project.

The project leader must manage the project within budget and time constraints. Since each project will inevitably be more complex than management believes, the initial estimates must reflect that reality. Costs in addition to hardware and software may run in the multiples of two to five times the system costs. These are made up of consulting fees, training, and internal costs.

The project leader must be coach, mentor, confidante, cheerleader, and visionary. He or she must reconcile the often conflicting needs of the user community, the technical team, the design group, and the steering committee. The beginning of the project will be a honeymoon period, when everyone concerned feels great about the project and is optimistic. No problem there. It is when the project team begins to develop substance in its recommendations that difficulties arise. Inevitably, something will not be right for someone. The project leader must be convincing and persuasive; he or she must sell the overarching goals to obtain the continuing support of the user management. And at times, he or she must be empathetic but uncompromising on critical issues, knowing when to ask for help from the steering committee.

Selection of a strong project leader is not the place to save money.

7.4 Structure the Project Teams

The project leader, in conjunction with the steering committee, will identify the number of teams and their membership that the project will require. The numbers and constituencies of these teams will change somewhat during the course of the project. It is generally recommended that each team (with the exception of the technology team responsible for the basis or technical architecture) be made up of two or three users for every one IS person. You must keep in mind that you are implementing a package: there is no development required. The decisions these teams will make are primarily about the business processes. These decisions will be expressed in terms of customization aspects, that is, setting table parameters, describing scenarios, configuring screens, and the like.

In some cases, the IS people who have been supporting a particular business entity are intimately familiar with the processes and have the trust of the user group. They will make good representatives to the project team. Some companies have reversed the proportion given above and used a majority of IS professionals as team members. The individual's title is not as important as his or her knowledge of the business situation and creativity to improve the flow of work. Nevertheless, using a high percentage of IS people to represent the user group may lessen the ability of that group to integrate the detailed knowledge back into the department.

Teams should contain from seven to twelve members. A team having fewer than seven members will not be able to do its work in a timely fashion. In addition, there will be fewer ideas put forth. Implementing R/3 requires a relatively high level of creativity. The number of people in a group is positively correlated with the number of ideas—up to a point. When groups reach a size of over fifteen, many members will not feel free to offer their insights. A few will take over the group, and many will feel intimidated or undervalued. The quantity and quality of ideas is then diminished.

The number of teams will be determined by the size of the project. Computervision, a relatively small company, established three teams—a business modeling team, a software team, and a networks/hardware team. Autodesk implemented R/3 in their entire company in two phases. They finished the manufacturing in December of 1993, and completed the financials and sales/distribution in February of 1994. For the second phase, they formed four teams—finance, sales/distribution, manufacturing production, and technology. They had a total of 45 people involved in the project teams—15 IS people, 15 users, and 15 people from the two consulting firms they used. In addition, they used some SAP experts to develop the technical architecture—what SAP calls the *basis*. Owens Corning has 200 full-time people devoted to their implementation. Each subteam has around thirty members. In groups of this size, the leader will need to subdivide members based on specialty or task, to effectively manage the numbers.

Other companies implement smaller portions of R/3 and have only one team. At Steelcase the general ledger project leader was chosen from the finance department. She completed the implementation using a combination of users and applications support people, with the addition of up to ten external people at the peak of activity. The team membership varied from twelve to twenty-five members, depending upon the need at the time. It was comprised of 60 percent users and 40 percent IS and consultants. She did not, however, have a more technical systems engineer available to the team who would have been helpful in terms of identifying what would happen when moving from the sandbox environment to the production environment.

SAIC is running lean in terms of project member numbers. They have five teams or *tracks*. The systems engineering track has five people. The training and help desk track also has five members; however, they will be augmented by additional trainers at the appropriate time. The remaining three teams have six people each. These are the finance, purchasing, and reporting and interfaces tracks. The project leader has assigned an experienced implementation manager to work with these three groups to ensure their work is integrated in terms of design and configuration. This grouping will increase the effectiveness and creativity of each track and individual.

Another company that is in the process of implementing nearly the entire R/3 suite has formed four teams, divided by function. They are sales, manufacturing, finance, and technology. They have already run into problems because they did not foresee the need to integrate the results of the several teams.

7.5 Integrate the Team Findings and Decisions

It is essential to provide integrative mechanisms in a large project having multiple teams. Most legacy systems are not, by definition, integrated. This results in different approaches to the information used in several systems. The numbers from the order processing system, for example, might not exactly match the numbers on the general ledger. Historically, the solution to this mismatch is for a finance person to develop a spread sheet that will analyze and combine numbers from various sources. The results are fed into the general ledger or balance sheet by a batch process. This is neither desirable nor possible in the R/3 environment.

However, if teams are off in their own environments establishing the rules of their business processes, they are likely to define some common fields in different ways. These conflicts will, of course, show up when the system is tested for integration. A more efficient way to handle the conflict is to surface it far earlier in the process. Sales order processing may define a product having a product number that means something to its way of doing business (a smart number), or may identify a subfield differently than does the materials management process. Many companies find that separate customer, product, or order numbers exist to identify the same entity.

If the order processing system, for example, defines the unit of measure as liters, and the materials management thinks of it in gallons, there is an obvious conflict. Implementing R/3 may mean addressing the question of whether you want to measure by the way you sell or by the way you store a product. You can decide on a base unit measure, and the system can automatically convert for the Sales Department.

Integration Mechanisms

Various mechanisms can be employed to discover these points of conflict early in the implementation process. They include: holding joint team meetings, presenting consolidated briefings to the steering committee and the user groups, having members of one team formally sit in on another's meetings, establishing a common working space for all the teams, holding formal integration meetings, choosing members who have a broad understanding of the cross-functional processes, and selecting methodologies that encourage multiple points of view.

> **Integration Mechanisms**
> - Joint team meetings.
> - Consolidated briefings.
> - Members sitting in on another team's meetings.
> - A common working site.
> - Formal integration meetings.
> - Members with multi-discipline experience.
> - Methodologies that encourage multiple points of view.

Several companies that have implemented R/3 noted that having a common work site or war room is a useful mechanism. The noise level may be high, but everyone has some understanding of the focus and efforts of everyone else. One team member, for example, may overhear another talking about the elements of a part number, and may wheel his or her chair over to inform the other that an entirely different perspective exists elsewhere. These two can then go to their respective teams to highlight the conflict.

With everyone in attendance, the teams can meet informally to resolve a perceived conflict. Both formal and informal joint meetings are essential for each team member to have an understanding of the whole system. Several teams may prepare a briefing for the user group periodically. This provides those departments with the opportunity to communicate to all their employees, as well as a chance to question a decision or a direction if it seems not to meet their needs. The resulting discussions can be very valuable for reinforcing the reasons for a change in the business process or to elevate a concern that has been missed by the project team.

Autodesk project team leaders met for two hours each week to discuss any integration issues of concern. This meeting was followed by a weekly status meeting. Potential conflicts were identified immediately for resolution.

Monsanto is in the process of a major initiative to redesign its supply chain. It will implement R/3 3.0 to automate the redesigned supply chain and financial processes. This project will be piloted in a major strategic business unit (SBU) of 5,000 employees. The project team expects most of the 5,000 will be affected in some way by the overall change. The implementation team assigned to this SBU includes approximately one hundred people full-time. This group is comprised mainly of users, reengineers, and information technology resources. They use a threefold structure with many built-in integration points. The structure is built around three key elements: people, processes, and technology. The largest number of people is involved in the process segment. This segment is comprised of three teams—supply chain, plant operations, and plant infrastructure. Members from each team are scheduled to attend the formal meetings of other teams. Formal integration meetings are held periodically. Each team has an expert in change management available in part to assist the integration efforts. The Monsanto approach to change management will be presented in greater detail in Chapter 11.

7.6 Set Objectives

The steering committee, in conjunction with the project leader, will need to specify the business results that are expected to be gained from the implementation. Some companies have a very clear idea of exactly what business problem they want to solve. They may say, for example, "We need an online real-time system for order management. We need to be able to tell our customers what we can deliver and when that delivery will be." Other companies are not as clear. They may, for example, say they like the idea of integrating their systems and that they are frustrated with the cost and time needed to maintain their old systems or to get consolidated reports. Most companies are somewhere in the middle, with some concept of what they want to accomplish. It is necessary to develop project metrics as a baseline prior to implementation to know whether you have made the right investment decision. After the fact, you will then be able to state clearly what advantages have been gained.

Some advantages will be difficult to measure, such as the ability to integrate the major systems running the company, the elimination of a systems request backlog, the ability to leverage reengineering efforts, or an enhanced state-of-the-art image.

One company believed its ability to generate a profit-and-loss statement in minutes, close the business in a day, or generate a credit report instantly would result in a greater ability of the finance people to analyze trends to help set the future direction of the company. Under its old systems, people did not have the time for such work, and much of the information to accurately analyze their company's position was not even available.

Other advantages will be readily measurable—usable to determine the success of the system. Battco, for example, believed it could reduce the time to ship from two weeks to two days, and that this would improve its competitive position. The company also believed it could improve customer satisfaction scores by 40 points on the survey used.

One company developed a list of eight key performance indicators to test the system and the related business process reengineering. These measures included total supply-cycle time, cost to manufacture, amount of capital employed, revenue growth, and customer service.

7.7 Develop Guiding Principles

It will be useful to spend some time at the beginning of the project to develop a mission, a vision, or a set of guiding principles. Some companies distinguish between these three and develop all of them. The picture of what you are trying to accomplish and how you intend to go about it will focus the steering and project teams, and will provide the essence of communication to the user community. It will help to increase commitment to the change. Any vehicle can be used to sell the change, and selling it is essential to acceptance.

One company identified the mission of the R/3 implementation as the ability to link together the corporation. This phrase *linking the corporation*, became the banner for all presentations to user groups and outsiders alike. Regardless of whether they actually understood what it meant, it sounded right, and people felt they were part of something important, a critical factor in the system's success.

SAIC developed four guiding principles in phase 2:

- Support the ultimate customers.
- Leverage reengineering efforts.
- Government rules of engagement shall not impact commercial business processes/procedures.
- All end users trained and working on the system.

The decisions and choices that companies make in the design and customization of R/3 will be guided by these principles. They speak to the outside customer, the employee, the business process, and their unique historical business environments.

7.8 Develop a Detailed Project Plan

The responsibility for the detailed plan will rest with the project leader. The steering committee will advise and finally approve the plan. In addition to the cost and time frame as identified earlier, the bulk of the plan will set out the many tasks, milestones, and approval cycles to be followed. Since implementing R/3 is a complex undertaking, it is essential to use a good project methodology. Every consulting firm has its own, and you may have one you use in-house. As long as it is robust, any plan will do. But you do need one. It will remind you of tasks you might have otherwise neglected. And you can always skip a portion that does not apply to your project or your company.

In developing the plan, the project leader and each of the constituents must keep in mind the iterative nature of the customization of R/3. Once into the detailed design, the process will loop and twist around itself until the result meets all the specifications. This is no linear approach. Understanding the relationship between the current situation (the *as is*) and the desired future (the *to be*), and creatively developing a business process/information system solution requires a new approach rather than the traditional systems life cycle of only a few years ago. If the members of the purchasing or order processing or materials management departments will work in new ways, so will the IS group in supporting the implementation of R/3.

7.9 The Case of Agrium, Inc.

The early stages in a project are critical to the final outcome. A detailed project plan should be reviewed from many angles before beginning implementation. Decisions that seem insignificant early on may result in major time delays or even possible incompatibilities between the system and the business requirements, as we shall see in this next example.

Agrium provides agriculture input to large farmers. Agriculture input is fertilizer which comes in a variety of combinations of four ingredients: nitrogen, phosphorus, potash, and sulfur. Farmers apply hundreds of pounds per acre during the growing season of March, April, and May. Since fertilizer is a commodity product the price will almost certainly change frequently during that period.

Agrium is located in Calgary, Alberta, Canada, and operates its primary business in Canada and the United States with an international division rapidly expanding into South America. It went live on R/3 3.0C November 1, 1996, with MM, PM (Plant Management), CO, FI and Consolidation. The company has about $2.5 billion (U.S. dollars) in revenue and employs approximately 4,500 people.

In order to prepare for the configuration of the R/3 system, teams were formed for each module, consisting of equal portions of U.S. and Canadian employees, along with the usual complement of consultants.

The primary point of contention was a difference between the Canadian and U.S. business processes. In Canada, fertilizer traditionally is supplied as needed during the busy season and the price changes are ignored until June. At that time, the company agrees with its customers on an average price and changes their computer system retroactively. The Canadian agriculture business is one of a long history between customers and vendors, resulting in a sense of loyalty. It is less dynamic and more stable than in the U.S.

In contrast, U.S. customers want price changes made immediately; the business is more dynamic due to more intense competition and the availability of more fertilizer choices.

Ultimately, the teams decided to structure the system according to the U.S. mode of doing business. Early in 1997, Dennis Kalma, CIO, remained unsure if the decision made in the early stages would turn out to be the right one. When implementing R/3 across different countries, or even divisions, the overall structure of the system must be the same. Agrium has only one instance and one database server. It would be awkward to implement R/3 in a way that would accommodate the differences between the two operating approaches. Thus the structure of R/3 itself has proven to be problematic with regard to the product pricing. Furthermore R/3 is structured to require one order for each mode of transportation and date of delivery. A customer service representative (CSR) will frequently field a call from a customer asking for 100 rail cars each with a different product mix. Rather than one order, SAP structures this as 100 orders. During the busy season this requirement of the system inhibits the CSR from giving rapid service. Currently Agrium is looking at some type of bolt-on, non-SAP spreadsheet, or reporting fix to enable them to be responsive to the alternative customer requirements.

The difficulties in SD (Sales and Distribution), specifically at the customer interface and management price analyses, were the only major ones in the implementation. Users are excited by the changes brought on by the MM and PM modules, and the financial people believe that, even though it took a full month to complete the first month's closing, the delays were mostly because they were so cautious and slow to trust the new system.

In retrospect, says Kalma, the teams should have been organized by business process rather than by module. For example, configuration decisions made by those in SD did not work for those in finance, requiring greater time (and thus cost) to sort out such conflicts than if the teams had worked together from the beginning. In addition, he discovered they had not allocated enough effort to testing the system prior to implementation. In some cases, the latter problem was caused by the former.

CHAPTER 8

Phase 2: Create the As Is Picture

8.1 Analyze Current Business Processes   168
8.2 The Case of a Systems Integration Company   170
8.3 Map Business Processes into R/3   171
8.4 Identify Data and System Interfaces   172
8.5 Inventory Existing Hardware/Software   173
8.6 Install R/3   174
8.7 Begin Project Team Training   175

At this point, you have in hand an assemblage of people and a detailed project plan. You may also have the results of a BPR effort. You have a number of tasks to accomplish in this phase. Many of them can occur in parallel. The major output of this phase is to understand, to the extent necessary, your current, or *as is* environment:

- Analyze current workflows.
- Map business processes into R/3 modules.
- Identify data/system interfaces.
- Inventory existing hardware/software.
- Install R/3.
- Begin project team training.

If you have completed a BPR, in all likelihood you have not assessed the current environment from a technical perspective. Regardless of the extent of your reengineering design prior to the implementation of R/3, you will need a concrete detailed understanding of all the existing systems, databases, and networks. These will be required by the technical team to ensure that the basis is sound and that all interfaces have been identified.

Your output from phase 2 is a solid picture of the problems and opportunities that exist in your company's environment, an understanding of which modules of R/3 you plan to implement, and an establishment of the foundation for the future work. This picture has two aspects, the business and the technical. Let us discuss the business side first.

8.1 Analyze Current Business Processes

As was stated in Chapter 2, your approach will depend upon where you fall in the scale/magnitude matrix. If you are far to the right, you have already accomplished as much of the analysis of the current work flows as your situation requires. If, however, you are more in the middle of the matrix, now is the time to collect detailed information about how satisfactory these processes are to their owners and customers (whether internal or external). You should also take the larger perspective and ask to what extent they accomplish your company's long-range goals. Using best practices as a guide, you may start to set out concrete goals for your company, such as three hours to quote a sales order or four hours to verify credit.

A computer manufacturer decided as a result of this phase that it needed to centralize all inventories, to consolidate all credit management under customer service, and to eliminate all customer service and planning department manual reporting. The company set a goal of completely processing a customer order in eight hours. It implemented sales and distribution, materials management, inventory management, and the financials, leaving out modules such as procurement and purchasing.

It may be useful to draw large flowcharts of the processes in question. Digital Equipment uses a proprietary process called *TOP Mapping* for this purpose. These maps illustrate the channels between organizations and the difficulties in moving information from one to another. Completed in a few hours, they can be nested, that is, illustrating greater and greater levels of detail in a particular area or department.

Along with the flowcharts, role mapping is a useful process. It will be necessary to understand exactly who is involved in a process. If the output goes incorrectly to accounts receivable, but no one noticed until the system is configured (or worse, implemented), you will have created quite a problem.

With an overall view of the set of issues involved, the team may use brainstorming to identify the key opportunities. This process of positively building on one another's ideas and including everyone's point of view is generally a high energy activity that gets the creative juices flowing. Often the really high-leverage concepts will develop from this or some other creativity-producing event.

A team can take either the viewpoint that it is identifying opportunities or that it is assessing risks. Many companies use a process of creative visioning to identify for themselves how they would like to be known, and further, how they wish to achieve their reputation. Creative visioning has two major benefits, it results in ideas that can generate excitement and energy, and it has more appeal than merely solving problems. Selling such ideas can generate enthusiasm in employees to carry out the vision.

At the same time, fixing problems that have hampered and frustrated employees at all levels can also provide motivation. The team can ask itself, "What is most broken? Where do we deviate from best practices? Where can we make the best use of automation?" and similar questions.

From these activities, the team will begin to develop recommendations which identify the highest leverage aspects with the most manageable scope to be presented to the user group and the steering team. These recommendations may appear to be the ones already defined in phase 1. They are not. Here the team must get into the next level of detail. This process of continually decomposing the problem set will continue throughout the first several phases of the project. To make a substantial difference in your company, you will necessarily have to delve into considerable detail. You cannot simply drop into that level right away; it is too overwhelming. Nor can you avoid it; R/3 will not allow you to be imprecise.

The recommendations required here will not change the overall objectives of the project; rather, they will better define them.

8.2 *The Case of a Systems Integration Company*

This company completed a BPR project prior to the R/3 implementation. It was motivated by numerous complaints about inefficient use of time and the considerable consumption of resources in the administrative process, especially the financial operations. A BPR team was organized. The members quickly recognized that simply automating the present process was not only useless, but would eventually be detrimental to the success of the company. They decided to narrow the scope to the procurement, accounts payable, expense reporting, and asset management processes.

The BPR leader decided to focus on the future vision, and use the current situation to check on the reality of the suggestions produced. She felt that an exhaustive study of the current problems would focus the team on solving present problems rather than taking a more creative approach. She began a series of two to three day meetings at various sites, involving customers (of these financial processes), the various professionals (the doers), and management.

Several of her team members attended each session. There, they began by discussing the overall project and the needs of the company. Since all had their own version of the procurement/accounts payable process, she had created generalized flowcharts for reference, but started by asking people to describe the perfect system. "If you were king or queen," she asked, "How would you design this process?" She was rigorous in stopping the group discussion when it began to simply solve current problems, and she refocused the group on what would be best for the company.

After each session the BPR leader wrote up the findings of the group, in categories such as policy, procedure, automation, roles, organization structure, and the like. This document went back to the session attendees for their responses. As session documents accumulated, the leader also created a cumulative findings document, which was also circulated to session attendees to stimulate more ideas.

The BPR project team assembled for a week to consider this large document that contained suggestions ranging from simple changes to complex reengineering suggestions. The team worked through which ideas to recommend, as well as its many concerns about how to implement these changes. The final results were given to the executive management for its approval (which was given), and handed off to the SAP project team. The BPR team had recommended the company accomplish such goals as generate commitment upon placing of a purchase order, adopt a one-approval release strategy, and consolidate accounts payable into one centralized organization. In addition, there were numerous specific automation requirements, as well as changes in the roles and responsibilities of people across the company.

Thus, the BPR team had answered the question, "How do we want to do business?" The SAP project team was next to answer the question, "How do we want to do business in the context of R/3?"

8.3 Map Business Processes into R/3

The R/3 project team will need to understand the selected modules of R/3 well enough to judge where and how the system will be able to accommodate the required changes. In the prior example, the two teams (BPR and R/3) worked with the recommendations to develop a document that identified which of the required functions would be provided by R/3. Of their 132 requirements, 11 were not provided by R/3. Requirements that were provided included, for example, complete purchasing history, asset inventory data, approval capability, patent notifications, asset classification for useful life, and the use of EDI to send orders to suppliers. Requirements that were missing from R/3 (Release 2.2) included the ability to notify requesters of deficiencies in requisitions, as well as several features desired in the employee travel expense module. The project leader does not believe these functions are available in Release 3.0. Also missing was the ability to validate available budget; however, the company had planned for this gap when they decided not to implement the budget module in their initial project stages.

With this level of detail available, the project team can communicate to the user group which features will be forthcoming and which will not. The team (with input from the users) can then assess the importance of the missing features and can decide whether to provide a work-around or to wait for a future revision of R/3. Work-arounds may be hard coded into the R/3 system, thus creating a potential upgrade problem, or can be handled via such off-line alternatives as spreadsheets. Many companies have created offline work-arounds to serve their specific needs when those requirements are minor compared with the advantages of implementing R/3 as it is presently configured.

8.4 Identify Data and System Interfaces

On the technical side, the project team must identify all systems and data feeds or outputs that touch or are touched by R/3. If you implement accounts receivable but not the general ledger, or if you implement billing, but not the order entry processes, the systems people must create interfaces to carry the information away from and into R/3. The old legacy general ledger system must receive the AR input in some form; likewise, the new billing system must receive information from the old order entry system that is compatible with R/3.

The technical goal must be to provide uninterrupted dataflows in both directions as long as legacy systems are being used, and to provide employees with at least as much data as they currently receive. IS must also be sure to provide dataflows between the company and any third parties that are connected in any way. Business must not be interrupted.

Baxter Healthcare Corp. is one of the first in their industry to choose R/3. In its case, the focus is on supply chain management. In particular, it intends to begin with materials management, sales and distribution, and the financials. In the initial stages of implementation, Baxter identified 159 interfaces its users feel are essential. This number was quickly reduced to less than 80. Even this number may be reduced, but the project team is concerned that it must keep the customers happy.

Steelcase is in the process of implementing the entire order management process. The project manager for that effort says he is going as fast as possible, but he has to be careful not to bring down the business. His team is implementing one SBU at a time. This approach has meant additional time spent in doing and redoing the interfaces.

SAIC identified 16 interfaces needed to implement the procurement process across the corporation. More than half of these are to external systems. Some of these will be temporary, to be replaced in the next phase of R/3 implementation; however, most are expected to be permanent. In one case, an interface must be written between two R/3 modules to circumvent the creation of a master record. The interface team estimates it will expend three person years of effort over a period of four months.

8.5 Inventory Existing Hardware/Software

The IS department should have most of the information regarding the existing hardware and software being used by the target population. At least this department knows the mainframes and networks, although not necessarily all the various PC solutions people have created to take information from the corporate systems and create their own databases. It will be important to inventory all this equipment.

Most IS departments today allow users to buy their own equipment from a short list of approved vendors and products. Outside of those guidelines, users will be on their own for support in using their equipment. As part of this limited option approach, the user is generally responsible to choose, purchase, and install his or her own equipment. The IS department will provide answers via a hotline in cases of malfunction of supported hardware or software.

With R/3 in mind, the IS department can issue minimum specification recommendations which identify which configurations can be used to run the R/3 front-end or desktop applications.

The user departments involved in the implementation of R/3 will need to depend upon local printers. No longer do IS departments run large print jobs at night and deliver the results in the morning. Therefore, the networks are the responsibility of IS, and must support some number of printers and print servers.

8.6 Install R/3

The IS department must determine the *basis* for the system. As we said earlier, this is the combination of hardware and networks that comprise the system architecture. It includes the system programs, the database administrator, the networks, the operating system, the data dictionary, and the language support for ABAP/4. It also includes such details as disk sizes and how the data are best laid out. The key issue is how to optimize performance. This will be determined by an analysis of existing equipment that can be used, the size of the eventual user population and the volume of transactions expected. Setting up the systems correctly is not a trivial exercise. It is a critical aspect of the overall project success. Too small a system configuration will significantly impact the response time. Too large a system will be overly costly. Some companies have found this to be a difficult process; others have not struggled with it. Experience in a client/server environment will be helpful. The IS people are more likely to express concern than are the users. This is to be expected, given the difference in perspective and expertise.

The IS team will install R/3 in several instances. (An instance is a separate installation of the software.) By setting up the system this way, you can provide different levels of completeness of the system. Most companies have a development or sandbox instance. On this system, the project team can experiment with different table settings, and explore the possible ways to achieve various goals. These changes would not be saved, and would not be considered final. You may set up a separate instance for prototyping. This instance would have more completeness, and changes would be saved. On this instance, the team could test their more developed concepts. Another instance might be for the purpose of testing the integration of a number of modules. When the implementation is complex, testing will start with the lowest level of detail and proceed upward to greater levels of detail. A module may perform exactly as expected, yet fail when tested with another module. This is not likely to be a fault in R/3. It would happen, for example, if table settings in one module conflicted with those in another.

Most companies have three instances, rarely more. It is possible to set up more than one client within a single instance. Some companies set up one client for quality assurance and another for acceptance testing within the same instance. They will load the configured system with live data and exercise it with users in as high a level of transaction processing as possible.

The R/3 system comes with several clients contained within it. For example, client 000 is the SAP Model Company; client 066 is set up for SAP to run system diagnostics as necessary; and client 001 is an empty/configurable client that is typically copied and used to create the company's version of the system.

Of course the production instance is the final, tested version of the system that needs to be protected in terms of version control, frequent backups, and security.

Each of the instances must be maintained separately. They may occur on the same physical machine; however, they are considered unique logical entities.

8.7 Begin Project Team Training

There is a great deal for the project team to learn about the R/3 system. The entire project team and the user management will be well served by attending the introductory seminars. The project team will require more in-depth training in the R/3 approach, as well as in the specific modules. Depending upon the modules selected, team members will likely be in class for four to six weeks. The technical team will need additional training for interfaces and reporting.

SAP is in the process of redesigning the training approach to shorten the time needed and to provide a business process approach via case studies. For example, a team may need to understand the customer order management process. The training then would follow this business process through sales and distribution, materials management, production planning, finance, and the like. SAP training tools will be available online after the actual training event. Team members will attend training sessions, and for best retention of learning, will be able to try out their newly acquired knowledge on their sandbox instance.

In addition to learning about the system and attempting to apply this knowledge to their specific business cases, teams that perform well will also receive training in team development, interpersonal communications, decision making, and conflict resolution. These topics will be addressed in greater detail in Chapter 10. These additional skills will be critical in the months ahead. Unfortunately this is an area that is often neglected by the project leader and his or her steering team.

Even companies that are sensitive to the potential change management issues for the users of the new system may forget that the same concerns will apply to the project team. High performing teams are those which have been given a common language to work out their problems, both technical and personal.

CHAPTER 9

Phase 3: Create the To Be Design

9.1 Develop High-Level Design   178
9.2 The R/3 Hierarchy   179
9.3 Gain User Acceptance   180
9.4 Detailed Design   182
9.5 Scenarios, Scripts, and Tables   182
9.6 Iterative Prototyping Using Tables   184
9.7 User Communications   190
9.8 Gain Final Acceptance   190
9.9 The Case of a Semiconductor Company   191
9.10   The Case of a Products Distribution Company   192

At this point in the project, you are ready to define the future for your business. The phase 3 task list is as follows:

- Develop high-level design.
- Define the hierarchy.
- Gain user acceptance.
- Develop the detailed design through proto-typing.
- Communicate.
- Understand the implications of the changes.
- Gain final acceptance.

You may already see the iterative nature of this process in evidence. If you conduct a BPR prior to the R/3 implementation process, you will already have in hand many of the ideas for the new approach that will be part of the final design. In creating the *as is* picture, a number of solutions will have presented themselves. In fact, you probably started the project with some ideas as to how you can improve your business. In each step along the way, however, the picture has become clearer, some ideas have been dropped because they were too expensive or unnecessary, and new concepts have been evaluated and added. Furthermore, as you develop each succeeding level of detail, there will be items at the higher level that will be modified.

A senior partner at one of the major consulting companies said that she first became knowledgeable of SAP when she was an IS manager for a company that implemented R/2. During the first implementation, she said, the company hierarchy was revised several times because in the process more and more details became known, and early decisions became obsolete, giving way to new ones that influenced the company structure. The same potential exists in any R/3 implementation.

9.1 Develop High-Level Design

You may recommend some substantial changes, such as closing a plant, centralizing or decentralizing a function, taking profit differently, or assigning cost using a different model. In these cases, it is clear that executive approval must be obtained prior to moving forward in your project. A high-level design will, of necessity, contain more detail than is usual for an IS project. You are, after all, implementing a form of reengineering.

The project team will need to prepare visual descriptions of the design, as well as bulleted descriptions of the process. One manufacturing company developed large flowcharts that covered the walls of a work room. The company had pictures taken and reduced to show to the user management. Another team prepared an extensive three-ring binder that included a great deal of information about the elements of the redesigned system. Three key user managers worked with the three project subteams to develop this material.

A Steelcase general ledger administrator at one of the divisions had been very vocal about the need for changes in the financial reporting. He was tapped to head up a team to investigate and recommend changes that were needed in the financial structure of the company. This process improvement effort resulted in a new chart of accounts, new methods, new organizational entities, and different ways to roll up the information. The design was approved, and the R/3 implementation began. The project team used R/3 to firm up the original design. At first the users blamed the system for their difficulties in making the change, however, after a few months of progressively smoother closings, users and management are pleased with the vastly increased ability to access critical information.

It is not unusual for R/3 to be seen as the cause of frustration with changes in the company structure or business processes. This blame is, of course, misplaced. The system merely automates the substantial changes that affect the everyday lives of employees. The communications effort regarding all the changes must emphasize the need for business changes to give employees the bigger picture.

9.2 The R/3 Hierarchy

One of the first steps in creating the *to be* vision is to define the hierarchy of the company. There are several tables that will be set up to identify the most basic level in the company. They include such elements as customers, products, the organization structure, legal entities, business units, and distribution channels. Defining these terms in complete clarity with regard to their relationships requires executive agreement on how the business is to run. And this must be done very early in the process. The executives must be aligned on the future operating model of the company in a detailed fashion. The more detail that can be identified and agreed upon early in the process, the fewer acceptance problems that will arise later.

A senior partner at CSC/Index advises project teams to think as far ahead as possible in creating the hierarchy. While users will be able to change some aspects of the system once implemented, it is difficult to change the basic structure of the company. Centralizing order fulfillment or accounts payable, for example, will be easier than decentralizing them. This is so, he explains, because once you have defined these structural elements as part of the field organization, they can be reconfigured into one source. If, however they exist only at the corporate level, it will be very difficult to reconfigure them to a field level.

Jane Vaughan is the national director for SAP services for Ernst & Young. She explains that in making the hierarchy decisions, company business leaders should evaluate alternatives and understand the business impact that each alternative implies. Even when only one business unit is implementing SAP R/3, consideration should be given to enterprisewide business requirements to prevent future surprises and possible rework as R/3 implementation extends to include additional business units. Critical to the hierarchy decision is the company's need to reorganize, divest, or acquire business units. Adding or eliminating business units or moving a business unit within the hierarchy structure is not a difficult task. The difficulty arises if the decision is made to move historical data associated with the business unit to the new position within the R/3 hierarchy. This task can be further complicated if the business unit will now be positioned at a different level of the hierarchy, because data elements are aligned with specific hierarchy levels. By working through the implications of anticipated business changes, the company can choose a hierarchy structure that will best support its current and perceived future requirements. If an unanticipated significant change in the structure of the company occurs, the value of moving historical data should be determined before undertaking the substantial effort that may be required.

Thus, an unplanned significant change in the structure of the company may require a substantial effort to reconfigure, test, and re-implement R/3.

9.3 Gain User Acceptance

Management must agree on the future operating model. The project leader must provide a vision of how the business will run in the future.

Enough detail must be included so that the business owners will have an understanding of the implications for their organizations. In addition to gaining approval, this task will allow the project leader to initiate the communications so necessary to final acceptance. The rule of thumb should be *no surprises*.

This high-level design will probably be presented at one or more executive briefings. Be sure to allow plenty of time for questions to arise. It is better to deal with them at this point, than when you are ready to implement. Some questions will need to be handed off to the project sponsors or the steering committee. They will have the power to answer such queries as "Do we really need to change the way we operate?" and "But we've been very successful doing things the old way, why change?" Employees often raise these questions, especially when a successful company realizes that changes are necessary to continue to compete effectively.

One of the companies we researched held such a two-day meeting. Some of the user managers had been part of the design process, and so understood the issues. Some didn't understand the implications of what was discussed and needed to be educated further. Some, however, began to comprehend just how much their lives would change. They were the ones who asked the most difficult questions.

In the purchasing process, for example, there was some concern about taking away the administrative people who research the purchase order information and enter it into the system. The new system would be inquiry-based and driven by the purchasing agent who enters much of the data about a certain order. Agents and managers were concerned that the change was, in effect, making them into clerks. They showed a natural fear about losing their status and spending time doing work that did not use their skills appropriately. What they did not appreciate was the new way that business would be carried out. Purchasing agents, among others, would, in the future, do their work on the terminal. Their job would be to inquire as to the status of orders, prices from vendors, delivery information, and the needs of the requester. Most of that work would be done online. Thus it would be necessary for them to be the ones to enter orders, massage them, and submit them to vendors. It is a very different way to operate, and a difficult transition for those trained the old way.

9.4 Detailed Design

So too, the process of developing the detailed design represents an entirely new way to operate for most project team members. The most successful way to accomplish this task is to log on to the development machine and begin to explore the details of the R/3 system. Many team members will be uncomfortable with this approach, preferring to define the system on paper just a little while longer.

Several implementation teams reported they had learned the hard way that going too far on paper represents work that will need to be redone on the machine. One semiconductor company had to throw away three months of work because the detail, while not incorrect, was in a form that was incompatible with the R/3 system. A chemical company conducted an elaborate reengineering effort, going to considerable detail on paper; however, the details of the redesign didn't fit into the R/3 structure. It was necessary to back up the reengineering effort, eliminating a significant amount of detail. Next the project team mapped the higher level design to R/3, thus gaining the level of detail needed.

How much detail is too much? Experienced consultants suggest a company not go any further than to develop scenarios on paper. At that point the most effective approach is to do table entries, and develop scripts while on the machine.

9.5 Scenarios, Scripts, and Tables

Scenarios identify how the business is actually carried out, where the bottlenecks are, and where the process can be improved. To build a set of scenarios, begin with the easiest case. In order management, for example, the team might start with an incoming order. First, assume the customer is known, the products are standard, and they are available. The team can identify each step of that process. Then it can move to more and more complicated situations. If, for example, the product is not in inventory, it must be put on back order. Thus the back order process becomes another scenario.

When the scenarios are built, *scripts* can be developed that walk a person through that scenario and identify the decision points with which an employee might be faced. For example, in processing the order, an employee might have to decide if the standard pricing is correct in this situation, or whether any discounts apply. The employee might have to decide if the back order scenario must become active. Essentially, the team is defining the details of a transaction. The scripts define the flow of how a person will do a job. They are useful for explaining to outsiders how the process works. They will also ultimately provide helpful input into job training documents and classes.

Many of the major consulting companies have tools to assist their customers with the development of scripts. Ernst & Young has developed a tool called *Mentor*™. This software uses case-based reasoning to assist the customer implementing R/3 to select scripts meeting or close to meeting the customer's needs from an extensive Ernst & Young script repository. Vaughan explains that the Mentor operates at the transaction level rather than at the broad business process level or the generic industry levels. This approach may be compared to the use of object-oriented design in that the detailed subprocesses or transactions represented by the script may be reused by customers within the same industry, or across industries. Of course, if your consultant provides a script that does not entirely match your business needs, you may modify it.

If the team members are working to develop scripts on the development instance, they can go through each transaction and make screen prints to identify each element. These can then be used to clarify definitions for each field. A *field* is a specific piece of data such as customer, product, or price.

It is essential that each field have a unique definition. Many companies run their various systems with differing field definitions. They have usually developed ways to consolidate or redefine the data when needed for corporate reports. The differences allow them to operate in different locations or markets according to their unique needs. If you intend to implement R/3 throughout your company, you will no longer be able to operate in this way. A company that is defining its financials as a first phase of R/3 implementation will find itself defining far-reaching business processes, regardless of whether it is aware of this impact.

Each scenario and script identify a set of *tables* that must be set up. The tables define the details of how the business operates. They allow you to set up the rules of how to obtain detailed information about a customer or customer type, a product or product type. Using R/3, you can obtain whatever analysis you want once you have set up the tables to do so. The user will be able to identify orders by time period, customer, materials, or distribution channel. Analyses can be obtained as long as the information structure was established as part of the system.

You will use tables, for example, to structure where in the company you will run a profit and loss and balance sheet. A product line might reside at the strategic business unit or lower organizational level. You could have as many profit and loss statements as you have products. Placing a product line at too low a level, however, may provide too much detail, or potentially cause a performance problem. It certainly will mean a higher cost in table maintenance. Someone has to manage the data in all the tables, and depending upon how they are set up, this can become a major task.

As with the hierarchy example, should the company decide to change the way it operates, the tables can be modified. Next, the data will have to be called up and the identifiers changed. Orders will have to be assigned to another division or sales person, for example.

One company in the midst of implementing R/3 decided it wished to maintain each product line at the plant level. That company wanted to have the ability to run a profit and loss by plant and by product line within plant. The consultants questioned whether this amount of detail was worth the price of maintenance. In this case, the company decided to pay the price for the greater flexibility.

The set of scripts in Figure 9–1 are taken from a real company. This example shows the user how to process customer orders that arrive without material reservation—that is, new material that has not been priced. This scenario is part of the activity that processes customer orders. It in turn is part of the customer order management portion of the customer fulfillment segment of the sales and distribution module. As of press time there was a question as to whether sales office and sales group were required or optional. This script actually continues on for 26 pages, covering all tasks that might occur in this, one of many, business situations.

9.6 *Iterative Prototyping Using Tables*

As the scripts are defined, the team members set up the R/3 system to operate in the way they want. This is called *prototyping*, and it will prove to be an iterative process. R/3 is a table-driven system. In Version 3.0 there are 8,000 tables. Many of these, however, are designated for system operation; thus, those actually configuring the system will not have to concern themselves with them. The real art in

SAP
Customer Order Management

Create Customer Order without Material Reservation
For New Material Without Price

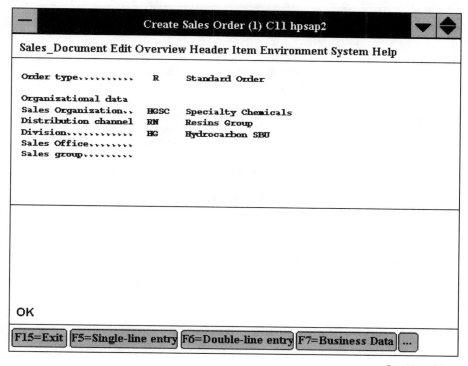

Copyright by SAP AG

Fill in the appropriate organizational data as follows:

Field	I	Action
Order type	R	Enter "OR" (Standard Order)
Sales Organization	R	Enter the code of the operating company (e.g., C106 for HGSC in the US or C550 for HGSC in Holland) for the specific legal entity.
Distribution Channel	R	Enter the code that identifies the Business Unit (e.g., RN=Resins, PG=Paper Technology)

Figure 9–1: Sample script for processing customer orders

185

SAP		Create Customer Order without Material Reservation
Customer Order Management		For New Material Without Price

Division	R	Enter the code that identifies the SBU (e.g., PS=Perozy, HC=Hydrocarbon Resins). If "XX" appears from previous DYNPRO (Create Customer Master) be sure to override this with the proper group, otherwise a verification error will be displayed.
Sales Office	OR?	Leave blank. Appropriate code will be selected automatically from the Customer Master. Represents the appropriate Sales Region. An entry on this screen will override the Customer Master.
Sales Group	OR?	Leave blank. Appropriate code will be selected from the Customer Master. Represents the appropriate Sales District. An entry on this screen will override the Customer Master.

Press F5 or press Enter for single-line entry.

Figure 9–1: Sample script for processing customer orders (continued)

SAP   Create Customer Order without Material Reservation
Customer Order Management   For New Material Without Price

Copyright by SAP AG

This screen now confirms the warning message encountered in the Product Selection screen displayed earlier.

The first line item (10) is a new material and shows a default price of zero because no standard list price has yet been attached to this product. In this example the assumption is made that a price is obtained from the appropriate authority and can be entered on the order.

Note: This will be a "on-time" price override and will not update the material list price in the pricing system.

The following additional information is displayed on the above screen

Figure 9–1:   Sample script for processing customer orders (continued)

| SAP | | Create Customer Order without Material Reservation |
| Customer Order Management | | For New Material Without Price |

Field	I	Action
Deliver plant	O	Enter the delivery plant from where goods will be shipped, if the majority of items will be sent from this plant. Although the plant is entered here, it can be overridden at line item level. If a product has only one source, the appropriate plant is selected automatically by the system at the line item level.
Item	P	System generated number of the line item, in increments of 10. This field may also be used together with "HgLvIt" to tie line items together.
First date	O	System generated date which identifies the preferred delivery date requested by the customer or the earliest proposed delivery date if a lead-time for order preparation is specified in the material master; can be modified, if necessary.
Plnt	R	Plant from where the product is shipped. This may be defaulted from the customer master, the material master or the delivery plant in the order header (in that sequence, with delivery plant in header being the final default). Enter plant code to override the defaults.
ItCa	D	System generated from a combination of Order Type and Item Category Group from the material master and defines the properties of a material on an order line item. Can be overridden on the order line item.
S	D	Indicates when there is insufficient material in stock for a single delivery of the specified line item. Not applicable for "orders without material reservation."
HgLvIt	O	Item level hierarchy; used as a link to the main line "item" to group products for pricing, rebates-in-kind, bundled items, etc. Bundled item products will default from the "Sales" Bill of materials after pressing enter.
CnTy	D	Pricing condition type (e.g., PR00-list price). Will default if a standard price exists. Can be overridden or entered manually when no standard price exists. **Note:** Use "PR00" as the condition type for manual pricing.
Rate	D	Gross unit price. Will default if a standard price exists. Can be overridden or entered manually when no standard price exists.
Curr	D	Billing currency. Defaults from the Customer Master/Pricing condition.
Net price	D	Net unit price. Will default if a standard price exists with a discount conditions attached. Can be overridden or entered manually when no standard price exists.
UoM	D	Pricing condition unit of measure for order-related discount calculations.

To proceed to the price override screen, see the next screen example on the following pages.

Figure 9–1: Sample script for processing customer orders. (continued)

configuring R/3 is in the manipulation of the thousands of tables. Thus, the implementation team will find that the key to success in the detailed design is the ability to set up these tables to produce the desired results. While there are some tools, these illustrate how SAP believes the process should operate. If you have a different view, your success will be highly dependent upon the skill and expertise you have available in understanding the particular modules that are of interest to you.

There is no tool yet available to pick out the correct table entries for your situation. SAP and some of their consulting partners are working to address this gap. You will have to decide the table entries that are right for you by a combination of experience and trial-and-error. There are numerous ways to obtain the same results, but it takes considerable massaging of the system to identify the optimal way. It will contribute to your success if the people who know the business choose the table settings while working with a consultant who knows the SAP module. Thus, the process designers (not the same as process owners)—the people who developed the new vision—must also be the ones to sit day after day at the terminal testing out various combinations to configure the system so that it will correctly carry out the identified scenarios. In addition, there will inevitably be a number of decisions to make that will affect many people in areas such as pricing, costing, commissions, and the like. The project team members must either be able to make those decisions, or have a fast track to the appropriate executives to have the decisions made immediately.

In prototyping, you test various alternatives. There may be two to five ways to accomplish the same task. You follow each through, look at the pluses and minuses, and then decide which to choose. Then you move on to the next scenario. Of course it is always possible (in fact, it is likely) that after you have completed several scenarios something will come up that causes you to rethink the earlier decisions. Sales, for example, may need credit information, but the credit and collections department had not planned for this, and may not want to entrust its information to other departments. At this point, the process stops until someone can work out a solution to what is actually an organizational issue, not a technical one.

Some experienced project teams state that the best way to approach interactive design is in stages. The first pass would set up the core functionality, and the succeeding passes would add increasing detail until the design is fully operational—that is, operational in the development instance, but not yet in a production mode. The system must be formally tested first. Prototyping is a preliminary testing process. The project team will set up hundreds of scripts, and in each case, will run through the script to test its logic. The team will enter some test data to try out various combinations. The full testing process, however, will await the next phase.

9.7 User Communications

Creating the *to be* design requires a series of communication efforts. The most successful companies use a variety of communication vehicles to ensure that users at all levels are aware of the nature of the changes to be implemented. This process should continue throughout the life of the project, growing more intense closer to the actual implementation. You cannot overcommunicate. Invariably when asked after the fact, many people say they knew little or nothing about the project even though it had been well publicized. People are involved in doing their jobs; often, they do not wish to contemplate changes that will affect them; and generally, they will wait to pay attention when the change is imminent. This is normal human nature. The communications people must be diligent in trying all available means to inform people of the nature of the change and its implications for the employees.

As the detailed design becomes more concrete, the project team should analyze the impact on organizations, people, policies, procedures, processes, and standards. These will not be evident to all those who will eventually be affected. It will have to be made very clear and explicit.

9.8 Gain Final Acceptance

Many companies hold formal design review sessions. The audience is likely to include the entire user management group, the steering committee, the executive sponsors, and other interested parties. At this session, the detailed design will be presented, along with the implications of the changes. All the major decisions should be reviewed, and any objections raised and answered. It will be costly to backtrack at this point; however, if the design results are unacceptable, the concerns need to be addressed before proceeding. If the project team has been careful to address each major issue as it arose, and to gain executive support for the decisions made, there may be some grumbling, but there should be no major disagreements.

9.9 The Case of a Semiconductor Company

This company (we'll call it *Semico*) manufactures and distributes semiconductors utilizing three manufacturing plants and 12 stocking locations (11 of these are international). The company's goals were to relieve the sales organizations from distribution concerns so they could better focus on selling. This led to a project to streamline the distribution operations. Customers were increasingly turning to multisourcing to keep down their costs. Providers had to improve their customer service, especially their ability to provide rapid delivery. Semico wanted to reduce their shipment time for in-stock items from 48 hours to 4 hours.

In this case, there was a long manufacturing cycle time, so the company could not make products to order. Most orders were scheduled out over a period of time. A customer might order 1,000 of a certain type of material to be delivered each month on a certain date. However, the manufacturing process was such that Semico did not know what the yield from any particular production run might be. This made scheduling shipments difficult. None of the legacy systems spoke to one another well, and the distribution department personnel spent endless hours projecting possible alternatives to meet the needs of all customers. The key drivers for selection of R/3 were its multilanguage, multicurrency capabilities and the ability to track *availability to promise*—that is, the difference between when the product was available and when it was promised. This was essential, since the old system produced weekly availability reports, and thus was out of date four days out of five.

The development of the *to be* design thus needed to incorporate inventory, ordering, internal ordering to supply stock rooms, shipping, and the financials. One of the questions the project team discussed for some time was the pricing process. R/3 provides a sequence to discover a correct price for a product. The team, however was not sure whether it ought to make the system continue looking for the best price after it had found a correct price, or to stop without looking further. Eventually the team decided to go for the best price, difficult as this decision was.

During this process, Semico discovered that R/3 did not provide the capability to capture and maintain the original date that was promised to the customer. Since everyone in this business also needed this type of information, Semico collaborated with one of its competitors to develop the software needed for this one important piece of information. This was an unusual move, but one that benefited both companies.

9.10 The Case of a Products Distribution Company

We have seen in the case of Semico, the iterative nature of the *to be* process as well as the nature of the decisions that must be made. In this next case, we will see that the pressures of ongoing business prevented the company from engaging fully in creating the *to be* design. The decisions regarding future changes were suspended until the system was implemented. In this case, the structure of the design will need to be changed and, as a result, much of this step will need to be redone.

This company distributes its products to several locations in South Africa. The decision to implement R/3 was made to enable the company—we'll call it Afco—to compete more effectively in the global market due to opening up of trade with countries outside South Africa. The company was particularly vulnerable in order entry and finance. The decision was made by the Finance and IT departments with input from all departments involved, although some felt the solution was overkill for their particular needs. The BOD approved the decision and the seven-phase implementation plan was drawn up.

Afco planned to implement MM, SD, and FI at five locations, followed by an HR implementation in all locations, and, finally, a PM and PP (Production Planning) implementation for all locations. There was no redesign of the company structure or business processes, although it is recognized by the project leader at one location, Jeremy Farrell, that implementation will force changes in structuring and planning processes. The project was designed to ensure that the company will work on a common standard and that financial reporting will be consolidated centrally.

In order to accommodate each locations' separate way of operating, the project manager allowed each region to determine its hierarchy independently and to run on its own machine. Each region was also allowed to develop its own plan and little coordination occurred among the regions. In addition, poor documentation and control of changes and design issues has hampered the ability of regions to learn from one another.

Compounding this disparate project organization, the consultants were expected in most cases to complete the configuration. There was a plan for all superusers (some taken from unrelated jobs) to come together for training and return to their regions with all necessary knowledge. The press of everyday business derailed this plan and ultimately a consultant was appointed at each site to drive the implementation. Success was only achieved when the consultants were dedicated to their sites. Amazingly, the users have responded favorably to the implemented system even though they still require considerable training.

Farrell says, "This company has spent a lot of money to implement a system which largely mirrors their current systems, either computer or manual. Due to lack of management and planning, the wheel has been reinvented in several regions. The inability to appoint real superusers in regions has caused design issues to be reviewed immediately after going live. Preparedness to push on without signed deliverables has resulted in incorrect assumptions compounding until final training occurs, and users tell you the system does things incorrectly."

Such a frustrating implementation effort as this only emphasizes the need to carefully construct the *to be* picture. It also brings up the issue of how best to use consultants. They can save your skin, but at what cost to the company in the end?

CHAPTER 10

Phase 4: Construction and Testing, and Phase 5: Actual Implementation

10.1 Develop a Comprehensive Configuration   196
10.2 Populate the Test Instance with Real Data   197
10.3 Build and Test Interface Programs   201
10.4 Write and Test Reports   201
10.5 Test the System   202
10.6 User Testing   203
10.7 The Case of Felix Schoeller, Osnabrueck, Germany   204
10.8 Phase 5: Actual Implementation   205
10.9 After Implementation   206
10.10 Moving into the Future   207
10.11 The Case of Chevron   208
10.12 The Case of Hydro Agri North America (HANA)   209

Project teams will find that the majority of their work is accomplished in the first three phases of implementation, although they must maintain focus on the goals of putting the system into production. They will need to spend time during the testing and actual cutover to ensure the system works the way they planned. However, much of the work of the final two phases either has been identified during the earlier phases or is of a technical nature.

We will cover the essential steps of the last two phases in this chapter.

10.1 Develop a Comprehensive Configuration

Now that you have a prototype version of the detailed design and it has been accepted, it is time to move the pieces from the development instance to a test instance. In so doing, you will construct the system from the various elements. The tasks involved are the following:

> - Develop a comprehensive configuration.
> - Populate the test instance with real data.
> - Build and test interface programs.
> - Write and test reports.
> - Test the system.
> - User test system.

For the first time, you will develop a comprehensive configuration. It should contain a full set of test data, which includes all possibilities (old customer, new customer, inventory available, back order, good credit, marginal credit, and so on). It is critical to test all combinations. Some companies move on to a quality assurance instance to accomplish this testing, and then to a full test instance for the stress test.

In this step, the system administrator, generally but not always an IS person, will establish the archive and version management procedures and prepare the various routines that will need to be run for actual production.

In implementing its general ledger module, one manufacturing company ran into a not uncommon event. Turnover at the executive level resulted in a new approach to the company structure. The team was in the middle of system testing when the new organization design was announced. The project leader reported that R/3 was able to accommodate the changes even though it meant some rework. The system was flexible enough to meet almost all of the company's needs. This misstep increased the confidence of the team and the user management in the system. They felt it would be rigorous enough to handle most changes that might occur in the future.

At the same time, the project team struggled with capacity planning. Not knowing what questions to ask and not having a basis or systems engineer available to them left them with a configuration too small for the eventual production system. Backups were very slow and response time was not what it needed to be. This problem was solved rapidly, and the leader and the IS department now have a better understanding of the system requirements.

Experience with R/3 results in faster implementation projects. Several companies noted that actually going live on the system was a minor part of the project. Autodesk, for example, is in the process of implementing the system in Singapore. The company brought together the international people and defined the requirements. Back home, the system was configured and demonstrated to the key users. Next, team members went to Singapore to set up a pilot system, made the necessary changes, and are ready to go live.

IBM Storage Systems implemented order entry, finance, manufacturing, and distribution in 1994. They chose to implement the system as it was—a vanilla version—and implemented the system below budget and three months early. Judy Johnson, the project leader, believes you can complete your follow-on project twice as fast if you replicate what was done in the first project.

10.2 Populate the Test Instance with Real Data

There are two types of data that must be entered to fully test the newly configured system. Some data are relatively permanent, such as pricing or discount tables, while other test files will have temporary transaction data. The master data files, such as employees, customers, products, and the like, have to be resident on the system before any processing can begin. Transaction data, such as manufacturing status or accounts receivable, must also be entered.

Setting up any of these data files is done via a temporary program that reads the data from the current production system and writes it into the R/3 format. Some master data will need to be entered manually; the method is typically determined by an assessment of the amount and complexity of the data. The project team may find some data reside only on paper or on an unconnected PC.

The team will also need to assess the similarity between the data. In some cases, R/3 has so changed the face of the data that it is difficult to translate from one system to another. The project team may, for example, have redefined the structure of the company so that sales or plant or product information no longer pertains to the old form of organization.

One company that implemented all the financials found they had to add capacity during their implementation process. One reason for this shortage was that they had assumed they would be able to develop a small set of test data. Instead, they were surprised to find they needed to replicate the entire set of master and transaction files.

SAIC identified 12 data population sets that need to be entered into the corporate R/3 system. They are shown in Figure 10–1. The conversion of numbers (customer, vendor, product, and charge) illustrates a potential hidden work load. If, for example, the vendor number is changed, each vendor has to be notified or a table maintained to match old and new numbers. In some cases, several years may elapse before all the old numbers are retired. (See Figure 10–2.)

Planning for the data migration involves such tasks as data cleanup, timing of transactions, and user training. It will be helpful to encourage the users to clean up the existing data prior to the conversion. Historical data that have never been removed, inconsistent records, incorrect records, and the like must be identified and removed or corrected prior to bringing them over to R/3. If this is not done it will compromise the new system. While the system is being tested, and prior to actual cutover, existing transaction data will be loaded and new transactions will be entered in a test mode. The project team must work closely with the users to ensure that all transactions completed on the old system are transferred to R/3, while transactions in process are held to be entered onto the live system. For example, if open purchase orders are not entered in one system or the other, accurate commitments data will be missing. Users must be included in the data population process, and of course, must be told exactly how to make the transition as accurately and easily as possible.

Phase II Conversion Diagram

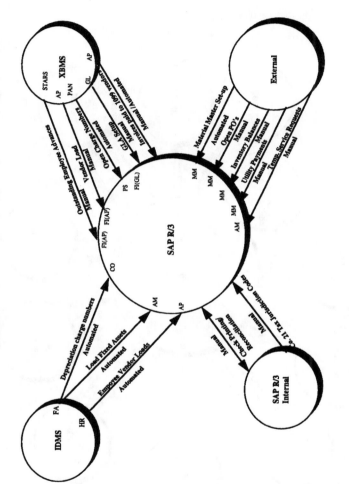

Figure 10–1: SAIC conversion diagram

Eagle PDR/Interfaces

Figure 10-2:   SAIC interface diagram

August 28 - 30, 1995

10.3 Build and Test Interface Programs

The interface team investigates the requirements for all the interfaces that will be needed. In this phase, the team will complete the coding for each interface. Next, each must be tested for all situations. Some interfaces will be in place only until the company can implement additional R/3 modules. Others will remain permanently in place to transfer data back and forth between external systems and the R/3 system. Figure 10–2 is the SAIC overview of the 16 interfaces required. It shows, for example, the ADP download. This interface will provide an automated way to provide payroll data to the external employee reimbursements process. In this project emphasis was placed on ensuring employees would have access to all data they normally obtain under the old system.

Some specialty software vendors have developed *bolt-on* systems that augment the functionality of R/3. In some cases, they provide an ABAP/4 interface; in others, the interface must be created. For example, several companies use ADP, the well-known payroll check processing vendor, to print their employee's paychecks. Others mentioned IXOS, a German company that provides a product which links to SAP offering a *jukebox* approach to report archival, that is, a way to select certain files for backup. This product eliminates the need for microfiche. It can also scan documents back into the system.

10.4 Write and Test Reports

The development process will identify the majority of the reports needed by the users. Old reports will be produced where this is possible and useful. New ones will be suggested by the project team in conversation with the various users. The definition of the new reports will come from an analysis of the data and system structure. In many cases, reports can be replaced by a query function. For many, the definition of reporting will be changed from being given information, to getting it yourself. People who are used to being handed reports will find it difficult to conceive of other ways to fill their needs. This will prove a major shift in thinking for many users.

Formal reports, whether online or printed, will be written and tested in this phase. Test reports that are relatively complete should be presented to users. It is difficult to imagine what a complete report will look like and to identify its value, when only a few lines are shown. This will mean that the report team will need to work from a set of databases that are more complete than are needed in developing the table settings and scripts.

R/3 will automatically provide many of the reports needed, through online queries and drill-down capabilities. Nonstandard reporting requests should be identified and prioritized. This analysis will provide the project team with a view into the users' mind-sets. In some cases, these requests can be met by queries. In other cases, the request will be unnecessary, and some requests will have to be met through customizing.

10.5 Test the System

Companies are generally extremely eager to put the system into production at this point, and may be tempted to skimp on the testing phase. Do not give in to this temptation. Testing is critical to the success of your implementation.

The system should be tested in two ways—by the individual units and by the integration of the units. The unit testing should proceed with few problems; after all, you have tested the pieces as they were being constructed. Set up a master schedule and be sure you test all cases of each segment. You will have hundreds of scripts to test, and it is easy to assume they will all work perfectly by this time. If you are rigorous in testing each possibility, chances are you will find only a small number of problems to be resolved.

The integration testing will be the more problematic. You must make sure each part is passing and receiving data correctly. One implementation team had overlooked a time variable. In an accounts receivable situation, when posting a payment to the financial system, the system failed to post the information correctly. After some research, it was discovered that the first part of the payment had occurred in period five, while the second part occurred in period six. The period six data overlaid the period five data and resulted in an incorrect total. The greatest difficulties will come in crossing certain functional boundaries.

SAP recommends completing a stress test as a final segment of the integration test process. Not only will this provide an opportunity to examine infrequent occurrences of special transactions, but it fully tests the system architecture. The stress test should consist of a simulated full load, that is, the master files and data files should be fully loaded, and the transaction per minute load should be high. Because this is not easy to organize, it is often overlooked. After all, where will you get people to enter all those test transactions when they are busy with their day-to-day tasks?

The stress test is extremely useful, especially when the implementation is a large and critical one. Companies that have had major difficulties during actual cutover tend to be the ones that did not do a complete stress test. If, for example, you run into bottlenecks in transaction processing or line speed, additional servers can be added to the system configuration. Making that shift will take time—time that is essential if you are running live. SAP can make available a team called the *Early Watch group*. This team will come in at this point in your process, review the system, and make recommendations for improvements in R/3, the operations parameters, or the database. It will review the backup and recovery mechanisms, the database administration, the system administration, and even the education needs of your employees.

Companies will find that they use the system differently in development than they do in production. Sometimes certain locations may go down. The system can be structured such that the site in trouble can be brought up elsewhere. Some companies in production will do more background processing, some more real time, and some will fluctuate between the two at different times of the day. The system should be optimized for all these occurrences.

10.6 User Testing

Users should be encouraged to experiment with the system as early as it can be made available. Since it is not likely to be accessible from their desks, the project team members should set up a demo room and hold periodic tours, explaining the system to groups of users. This will help in increasing understanding of both the general purpose of the system and the details of how it will work.

The users will be essential when conducting the stress test; therefore, they must be trained prior to that event. Earlier tests can be conducted by smaller groups of selected users. While setting up this level of user involvement may seem cumbersome, it will pay rich dividends during phase 5, actual implementation.

10.7 *The Case of Felix Schoeller, Osnabrueck, Germany*

The series of testing steps in phase 4 is critical to the success of a project. Phase 4 is a technically focused set of steps which will place great emphasis upon the skill and knowledge of the IS team in particular. Here they will discover the intricacies of R/3. Stress testing is the best method to identify the types of learnings shown in this next case study.

Felix Schoeller, Jr., produces 60 percent of the world's supply of photo paper in four plants. It also produces decor paper in three plants and imaging paper in two plants. The legacy materials management and financial accounting systems needed to be replaced and the company chose SAP R/3. The first step was to implement MM, FI and CO. The next step was SD; PP and PI (Process Industry) are planned for 1997. The company is replacing its formal departmental structure with process oriented teams and R/3 was seen as a way to accomplish this redesign. From a technical perspective, the team discovered the following important learnings:

- Success requires good connections to SAP and special SAP consultants.
- You must be careful with version upgrades during the end of the test phase because each upgrade brings new bugs.
- You will need a production system, a test system and a play system.
- You should be careful when transporting customizing changes to the production system. Sometimes only parts are transported and others are not.
- Try to keep the system knowledge in-house; use few consultants.
- Check the user privileges when going live. In the test system the user privileges are often different than they will be in the production system.
- Connection between teams scattered around different plants is critical.
- Early information and education for users is important.

The technical team found connection between their PCs and R/3 difficult to achieve. The technical people first tried the remote function call (RFC) approach. They discovered that Visual Basic modules can be generated in R/3 for function modules, but they are hard to change because the data structures are hard coded in the source. When they upgraded to 3.0C, they found a better way. The SAP OLE automation server worked better for them because the data structure is read at run time and the RFC is encapsulated as an object. With a few lines of code the team members could call every SAP module from Visual Basic, Excel or Access.

This company is pleased with their choice of software. All plants are connected on a single R/3 system improving business results. For example, inter-plant deliveries are easier and faster because of R/3.

10.8 Phase 5: Actual Implementation

The technical team is responsible for ensuring the system is available at every desktop. This team will set up the networks appropriate to the expected load on the system. Team members will encourage the users to acquire the recommended (or at least, minimum) hardware and software. Since there are likely to be problems if there are many users, the team will want to set up the infrastructure in advance of the system cutover. Their tasks will be the following:

- Build the networks.
- Install desktops.
- Training and support users.
- Communicate.
- Populate the production system with real data.
- Go live.

The training team will identify the number of sessions that must be held. As we have said, these should be scheduled as close to actual implementation as possible, since people will not remember all the details for long. When there are many users involved, it is inevitable that some will be trained earlier than others. A strong user support system must be put in place, including online help, a hot line, power users, and job aids (usually a one-page description of the essential tasks).

In addition to the formal training, the communications effort must intensify as implementation approaches. The purpose of the new system and other process changes should be repeated, as well as the details of what the user should expect when the new system is live.

On the appointed day, the system must be populated with the current data from all master files and transaction databases that relate to the modules being implemented. All system switches must be activated to point users to the new system. Then the project team will wait to see what actually happens. One hopes that users will take to the new system, and that any problems will be minor. However, experience with large-scale information system implementation tells us that some problems are to be expected. The team will need to stay intact to deal with them, knowing that some problems will not surface for days or weeks into the implementation.

Preparations must be made for long-term support, both of a technical and a business nature. In addition to solving problems, the technical team must identify ongoing production and optimization mechanisms. The technical team is well advised to set up automated tools to document and manage interfaces and revisions in an ongoing environment.

In addition, many groups, such as the NEC Technologies team, will re-form and take on a longer-term mission. In many companies, individuals with experience in implementation are asked to assist with subsequent projects. Several companies indicated that many of the project team members had essentially changed career paths, forming the nucleus of a change management department.

The final phase in the R/3 implementation process will take less time and fewer resources in comparison to other system changes. This results from the intense amount of detail and planning required at the beginning. The costs are front-end loaded. In most cases, the actual implementation was reported as a relatively simple step. Project leaders said, in essence, "And then we turned on the system. We had a few problems, but we solved those relatively easily. We set in place a support team, and the rest of the people either went back to their jobs or turned their attention to the next project."

10.9 After Implementation

Production support and user support are two areas that must be addressed to move the system into a maintenance mode. The production support team must continually work to optimize the system usage. In some cases, companies have found a need to add additional capacity they had not anticipated, due to the growing size of the system. This team will be required to manage all revisions, upgrades, and new releases, as well as the periodic back-up processes.

The user support group may be folded into the normal line management set of responsibilities. New employees must be trained. It is to a company's advantage to stress continuing system education even for those who have been using R/3 from the beginning. There are inevitably new ways to accomplish old tasks, as well as new tasks that need to be defined.

Once employees have been assigned roles in the support positions, the question arises as to the future for those involved in the project team effort. There will still be a demand for experienced R/3 project team members from both the IS and the user communities for several years to come. Such people are aggressively recruited, and the project leader and steering committee must make plans to address this issue. It is very likely you will lose one or several people. Many who were interviewed mentioned this concern. In most cases, they had developed plans for keeping their star performers. Many user project team members return to their organizations with enhanced responsibilities. Providing promotional (and salary or stock option) considerations is a key element in your plan. Each company implementing R/3 needs to develop its own plan. In some cases, you will need to plan to lose people if keeping them will result in compensation inequities beyond your tolerance. Executives experienced with the implementation process stated they expected this swing to level out, and note that it is no different than any other new popular technology expertise.

10.10 Moving into the Future

The competitive edge gained by R/3 is in two areas. First, a company will find itself ahead of its competition when it implements the system well, paying attention to all of the critical success factors we have discussed. Second, companies vary in their ability to actually use the system. In some cases, users do not explore the possibilities and limit themselves to a few defined activities. In others, the users discover numerous possibilities for data analysis and business planning. R/3 solves a major business problem by providing the technical base and infrastructure necessary to run the basic functions of any company. Once users have learned to use the system effectively, most implementation teams indicate that attention and effort can be applied to the next interesting business challenge.

We'll conclude this section on the implementation process with stories of two companies that feel they have made significant advances in their ability to operate, based on implementing R/3.

10.11 The Case of Chevron

Chevron is a $36 billion oil behemoth doing business in 70 countries. It is often either near or at the top of the Fortune 500 list. It is composed of 15 different operating companies that are subsidiaries. In 1992 the corporate entity kicked off a nine-month project to explore ways to reduce costs and improve profitability. A team of 30 members was convened, using individuals primarily from the top five companies. They formed into six process teams and set out to identify the best practices in these processes. They focused on the procurement-to-accounts payable process, as well as the project management process. Their investigation included such aspects as procurement of materials and services, capital project tracking, and fixed assets, as well as other financial accounting processes.

The team began with focus groups, from which it developed flow charts and maps of the processes then under examination. Team members gathered such data as: costs to process, which processes were time intensive, who carried them out, what were the labor costs, and what IT support was required. They next visited a series of companies in various industries who were reputed to excel in each of the identified processes. Two companies were visited for each of the processes being studied. From this effort, reengineering goals were defined for each of the financial processes within the project scope. The team identified target metrics and potential business benefits.

The business case was presented to senior management and met with their approval. The next stage was an R/3 pilot project. Warren Petroleum, a subsidiary of 900 employees, was selected. The business case team was reorganized into an implementation team of 50 members. The majority of the members came from the original project team. This team was again divided by business process for the design phase. The team moved into greater detail to develop a common process and system configuration that met the goal of a corporatewide standardization of these business processes across all subsidiaries. During the design phase, 70 percent of the project team members were business oriented, while the actual implementation activities (conversion and cutover) were carried out primarily by the team members having an IT background.

Of the 900 employees in the pilot project, some 300 would be actual users of the AFIS (Advanced Financial Information System). Of these, one-third (100) were expected to be heavy (constant) users, and the rest were part-time or casual users. These numbers provided a solid but manageable test environment.

The project was supported by the steering committee, a team of senior managers from Warren Petroleum and the corporation who espoused the concept of providing common financial processes throughout the corporation. In addition, the project team utilized a larger community of process experts and change advocates, members of the various organizations affected by the changes. These individuals were spokespeople for the project and liaisons for the project team at the various field locations.

The Warren implementation was completed in nine months and met the cost savings goals set for it. The project team was given approval to expand into the remaining operating companies. As of this writing, the system had been implemented in three companies, and four were in process. The next large target is a company having 3,500 users, which will provide a challenge in scope. Jim Zell, the project leader, reports that Chevron expects to complete the implementation by the beginning of 1998, at which time there will be an estimated 10,000 end users.

To date, there has been a reduction in process costs of 25 percent. In addition, the intangible benefits, such as better information, are difficult to quantify, but are supported by anecdotal evidence. Zell says that if the companies and individuals did not see the benefits, they would have slipped back to using the old processes. He emphasizes the need to make the users the owners of the project. This was done by a concerned focus on business benefits and a process of holding people accountable to accomplish those targets.

10.12 The Case of Hydro Agri North America (HANA)

HANA is a $600 million company that distributes agricultural chemicals across the Americas to large-scale farmer cooperatives and wholesalers. It came together with the acquisition of four separate companies, each with its own history of growth, unique culture, and individualized computer system. The largest company operated on a batch system providing correct inventory data only at the end of the month. HANA faced a challenge in its ability to manage inventory and logistics across its geographies. This required the four companies to truly merge and operate as a single entity while preserving the unique aspects that served the customer base.

HANA began its integrated systems project in November of 1992. The team identified information technology as a strategic advantage and a mechanism to consolidate four independent companies into one. The second phase of the project was process reengineering. In this effort, the team enlisted 75 percent of the users to define best practices. Early on in the project, it was decided that the software decision would be up to the users, in an attempt to remove traditional boundaries and to encourage cross-functional activities.

A set of detailed system requirements was drawn up, and the vendor selection (SAP) was made based on its ability to meet these needs. The company felt speed was essential, and it implemented financials, controlling, sales and distribution, and materials management in the largest HANA segment in nine months. The entire newly reformed organization went live in January 1995.

In a pseudo trial run prior to the first implementation, users discovered that the information now available was a quantum leap above their old data. This led to the decision not to bring the historical data into the R/3 system. It was incompatible and would take too long to convert. For their uses, there was little value in the history. The old system was kept online for a period so that inquiries could be made where necessary. This capability was soon phased out.

The new system solved numerous business problems—from the dot matrix printer that jammed every few checks it printed, to the ability to strategize at the executive level about the use of ammonia, a basic ingredient in all the companies. Overall, HANA saved $900,000 from the centralization of the back-office functions.

And the project helped to unify the culture. Many people from different groups were involved in rethinking the business processes and defining how the business should operate. The core project team members believed that once implemented, the common systems and data would bring people together. They were surprised to find that the process of implementation itself played a significant role in meeting this goal.

As one can imagine, the political issues were the most difficult to resolve. The president was instrumental in bringing the leaders together. He traveled around the country appealing to his managers' desire for an improvement in operations. During an SAP day, he personally demonstrated how he already used the system to gain improved business data. This story became part of the corporate myth and influenced many to accept the change.

The next phase, according to HANA, is learning to make the most out of the system. Executives reported that they felt as though they had purchased a Ferrari, but couldn't figure out how to get it out of first gear. As many other implementation teams have discovered, the ability to use the system is a challenge. Meeting that challenge will provide any company the ability to move ahead of its competition.

SECTION 3

Mitigating the Risk

CHAPTER 11

Managing Change: The "Political" Challenges

11.1 Why Companies Change   216
11.2 The Case of Monsanto   216
11.3 Key Principles of Change Management   219
11.4 Change Management Learnings   225
11.5 Multinational Implementation Challenges   227

11.1 Why Companies Change

The impetus for change comes from a sense of dissatisfaction with the current situation, a realization that there are opportunities not yet captured, or both. Today, executives manage change efforts larger in scope than were attempted previously for three reasons:

- Economics drives it.
- Competition requires it.
- Technology makes it possible.

Companies can no longer be complacent about their ability to sell their products. Customers are price sensitive, time sensitive, and quality sensitive. This has placed a burden upon many companies that assumed the opposite in years past. The company that does not utilize best practices in most of its business processes will find itself lagging in sales and earnings. Thus, the requirement to make substantial change is obvious to astute business executives.

Ten years ago, companies felt the need for change but were hard pressed to find the technological solutions (both hardware and software) to truly accomplish what they envisioned. Some experimented with combinations of networks and systems; others waited for the technology to emerge. R/3 is the first out-of-the-box solution that enables companies to tie together all their disparate corporate entities. This allows them to conduct all facets of the business more rapidly and with enhanced quality.

This opportunity creates specific change management issues. To take a closer look at these issues, let us examine the effort-in-progress at Monsanto.

The change management portion of this massive effort is exceptionally well structured, and will be used to illustrate the key principles of change.

11.2 The Case of Monsanto

Monsanto is a global company having annual revenues of over $8 billion. It is comprised of 14 strategic business units (SBUs), whose sales range from less than $100 million to over $1.5 billion. Monsanto's chemical SBUs account for about half of total company sales. In 1991, Monanto's chemical SBU executive management realized that significant change was required to compete effectively in the future. As a result, the chemical SBUs launched over a dozen reengineering initiatives, all focused on radical and lasting improvements of key work processes, with success measured ultimately in hard dollars taken to the bottom line.

One of these initiatives was called *Worldwide Order Fulfillment* and was termed *WWOF* (pronounced *woof*). It kicked off in early 1992, but as it matured it grew in scope and became known in early 1995 as *Worldwide Operations and Financials*. In its current scope, WWOF is chartered to completely reengineer Monsanto chemical SBUs' supply chain processes and all financial processes for the entire corporation. SAP-integrated software has been selected as the technology tool.

In 1992 and 1993, the focus was on improving the individual business processes, and in this effort Monsanto gained considerable benefits. As Jack Hanley, WWOF Director of Change Management puts it, "We gathered all the low hanging fruit we could, and because we had been so successful, there was quite a bit of fruit to gather. However, we recognized that going beyond 'early wins' required adding another dimension to our redesign tool kit—integrating technology."

At that point, Monsanto management and the WWOF team identified technology as the next area of opportunity for greater business returns. In mid-1994, SAP was selected as the integrating technology that would enable Monsanto to carry out a major supply chain and financial redesign. One hundred people from various functional organizations were recruited and asked to join WWOF for a three- to five-year period. The teams were told to create best practice models to be applied in a common fashion across all SBUs, allowing only minor modifications within SBUs to reflect unique business requirements. The teams dedicated themselves during this enterprise design phase to developing best-in-class processes for customer service, integrated planning and scheduling, procurement, logistics, manufacturing, maintenance, capital project management, and finance.

The next step was to integrate each of these designs. This was not an easy process. Perhaps in hindsight, Monsanto ought to have built in more integration points; however, the task was completed, and in June 1995 Monsanto's chemical SBUs started supply chain and global financials configuration of R/3. Throughout the enterprise design phase, the teams were driven to create best practice processes; the intent was that they not be driven by the technology. In addition, the

WWOF leadership team made a key decision early in the project—no customizing of SAP software.

By the end of September 1995, the WWOF project team completed the configuration and delivered the proof of concept. Its members had proven to themselves and their executive leadership that R/3 could deliver most of the redesigned processes. They achieved an 80 percent fit to R/3 Version 2.2. Of the remaining 20 percent, a few areas are critical, and they are now testing SAP Version 3.0 to determine how much of the necessary functionality 3.0 will deliver. What is not available in 3.0 will be supplied by bolt-ons that fit within the R/3 structure. For example, the sales and operations planning capability is not robust enough for their needs. They have already identified a vendor who can deliver against their specifications.

The Monsanto chemical and fibers divisions were the first to implement the redesigned supply chain processes. Implementation began with the general ledger, since it provides the transaction foundation for all the other SAP modules. Cutover to the general ledger and asset accounting for the U.S. was accomplished in January of 1997. This event was followed in April with a big bang implementation for 3,500 users of all the modules that support the best practice supply chain. This event included the implementation of their Enterprise Reference Data (ERD), a repository for all master data common to North America and Europe. In order to maintain the integrity of these data tables, Monsanto instituted a stewardship function to make final decisions regarding data standards.

Full SAP implementation for the chemicals/fibers side of the operations will take until the end of 1998. Monsanto expects to complete implementation for all in-scope SBUs, world areas, and functions, by the end of 1999, applying lessons learned from the pilot SBU and sharply compressing the amount of time required to implement.

While this rate of progress may seem slow to some, it is important to understand the scope of the project. The pilot SBU alone is as large as many good-sized companies. There will be over 4,000 ultimate users just in that SBU. In addition, Monsanto as a corporate entity continues to struggle with the issue of commonalty across a very large corporation. Further, because of the project's width and breath, virtually everyone in the company will see substantial change, so great attention has been paid to change management.

The WWOF team has built its organizing principle around people, process, and technology. The *people* side of this triad is change management accountability; however, it is important to recognize that the three aspects are inextricably interconnected.

Dan Dolger, WWOF Director of Organization Development and Design says that, in his considerable experience, many large-scale change efforts fail or are disappointing because of lack of attention to the people component. The key drivers identified by the WWOF change management team are leadership enrollment, communication, training, organizational roles and structure, performance management, and management practices. We will examine each of these critical elements in turn.

11.3 Key Principles of Change Management

- Leadership Enrollment
- Communications
- Training
- Organizational Roles and Structure
- Performance Management
- Management Practices

Leadership Enrollment

Many project teams struggle with this issue. They are asked by management to complete a certain project; yet they either feel abandoned or ignored by that same management, or are hesitant to go to them for help, fearing they will look weak. For their part, management has turned their attention elsewhere, thinking the problem is being solved.

A first step in maintaining senior focus is to create a management steering team comprised of the individuals who have a stake in the success of the project—the *stakeholders*. These people must be kept informed and involved if they are to truly be useful to the project. And they must be trained. Since executives are generally resistant to spending time in a classroom, the training should minimize this approach, with the exception of the R/3 orientation training. Other topics, such as change management, should be introduced in the same manner as we suggested the team training be delivered—just in time.

In addition to the executive steering committee, Monsanto created a Program Direction Team, a group of director-level sponsors, most of whom worked closely with individual teams, encouraging, guiding, and challenging their respective teams. The Program Direction Team also met with WWOF's leadership team on a frequent basis to help resolve tactical issues that impacted the project as a whole. Finally, Monsanto's WWOF redesign teams recruited stakeholders, functional experts who worked closely with individual teams, providing hands-on assistance in the creation and validation of the best practice processes.

Thus, Monsanto's approach to leadership involvement began at the executive level (steering committee) and included middle management (program direction team) and end users (stakeholders). It is critical to success that the managers of the functions involved understand the implications of the new design fully. It is the responsibility of the project leader, in conjunction with the steering committee, to ensure all parts of the organization are included in the initiative as early as possible.

Communications

An effective communications strategy is a two-way process for understanding the needs of the target audience and conveying the extent and nature of the coming changes. A project team can successfully accomplish this by identifying the most used communications vehicles and assessing the types of messages they deliver well, such as general information, project overviews, detailed analyses, and the like. The team must then target the various audience segments and their preferred mode of obtaining information.

Effective communicators know that getting across a complex or difficult message requires a variety of methods repeated several times for each person. Thus, a good presentation will include bullets, pictures, an enthusiastic presenter, and the presence and support of a senior executive. In this way, the presenter will appeal to several modes of learning. People will need to hear these messages a number of times before they can integrate them into their thinking.

The change management people at Monsanto say they are taking a disciplined approach to communications. They analyze the message, the intent, the audience, and the vehicle. You have to start early, they say, to inform the users about the new system—tell them what it is and what it is not. This is important because, otherwise, people stay in denial, believing the system is simply the *program du jour.*

It is hard to find the right level of detail. Of course, you start with an overview, but you have to get quickly into the details so that people can be prepared. Each company will need to develop the approach that will work best for them. If in your follow-up conversations, you discover that users have not paid much attention to your messages, you may want to increase the sense of urgency and the detail concerning how the system will change the way people must work together.

The most important communication of all is the reason and purpose for the change and how the change will manifest itself at the individual employee level. Strangely, this is often overlooked. When employees understand the ways in which the company will rely upon the new system and their roles in its success, they are more likely to adjust easily. Early, consistent, and continuous communications of the vision and the goals are essential to eventual acceptance and thus success.

To the extent possible, it is best to tell people exactly what will happen to their jobs. Again, this message is often overlooked or understated. Treat people as adults, and expect they will act in the same way. People will generally respond well to being told the truth. And if you are not yet clear, tell them that. Truth generates trust.

Training

For some companies, training is considered a low priority, an expense that can be reduced or eliminated in hard times. It is more effective to think of training as an asset. After all, the skills and knowledge of your employees are what make them valuable. You invest in their development just as you invest in building your product.

A good training program should begin with an analysis of the needs of the users. SAIC, for example, completed a survey and observation of employees who had participated in its pilot project. From that initial information, the SAIC project team created a corporate end user survey and conducted several focus groups. Team members interviewed each of the user managers and analyzed all the documentation provided by the project, as well as feedback from the demos and road shows.

The purpose of this analysis is to understand *what* to present and *how* to deliver the information. From the results of the analysis, the training team can identify the number and types of training courses. It will know the number of users to be trained, their locations, the number of days for each course, the number of courses to be delivered, and the number of trainers needed. The media to be used may include computer-based training, video presentations, manuals, and online help.

Most companies having a large number of users to be trained will use internal people to deliver much of the training. In Monsanto's case, WWOF is in the process of recruiting ten enterprise trainers, each of whom will be an expert in a best practice process and in the SAP modules that support that process. The enterprise trainers, in turn, will train super- or power users, all of whom will be accountable for training end users. The super- or power users will come from the *line*, and will continue in their line jobs. A key benefit in this approach is that, once initial end user training is done, end users will work side-by-side with the people who gave them their initial training. All trainers should be selected carefully; they should be natural teachers, must be experts in the business processes they are teaching, and must recognize and understand the relationships between their processes and all the others. In brief, trainers are in the business of transferring knowledge, and it takes time and experience to learn this skill. When using internal trainers, courses should be developed that are easy to teach. The combination of the trainer's business experience and the course design should deliver the most effective learning experience possible.

Organizational Roles and Structure

Reengineering major business processes—such as the supply chain—results in new organizational structures and new job roles for many people. To prepare for such a massive change, a company should begin by assessing the readiness and capability of the user population. Even when there is no downsizing involved, there will be people who cannot fit into the new organization and need to be redeployed. The company needs to understand the difference between existing competencies and those required by the new process and new system.

Make no mistake, the new competencies are complex. They go well beyond simple tasks such as learning how to do an inquiry into the system to gain customer or product information. When a business process is changed, it results in significant changes in the way people work and are managed. In the Battco case, for example, the order entry clerks would become customer advisors rather than typists. Assisting customers to order the best solutions for their business needs is a far more complex task than copying order information from one medium to another. In many companies, including Monsanto, teams will be formed to be responsible for major pieces of work. Not only are there team skills to be learned, but the managers of these work groups must learn a new way to lead them. They will have to learn to advise, more than direct the team's activities.

Companies that are shifting to a process view rather than a functional view of structure will find there are substantial changes to be implemented. There is significant resistance, particularly in companies that have been organized tightly around functional departments. Some managers will feel their sphere of authority is being altered in ways that seem detrimental both to the company and to themselves. In Battco, the finance manager had a difficult time seeing how she could do her job of controlling sensitive information if it was available generally. In addition, adding a new customer to the customer master file (originally her responsibility), would pass to the order entry department. She felt a loss of control over information that was critical to the success of the company. It is difficult to change one's view of responsibility to include a horizontal rather than a vertical view. Monsanto (along with some other companies) has identified *process owners*, senior managers who are held accountable for their cross-functional process. They are expected to be measured on the implementation of best practices, continual improvement, and corporate commonality.

These shifts represent some of the most difficult faced by companies that are reengineering their business.

Monsanto began by developing a diagnostic tool they called the *Change Readiness Assessment*. They interviewed senior managers to gain an understanding of their feelings about the upcoming change. They documented the results. Here are a few sample quotes:

- "After all, it's only a systems project."
- "This is a cultural change not a systems project."
- "It will impact a lot of people, but I don't see how it will impact me."
- "We may not have the right people for the new way."

From these interviews, the change management team saw where the education effort needed to be focused.

Next, the team completed an organizational profile in the pilot SBU. From the best practice processes, it extracted the attributes, competencies, and skills needed in the new way of operating. These data were developed into a survey which was administered to fully 20 percent of the SBUs' workforce, so that the results would be statistically significant. Individuals were asked to judge where they were today and where they would like to be with regard to each attribute or skill. The change management team then compared these scores with the goal required by the new system. The team was pleased to see that, psychologically, people wanted to upgrade themselves, although they did not quite understand the extent of the change required. But they were moving in the right direction.

From these results, the change management team created a prioritized change plan. It will address such issues as reward and recognition, role definitions, key performance indicators (KPIs), effective teamwork, and effective communication.

Performance Management

We will discuss this topic in the next chapter. It is one of the elements of effective project management. Here we take the larger view. Performance management is critical to the organizations affected by the reengineered business process and the system making it all possible. Employees (including managers) must be given clear targets for their actions. How else will they know if they have succeeded or failed? During a time of transition, when shifting from one way of operating to another, it is particularly critical to provide clarity. Part of the change management effort, then, will be to ensure that there is a clear and direct linkage between the work people do and the rewards and recognition they receive.

In addition, managers must identify the overall objectives or key performance indicators (KPIs) for their departments. Indeed, a team's performance evaluation should be linked directly to KPIs, which in turn should drive the team's rewards and recognition. At Monsanto, for example, an SBU president will look at cash flow as one measure of the financial health of the unit. Cash flow can be broken down into its component parts of accounts receivable, accounts payable, revenue, and inventory. Inventory and revenues are two KPIs that will be applied to the sales and operations planning team, a cross-functional team of supply chain representatives accountable for short-term planning and execution of a unit's business. The accounts receivable department is measured by the day's sales outstanding (DSO). This KPI shows the average age of receivables. For example, if customers are allowed to exceed 30 days regularly, this means that much of the unit's cash is not available. Thus, the lower the DSO number, the more effective is the unit's ability to collect the cash it is owed. Just the opposite holds for payables, measured in days payable outstanding

(DPO). The greater the DPO, the better it is for a company's cash flow.

Thus, inventory, receivables, payables, and revenues are components of cash flow that should be managed by the individuals and teams that can affect them. In cases where people cannot understand how their behavior could possibly influence a KPI, it is useless as a performance metric.

The change management effort associated with a major R/3 project, which will significantly revise the ways in which people work and are measured, should be responsible for ensuring that those changes are identified and implemented along with the new system. Quoting Jack Hanley of Monsanto, "Tell me how you are going to pay me and I'll tell you how I'm going to work."

Management Practices

Clearly, when a business process is revised, there is a major impact on management practices. The job of identifying and implementing changes in operations does not fall to the project team alone. Ultimately, it is the responsibility of the department or process manager.

Thus, change is often accelerated when it is leader led. Managers must be able to provide the type of direction that will encourage and challenge their teams and individual employees to operate successfully in the new way. The entire model of management has shifted in the past several years toward leadership. Managers are expected to coach, counsel, encourage, and challenge their employees. They must be able to operate in a cross-functional collaborative fashion using influence far more than outright commands. Managers must understand how teams function, to best support the teams for which they are accountable. They must be able to provide a higher level than before of conflict management, problem solving, and joint decision-making, and management must forsake micromanaging and practice greater measures of trust.

The change management strategy must include plans to deal with managers who will not or cannot make this shift and reward the ones who do.

11.4 Change Management Learnings

We see from this discussion of the key drivers in change management that there is far more to consider than merely training and communications. Unless the broader issues are addressed, managers are on their own. When this is the case, some will succeed brilliantly, some will fail, and the majority will languish somewhere in the middle.

How will an organization know if the changes have really been successfully integrated? The only way to really understand the nature of success and completion is to study the results after the fact. We found no instances where this has yet happened in a systematic way.

In the absence of such data, there still are some lessons that can be learned:

> - Magnitude of change will be greater than imagined.
> - The most resistance will not appear until after implementation.
> - Managed change may be expensive, but the costs are minor compared to unmanaged change.

Many companies want to revise their operations with a process view in mind and choose R/3, because, even though it is organized functionally, the integration available supports a process orientation. However, in implementing R/3, many companies have set in motion changes with greater implications for employees than they first imagined. In the example of Monsanto, we have illustrated many of these role and skill implications for all employees including managers. Monsanto was aware from the beginning of the nature of the changes the project had caused. Many companies are not. The attitude of many companies is that all they need to do is to change the screens and people will change their behavior. This is potentially a dangerous and costly way to proceed.

When employees are faced with the need to take on more accountability, or a different role; when their job changes so they feel they no longer have the skills required; when employees at any level feel they no longer have any control over their own domain, then the change manager will begin to feel resistance.

It is true that much resistance brought on by the novelty will dissipate with time. People will eventually learn how to operate in the new way, will apply the training, and will teach one another new applications they have learned themselves. This is not the resistance that is of the greatest concern, and it can be dealt with primarily by communication and training.

The deeper issue, however, is the massive change required in attitudes and approaches that is brought on by different ways of operating. In cases where the existing processes are not changed, but merely automated, these changes are never triggered. However, since so many companies have recently "discovered" process improvement, the nature of the change is yet to be fully explored.

Companies like Monsanto have taken the managed change route, and are preparing their employees for the new attitudes along with the new skills required. Others will find themselves in the unmanaged change category. They will discover that the cost to repair broken processes will rise over time, because incorrect and inaccurate perceptions and attitudes will become entrenched.

Happily, the way out of this dilemma is to pay attention to the various issues inherent in change management from the beginning of the project. The cost will be lower in the long run, and the project will be far more successful.

11.5 Multinational Implementation Challenges

Along with consolidation of acquisitions, the greatest change management challenges arise with multinational implementation projects. There are three approaches to this set of challenges: the export model, the partnership model, and the global model (see Table 11–1).

Table 11–1: Implementing systems internationally—multinational approach

	Characteristics	Advantages	Liabilities
Export	• Develop business/IS model at home • Implement with input from other countries	• Reinforces corp. identity/culture • Management can understand/explain approach • Focus on similarities	• Change may not fit country cultures • Resistance may be higher

Copyright 1996 Bancroft, Brite & Associates, Inc.

Table 11–1:   Implementing systems internationally—multinational approach (con't.)

	Characteristics	Advantages	Liabilities
Partnership	• Only a few countries involved • Closeness in geography, language, culture • System developed collaboratively	• Develop collaborative business/system model • System accepted by those involved • May increase mutual respect/trust	• Team may not choose the best approach
Global	• Company sees itself as a global enterprise • Corporate best practices are chosen as business/system models for development • Integration across countries seen as a business imperative	• Corporation implements the best approach • Business/system processes tied together with corporate requirements	• May be difficult to deal with corporate complexity • Integration challenging • Buy-in may take more time to achieve

The export model arises when a company decides that its corporate headquarters is best positioned to define the elements of the information systems required in other countries. Teams are generally made up of a majority of people from the functions within the country of origin. The design of the system is completed with as much input from the affected countries as is possible, depending upon the distance from the country of origin and the political ties. The actual implementation may be completed either within the country of origin or at the user's site. The key differentiator here is who has the greatest influence over the final design. Whether the territory involved is across several European countries or from the U.S. to Europe or the Far East, this model is the most frequently used. It is assumed by management that similarity of systems (with flexibility for local tax laws for example) will be the most efficient approach. A number of companies we studied fell into this category. We'll describe the Digital Equipment experience below as an example of this approach.

The *partnership* model is used most often when there are only a few countries involved. Teams are composed of equal members from each country and, while the design work may be accomplished primarily at the location of the country of origin, the design is a true collaboration. Chapter 5 included the case of Agrium, Inc. It is an example of this model. The project team was comprised of equal numbers of U.S. and Canadian members (the South American effort has not yet been started). The team met in Canada and finally adopted the U.S. model of pricing while other decisions were more easily and collaboratively made. Below, we'll describe the Samsung, Korea implementation in the U.K. as another example of this model.

The *global* model is used when there are many countries involved and the general philosophy of the corporation is that the company entity is truly global. Executives think of themselves as part of a corporation that just happens to be spread across the globe rather than one that started in a certain country and opened subsidiary offices in different countries. Companies in this third approach are generally very large and have been in business for many years. Proctor and Gamble, Coca-Cola, Dow Chemical, and General Electric are examples of such companies.

The Case of Digital Equipment Corporation

Digital is an example of the export model of multinational implementation approaches. Digital went live with SD, MM, FI, and PP for the PC business unit, a $1 billion business, in its European region in February 1996. It is currently running Release 2.2F using the Digital Alpha Servers, Unix 3.2, and Oracle 7.1.6. The implementation includes 39 business operations locations in 63 countries including the Mid-East and Africa. There are 200 concurrent users. The entire system is actually run from two data centers in the U.S., a main center and a duplicate fail-safe center. Dan Hamel, the CIO for the PC business unit and the project leader, feels that the success of this effort is due, in part, to the speed and reliability of the Alpha test version.

Digital had been running some sixty to seventy different applications in the European region. This region was the most complex and it was felt it needed immediate attention. R/3 contained all the salient features required for the project and, in addition, SAP was considered to have more momentum than its competition and to provide a leadership factor. The decision to choose SAP was made by the management of all the company's business units which will migrate to R/3 as soon as practicable. The PC unit was chosen to provide the base line for the company. Retiring the many legacy systems was a major future benefit to the choice of SAP.

The project teams, a total of fifty to sixty people, were formed with representatives of all affected functions. From thirty to thirty-five of these were Digital employees; the remainder were consultants. The team spent a year working together at a site in the U.S. to complete the project. There were numerous reviews with the European Region management. The team decided to spend six months doing unit testing and eight weeks of full integration testing in order to ensure success at final implementation. Twenty-six people who would be in the new organization were moved to Reading, England for final testing and training. The original plan was to centralize the order desk in one location with inquiry capability in the various countries.

When the countries began to realize what this would really mean to them (toward the end of the testing), they appealed for a change, and the system was reconfigured to allow order entry from each country. After several months, management began to see that the original plan was the best in terms of cost-effectiveness and co-location of order entry experts for communication and problem solving. The project then re-reconfigured the system (back to plan A) for centralized order entry in Scotland.

Even though they had been involved in the design, the local managers did not have much time or incentive to focus on the change they would feel. The pressure of everyday business made it difficult for them to internalize what would actually happen. When cutover time neared, the local management finally began to suggest changes in the design, and when major conflicts arose, the decision was sent to the steering committee. Because of schedule constraints, the decision generally was made in favor of the existing design. This caused problems after they went live, especially when the workers were actually given the system. Digital has a history of strong independent thinking and decision making. The precept of the founder, Ken Olsen, was "Do the right thing." Employees, even today, have a tendency to revert to their old ways even though policies and procedures have been written to reinforce the new system and the new ways of operating. Clearly, the problems Digital had were business and cultural ones, not system ones.

The decision to accede to the desires of the users and allow order entry to be carried out in the separate countries was the right approach given the culture of the company. That they came to see that the original plan was the best one was a tribute to the flexibility of the employees. Even though time was lost and the level of frustration was high, in the end the project management made a series of good decisions.

The Digital example is a clear case of a company using the export model for multinational implementations. Not only was the entire project completed in the country of origin, but the actual hardware installation was completed and is intended to remain there. The local management and users were invited to participate; however until the final implementation was close, they were not able to give the project much attention. The project leaders gave as much attention as they could to the needs of the local employees, and compromises were made if they did not have an impact on the deployment schedule. However, many of the previously established processes were ultimately changed in favor of the new SAP processes. In multinational projects, accommodations must be made by everyone involved.

The Case of Samsung Heavy Industries

Samsung Heavy Industries (SHI) is located in South Korea. In 1995 the company decided to expand into Europe, and its first step was to build a new plant in the U.K. Since this was a greenfield operation, there was no existing set of policies or procedures other than the South Korean business processes. The decision was made to choose a packaged system that would provide an efficient solution to the several modules that would be needed, as well as provide roll-up data to headquarters. Among the enterprise resource planning (ERP) packages, SAP R/3 was seen as having the most integrated and most popular system. In addition, SHI Korea has a master plan to implement R/3 in the future. Thus R/3 was the clear choice. Samsung implemented the modules SD, PP, MM, FI, and CO.

Members of the business processes involved and Samsung Data Systems (SDS) were sent from South Korea to the U.K. from July 1995 to April 1996. There they teamed with the newly hired Samsung U.K. personnel and the SAP consultants. Since there were no legacy systems to transfer, there was no problem with data conversion and no resistance of users. The approach was a new design, thus they were able to begin with the *to be* stage. The team used the Aris Toolset to define the design concept. The team was relatively small and were able to be seated in one room.

Most problems arose from the modular approach the team took to design. One subgroup would design a module, but upon testing, would discover that configuration decisions they made negatively impacted other modules. And some of the company requirements could not be handled by R/3. For example, engineering changes were maintained by product serial number, but Samsung products are configurable, needing material delivery to each work center. The team used the consultants to develop ways to work around in order to accommodate the delivery of stock to configurable products, as well as the high number of product modifications.

The team started training in May 1995 for three months to gain a good grounding in each module. As part of that training process the basic SHI business process was described to all members. The entire team was sent to Germany in August for additional training. Modeling was accomplished from August to October, and prototyping was done between November 1995 and January 1996. The next two months were spent on testing, and they went live in May 1996.

This team used the partnership model, operating in the U.K., with the employees who would run the new plant and those from the parent company working together to define a new system. This does not mean, however, that there were no problems. In addition to the language problems (some from South Korea did not speak English well), there were religious differences. On Sunday many went to church, while the Buddhists did not. These differences were not material to the project content but they degraded team morale. Team members were drawn to like or dislike others based on similarity. This made communications and decision making more difficult.

H. B. Park established the master plan for the R/3 project, organized members and contracted for needed expertise. He was also actively involved in each phase of the project. His conclusions are that all team members must be expert in their own functional roll; in addition, IS team members must understand the business process while users must be open to understand systems issues. When this is the case, the project will be successful.

CHAPTER 12

Team Formation and Development

12.1 The Essential Elements of Successful Teams   234
12.2 The Gap between Strategists and Implementers   241
12.3 Setting and Maintaining Expectations   243
12.4 Team Training   244

12.1 *The Essential Elements of Successful Teams*

Today, many companies have organized employees into work teams to tap the potential of human energy and apply it to business tasks. When set up properly, these teams can be extremely effective. Teams may be relatively permanent or temporary in nature, and often some form of team training is conducted to teach team members the skills of working effectively in groups. The essential elements of successful teams are:

- The right team members.
- Excellent project management.
- Clear goals.

In the case of temporary teams, managers often assume they have done what is needed simply by organizing the team, and do not give the team process another thought—unless a problem arises.

It will be far more difficult to solve a problem later than to forestall it in the first place.

Because the core team members for an R/3 implementation will be together for an average of six to twelve months, experience shows that attention to the three simple essential elements of good team processes will pay enormous dividends. They are simple but not easy. Sadly, all three elements are usually assumed to be in place, when they are not.

Choose the Right People

The five characteristics of effective team members are:

- Expertise.
- Respected by others.
- Vision and problem-solving ability.
- Openness.
- Ability to support the group decision.

Team members are usually selected from the user organizations because of their business process knowledge. Team members must reflect the expertise of the groups they represent. In addition, they must be well respected throughout their organization. If the person is isolated, he or she will not provide a credible conduit for essential information to pass in either direction, and ideas the individual brings back from the project team will not be listened to, much less accepted. At the same time, information on critical business needs will not be heard by the team.

It is essential that the team position not be used to solve performance or job assignment problems, even though it may seem tempting to the user manager. Only rarely will this tactic work to your advantage. In general, it negates the credibility of the project. If you want the project to be successful, assign your best people. There is no way around it.

Team members must be able to see the larger picture and contribute to the development of the redesign of the business process. And they must be good problem solvers. These skills are not the same. They require different focuses; that is, both divergent (the ability to see more possibilities) and convergent (the ability to focus in to the essential elements of a problem) points of view. They will need to have the patience to sit at a terminal and work through the iterative design of the new system until it meets as many of the needs as possible. R/3 will generally provide the ability to achieve your goals, but it may require considerable experimentation to discover the path. If team members simply give up and decide a module must be written to provide a feature that is desired in the overall design, they will, by that action, create IS maintenance problems for the future.

Each team member must listen to the others to understand their point of view. Project teams will necessarily be comprised of members from different departments and disciplines. Thus, each member may speak a different business language. IS, finance, manufacturing—each has a unique perspective and approach which must be honored. Good team members are open to the viewpoints of others, especially when opinions differ from their own. Effective team members are persuasive and nondefensive. They are able to explain and illustrate their own view, question assumptions (including their own) and are able to "walk in the other's shoes" to help the team reach a consensus while avoiding "group think," the process by which groups of intelligent people make terrible decisions.

Finally, an effective team member has the ability to support the group decision fully. As individuals, they must be able to put aside any reservations and accept the group decision. This does not mean members should not work to bring to attention decisions they believe are unwise. However, having had their say and having heard the opposing viewpoints, they must set aside their own desires for the good of the whole. Team members must be able to communicate team decisions back to their organizations clearly and convincingly. If the team members are not convinced, they will not be able to convince.

Provide Excellent Project Management

The demands of managing a project will fall most heavily upon the project leader. He or she must provide discipline, structure, diplomacy, and performance management. These are the four essential elements of effectively managing a project team. Team members are also responsible for ensuring that these elements are effectively applied. Experience has shown that a shared leadership model will work more effectively than a strict hierarchical one. If each member reminds the others of the four elements, the group will stay on track. The four elements of effective project management are:

- Discipline.
- Structure.
- Diplomacy.
- Performance Management.

Discipline

Discipline is the ability to direct, support, and manage differences within the team. Directing involves clearly communicating the desired outcomes of project tasks, setting and enforcing deadlines, keeping the team on track, and encouraging participation from all members. It can be seen as providing the *task* side of the task-relationship equation.

On the *relationship* side is the skill of supporting. The project leader must listen to all team members to understand their varying opinions. He or she must help people to clarify their thoughts and provide equal time for minority opinions. Supporting team members also requires confrontation of a team member's approach or attitudes when they are not helpful to the others, or of outside distractions that throw off the team from its focus.

Managing differences means allowing for productive conflict to expose all viewpoints so that an informed decision can be made. In this regard, all input is valuable. One person may argue for an approach that will rapidly cut costs. Another may argue that the users will be frustrated and confused by that approach and a phased solution may serve the organization better in the long run. It may be possible for the project leader to assist the members in developing a solution that is both cost-effective and attentive to the needs of the users.

The project leader will do a better job at managing differences if he or she is aware of his or her personal biases, and helps others to become aware of theirs. One member, for example, may have a bias toward the most simple approach to a problem, and another may prefer to provide as many choices as possible. There is no correct answer; however, if individuals realize these differences are not essential to success, but are merely preferences, conflict can be minimized.

The most successful project leaders keep a balance of task and relationship behaviors, managing differences with an even-handed approach. They strive for congruence in words and behaviors, and tend to be calm in the face of chaos.

Structure

The project leader is responsible for providing structure for the team members. Structure will be found in the project methodology, team meetings, and communications outside of the team. The methodology for an R/3 implementation must be a rigorous project management tool: there are a number of effective tools available. It should include timelines, task breakdowns with team member assignments, task interdependencies, and an indication of the critical path.

It takes discipline to use a project management tool well. Updates must be entered in a timely fashion and changes made when they occur. There is no benefit to going off on a sidetrack to gather enough information to make a proper decision without adding the task to the chart. That way, you will see the changes in the timeline, and you *do* want to see them, even if the news is not good.

Meetings must be organized events. Each one should be scheduled, with an agenda and expected outcomes. A useful, though underused, approach is to set an agenda with time frames for each segment. An announcement could take five minutes, questions to clarify it could take 15 minutes, and the discussion could be set for 40 minutes, if it is a difficult subject. Should the discussion reach the 40-minute mark with no signs of any conclusion, the meeting should pause. The attendees should then decide how much more time should be allotted to finish the discussion, and what to do about the remaining items. Do not decide that five minutes more will complete the subject, because it is usually not adequate. Teams have used this technique and added five minutes, then five minutes more, and so on, until they had discussed the topic for another half an hour. Be reasonable in resetting your goals. When a meeting must end at a certain time with a particular decision made, most groups will manage to eliminate the fluff and spend the time on the substantial discussions leading to an informed decision. Using a structured approach may not feel as nice as you would like, but it will get the job done on time. When they get used to this approach, team members generally prefer it.

Meeting minutes should be shared with all attendees, as well as with those who had to miss the meeting. They should be filed as part of the documentation of the project process. This task can be circulated among the members.

In the same way, a structured approach to communications outside the project team is essential to maintaining a focus on the overall goals, and to keep the users and executive management aware of the impending changes. Each communication vehicle should be assessed for its ability to deliver exactly the desired message to precisely the right people. A wide variety of methods should be employed, from one-on-one meetings to group briefings, to the company newsletter. Maintain records of when each was used and what message was delivered. Then you will easily be able to see where the gaps might be. Overlaps are fine: you can never communicate too much.

These techniques will create a sense that the complex and difficult project process is under control. It may not feel that way to the leader or team members at all times, but the various elements of structure will pull a group through the inevitable "down" times.

Diplomacy

The third key aspect of project management is diplomacy. Again, this task falls mainly to the project leader, although all team members are responsible for their part. The most difficult aspect of any large change project (and that certainly includes R/3) is dealing with the political issues. Conflicts must be identified and resolved when they occur, or they will cause the project to be late or over budget. The project leader must deal effectively with all cross-functional issues and manage the senior management.

Implementing a common system across departments or divisions that have historically operated independently cannot fail to raise serious turf issues. Each department will want to have the system reflect its way of doing things. If the system will change a business process, tasks and responsibilities will disappear from one department possibly to reappear in a different form in another. Managers will strive to maintain control over their areas of expertise. A financial manager, as in the Battco example, may resist having the credit information made available to the order entry person, for fear it will be used incorrectly. When a person's career has been focused on maintaining certain standards—in this case, of fiscal responsibility—it is difficult to change perspectives quickly.

The art of diplomacy turns on the ability to manage conflicts, especially cross-functional ones, early and rapidly. Further, the successful project leader will be able to do this in a way that is perceived as fair and firm. The finance manager who has lost the battle regarding control over the credit information will, in the best case, realize the greater good that will accrue from the change and feel that the project leader listened to her concerns seriously even though the decision was not what she preferred. The only workable way to manage these issues is to address them as soon as they arise. If left to fester, they will become seemingly intractable and thus far more difficult to solve. If, in our example, the finance manager's concerns about the volatility of credit information were not addressed, her level of support for the new system would drop, and she might insist that even though the credit information was online, her people would have to have control over what information was given out to the order entry people.

The real difficulty with resolving these conflicts arises when the problem is not expressed to the project leader. Overt resistance is far easier to manage than covert resistance. For this reason, the project leader will be well advised to spend time with the various user managers explaining the system and gaining their confidence. The managers will be more likely to raise concerns before they become life-and-death issues.

Managing up is an exercise in influence and suggestion, rather than direction. Senior managers are not likely to be personally involved in every twist and turn of the implementation project. That is not their job. However, the old saw applies: Out of sight, out of mind. And that is dangerous to the health and success of the project. The senior managers may have every good wish for the success of the project, and their active championship of the cause will have significant impact upon the timely success of the venture. The project leader must be proactive in managing up. He or she must meet frequently with senior management to discuss the status of the project and report significant successes or potential problems. The senior manager will usually have to be coached as to what to say in a public forum about the project, and perhaps even handed a script or brief outline (one page, please) about the essential facts of the project.

In one implementation project, the project leader, frustrated that the user managers had not attended the project review meeting and feeling that they did not fully understand the implications of the changes he was asked to complete, set up a series of mandatory training sessions. In his culture *mandatory* did not carry a positive connotation. Within two hours of his sending out the email establishing the dates of the sessions, the executive sponsor for the project sent out *his* email supporting the need for everyone to gain a better understanding of the system and requesting that everyone sign up to attend the informational meetings. This is an example of rapid support from the executive level that is required.

Performance Management

The project leader will need to ensure that clear, obtainable objectives are set for each team member. With regular status meetings, the leader will be able to discover if there are any missed deadlines. When the problem is a lack of training, that need must be met immediately. More likely, the cause is an overload of work that causes the team member to be unable to complete a task on time. When this is the case, the schedule must be assessed to see if tasks have too many subtasks or were not evaluated correctly in the first place.

The project leader must stay on top of such problems and troubleshoot them immediately. Don't bury or excuse missed deadlines. The problem may not be resolved by training or reducing the workload. Any inability to perform must be assessed and dealt with so that the overall project schedule is not negatively impacted. This requires a combination of empathy and strictness.

The key to managing team performance is creating a balance between team and individual responsibilities. For instance, the team may have to come to consensus on a particularly difficult decision that requires full participation from all. Certain team members may need to complete tasks or conduct research to make the decision. It is the team's responsibility to insure that decision process is conducted with integrity. It is the individual's responsibility to deliver his or her assignments on time.

The more the project leader can induce the team members to manage their collective performance, the easier his or her job becomes relative to managing individual performance. This balance is accomplished by setting clear goals and expectations, and establishing consistent feedback mechanisms.

Establish Clear Goals

Finally, the project goals themselves must be very clear to everyone involved. Often, organizations find themselves in difficulty over this admonition and cannot understand why. The cause may be the difference between the level of understanding in the executive's mind and in the project team members' minds. For example, the sponsor of the project may have charged the team to improve the way that the materials management process at one end of the manufacturing process interacts with the daily inventory status at the other end, so as to result in more accurate quotes to the customer. At the initial meetings and in the resulting project definition documents, sponsors and project team members may have believed they had a clear picture of the project goals.

Difficulties arise when the project team explores the details of what it will take to improve these processes, because the goals may change. The team may find out that to change materials management and inventory, it will have to change the manufacturing system. Since that was defined as outside of the scope of the project, the team members are left with a conflict. They will not be able to make as much improvement as was originally expected because they are constrained by the exclusion of manufacturing.

12.2 *The Gap between Strategists and Implementers*

There may be a major disconnect between the strategic intent of a decision to implement a certain system and the resulting actions that must be completed. The matrix in Figure 12–1 illustrates the reasons for such potential conflict. Here we have the two levels on the vertical axis—the strategists and those who are given the responsibility to implement the strategies. On the horizontal axis are shown the two focuses of these individuals. Strategists are terrific at setting the

@ 1993 Bancroft, Brite & Associates

Figure 12–1: The strategist/implementer matrix

context of a strategy. They define the overall direction to be taken by the organization in general terms. Implementers, in contrast, excel in carrying out the activities (the actions) that are required to implement a plan. The difficulties arise in the upper right and the lower left quadrants. Strategists seldom understand the implications of the actions suggested by their strategy, and it is in the details that a plan lives or dies. Implementers generally believe they understand the context for the strategy, but often are not aware of the full intent because it was never communicated, often because the strategists assumed everyone already understood it all. Implementers in such a position will create their own context for their actions, possibly resulting in a set of actions that do not achieve the true goal.

All the heads at the sales meeting may have gone up and down, but when the decision begins to be implemented and the next-level managers understand what they are being told to do, their heads may start to go sideways. Managing the differences between the original strategic context and the resulting actions that need to be completed correctly is an exercise in political expertise. The skills required are difficult to find.

Thus, goal setting becomes a process of goal adjusting. As before, the solution is to address the discrepancies early and rapidly.

Managing expectations is key to keeping those who are funding the project satisfied.

12.3 Setting and Maintaining Expectations

The model we use to explore expectations, and to set and reset them, is also used in a team discussion of dealing with conflict. The issues are the same. Let us consider the Pinch-Crunch model originally developed by Jack Sherwood.[1] In this model (Figure 12–2), we see that the first step is to share information and negotiate expectations. We do that in good conscience, knowing that there is information that is yet unknown. We identify the roles each will play in the project, and each player commits to achieving the goals. This results in a period of stability for a time. Soon however, as we get into the project, we start to wonder if everything will indeed turn out the way we originally thought. The team members find little discrepancies from the grand design. These minor difficulties are like a little pinch. They don't so much hurt as cause minor annoyance. Now we are at a choice point. We typically either ignore or deny we feel pinched, and pretend to return to stability.

Unfortunately, over time these little concerns mount up and eventually, we find ourselves realizing that we no longer share the same expectations. As in the example above, the team realizes it will not be able to obtain as much benefit by changing the external processes and ignoring the inner process (manufacturing). Suddenly, the team members and its leader realize they have a major problem. This leads to a crunch! The project leader must go to senior management and confess that the expectations will not be met. Again there is a choice point, but this time one with a great deal of emotion involved.

People may feel angry, let down, defensive, and so forth. The choices are to terminate the project (not likely to happen after all the announcements and money invested), a pretend return to the original commitment (that's the "you guys can do it, I know you can" pep talk) or a renegotiation under duress.

It is obvious from the diagram that the most successful way out is to renegotiate early when the first signs of trouble arise. This requires

---

[1] This model was described in an unpublished paper given to me by Jack Sherwood in 1982.

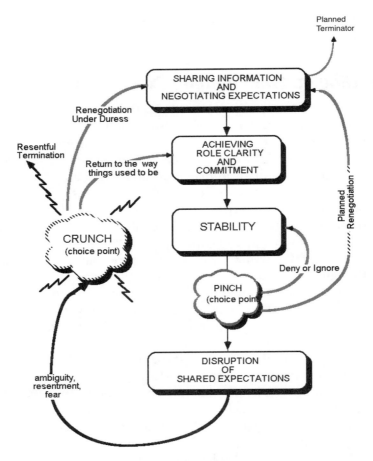

Figure 12–2: The pinch/crunch model

a calm discussion with the sponsor about the concerns and their implications, and a warning (usually based on experience) that these concerns do not generally disappear. The individuals involved can then
make an informed decision as to the best course available. This is the
process of goal adjusting. The overall goals generally remain stable;
their details will inevitably change as the project matures.

12.4 Team Training

The R/3 project teams will, of course, receive a great deal of training.
They will attend overview courses and courses in each module. As was

stated before, SAP is in the process of modifying its training to reflect a more interactive process approach; however, until that is available, the original module-based training will be necessary. The training will take up to three months, during which the team will be available for some assessment of the *as is* situation.

Many companies, justly feeling that they have spent enough time and money on R/3 training, will assume that nothing more is needed. Other companies, depending upon their goals and general approach, may provide the team with some additional training. Such subjects as the cycles of team development, interpersonal communications, learning styles, conflict management, and facilitation may be presented. In addition, some companies feel their teams benefit from off-site team-building sessions.

Often, when interpersonal problems arise, some will bemoan the fact that these topics were left uncovered in the press of time. It is impossible to know if such a session would have made a difference. Certainly, trying to resolve knotty problems when they have settled in is a difficult undertaking.

One day's worth of training for those who will select and manage the project team is worth three weeks of team training. Becoming proficient in the topics presented earlier in this chapter will forestall many (not all) of those interpersonal problems.

Should the team need help in a topic such as conflict management, the best approach is just-in-time training. In my experience, presenting the team with a two- to three-hour module on one of these topics when they begin to show a need for such input is far better than a formal training course. The preferred approach is to briefly present some conceptual material, such as the pinch-crunch model. The remaining time should be an immediate application of the model to the work in which the team is currently engaged.

This approach has two major advantages. First, it is an efficient use of the team's time. Two or three hours are spent rather than traveling off-site for a day or two. Second, it delivers the information and its application exactly when it is needed. Thus the learning is vastly enhanced. Adult learning theory informs us that most people will learn what they want to know when they need it. Further, people will retain a brief piece of information followed by a chance to practice it far better than a longer session of conceptual material.

Finally, it will be an effective use of time to hold an initial orientation team meeting, as well as several formal interim review meetings. These meetings should concentrate on the project itself with a statement of the project goals, a review of the schedule, and a statement of major milestones completed. Topics of general interest can be included if they are kept brief and to the point. For example, one team became so involved in designing a new financial system, that its members hardly had time to read a newspaper or listen to the TV. Periodically, the project sponsor would take an hour to review the company's financial status, explain the latest theory in science or mathematics, or present a session on creativity. The team members loved these sessions and talked about them for months after the project disbanded. They found it useful to take their minds off the project at hand for a brief period of time. And they felt they came back to the knotty problems with a renewed sense of excitement.

And that, in short, is what good team work is about—maintaining a sense of excitement about the project. Nothing is more motivating.

Implications of the "New" Technologies

CHAPTER 13

Changes in User and IT Roles

13.1 The Four Challenges 250
13.2 Meeting the Four Challenges 254
13.3 The Case of NEC Technologies 256

Success in such projects as the implementation of R/3 seems to be based on a shift in roles of both business and IS professionals away from traditional expertise and toward a greater understanding of one another's perspective. Furthermore, the language each uses is expanding to include words and phrases that come from both worlds. Line managers speak of line speed and response time, while IS people concern themselves with resolving customer queries or shipping correct orders the first time. These are trends that are encouraging. Not everyone, however, will be able to make the more substantial changes that underlie these surface aspects.

Project leaders are required to be able to deal as effectively with political issues as with business requirements and technical demands. Teams need to be trained not only in the new technology, but in such issues as change management approaches, team development cycles, and selling skills. Users are expected to learn how to learn better, that is, to discover how to gain the information they require, not just by using the query or reporting modules, but also by exploring ways to capture and compare pieces of data.

These role changes were identified as far back as fifteen years ago; however, the rapid deployment of R/3, with its consequent necessity for reengineering, has virtually forced companies to abandon business-as-usual and take control of IS projects in new ways. In this chapter, we will explore the ways in which changes in information technology and its strategic use by business managers have driven a need for significant reskilling of IS and users alike, as well as a reconceptualization of the IS project process.

13.1 The Four Challenges

We will examine the four challenges that have evolved out of the latest trends in information systems strategy and implementation:

- Reduced need for programmers.
- Reliance on complex technological architecture.
- Higher user involvement.
- User ownership of data/systems.

Reduced Need for Development Programmers

In the old days (still the norm in many companies), users would request a new system or a modification to an old one. IS (when the request made it to the top of the priority list) would analyze the business needs, and develop the system based on the traditional systems life-cycle model of analysis, specifications, coding, testing, and implementation. The user was asked to review progress at certain portions of the process. Everyone hoped the result would meet the needs. This work process resulted in large numbers of programs that needed to be maintained because of new computers, modifications in other programs, and business needs changes. Together, these are the legacy systems that exist in nearly every company.

Most companies hired development programmers and systems analysts, because they knew the programming languages and the hardware and network platforms used by that company. Programmers and analysts typically prefer new development over maintenance, because it entails design and coding from scratch. They tend to be people who look for situations where they can be creative and logical. They place a high value (higher than other professionals) on skill variety, task identity (completion of a segment of work such as a program or a system), autonomy, and job feedback. These elements have long been identified as basic to the structure of good job design. In addition, they generally score low on their needs for social interaction.

But the IS world has changed dramatically. Today many companies have made a strategic decision to purchase packaged software products. They generally prefer not to modify the code, but to customize only. Where the package does not meet the business needs, either the business will change, or a bolt-on module will be purchased, or as a last resort, developed in-house. Changing the code in R/3 is definitely not recommended.

Thus, the job content of the systems analyst/programmer has been changed to customizing, writing interfaces to send data from one SAP module to a non-SAP module and back again, and creating reports. The programmer is almost never allowed to get at the code, which is exactly what he or she prefers to do. One manager offers the opinion that many of the programmers who are truly creative have left the corporate world and have gone to work for the companies who develop all this packaged software. That's where they find job satisfaction.

One can easily see, in any case, that the need for large staffs of development programmers has diminished. They have not gone away completely, since there still remain many legacy systems to maintain, and there is interface and reporting work to do, but the preferred development projects no longer exist in any quantity.

Some have made the leap to the business side, where they provide support services helping with networks, PC questions, queries, and reporting needs. They are very useful in that capacity when corporate IS implements a new system complete with new hardware that the users don't understand.

In general, however, the role of the systems analyst/programmer has changed from that of an expert hands-on doer to more of a facilitator/advisor with an expertise in the technology. In any implementation of R/3, the project team has need of a number of members who understand the platform technology and the business and data structures and processes. The best team members operate collaboratively. They discuss options and make group decisions, a role not every IS person is capable of or desirous of taking on. It requires a significant change in job design elements. Most people find it difficult to change the aspects of their work that provide job satisfaction and motivation. Training people to become more interpersonable is difficult.

The best IS professionals will continue to be recruited for membership in project teams. The most successful ones will be able to make the leap toward a more collaborative, less independent work style. The customization needed in R/3 is extremely interesting and should provide enough challenge for the interested IS professional.

Reliance on Complex Technological Architecture

IS shops have, in addition to the programmer/analysts, a large segment of their population dedicated to the actual operation of the banks of computers. These system operations people are generally more involved with the actual technology than are the programmer/analysts. They speak the language of network protocols, optimization techniques, and reliability factors. This world has changed as well.

A recent advertisement for a data systems engineer (for an R/3 environment) requested experience in SAP procedures and forms maintenance, SAP system level install and upgrades on SAP servers, backup support to UNIX and Oracle DBA, database reorganization, data dictionary maintenance including data dictionary objects migration, data modeling, 4GL language, object-oriented systems analysis and design, RDBMS programming, and much more.

Some programmer/analysts have migrated to this world, where they will concentrate on the latter portion of the abbreviated job description above. The IS department of the future will provide a combination of specialties. IS professionals will need to be proficient in client/server fundamentals, databases, networks, development tools, and object-oriented approaches. They will also be expected to have a good understanding of some aspect of the business, materials management, human resources systems, or financials, for example.

The content of the operations-oriented portion of the job has changed significantly from the old IBM CICS days, yet the job goals remain essentially the same. Providing job satisfaction for these people is easier than for the development programmer/analysts since, the IS operations world remains one of managing the data and networks so that the users are able to easily and quickly process their transactions and obtain the data to make business decisions. Keeping the systems running and optimizing the performance remain the goals.

The changes in the technologies alone represent a significant training challenge.

Higher User Involvement

Project teams for R/3 implementation projects are typically made up of a majority of users with the addition of some IS people. The inclusion of IS is for one of two basic reasons: to ensure that the decisions made will be implementable in terms of the data structure and the architecture, or because the IS person is the SAP module expert. Whether the decisions are implementable in R/3 terms will become the province of the team as a whole in conjunction with the SAP module experts (who may be hired as consultants). One need not have an IS background to become an SAP module expert. Stories abound that illustrate the reverse. One secretary, for example, felt she could take on more responsibility, and was trained in the sales and distribution module. She was instrumental in configuring it as a member of the project team and was eventually hired away, thereby increasing her salary threefold.

Those interviewed concurred that users are well suited to make the configuration decisions because of their business knowledge. Users have always been involved in systems projects to some extent. In the case of R/3 they typically (although not always) drive the project.

Five years ago in one pharmaceutical company, users were appointed to the project team in equal numbers to the IS people. The

IS people, however dominated the process, because users understood neither the system development process nor the technology being employed. IS members continued to use programming logic language, and users who did not understand technospeak and who wished to help develop a system that would solve their business problem were frustrated and ineffective.

Today that scenario is quite different. If that same project were being implemented today using R/3, users would not only outnumber IS members, but the language spoken would be SAP, which all members would learn together. Users would find it easy to bring their expertise to bear on the issues confronting the team.

This change represents a shift in responsibility and in power. Users are in control of their business solutions, and correspondingly, must carry the blame if the system is late, over budget, or does not solve the problem. Since users generally are not used to assuming responsibility for their information systems, this brings about a need for a change in perspective and the addition of new skills to be acquired and managed. It also means that IS no longer has control over the design of the system.

User Ownership of Data/System

Along with their increased involvement in implementation projects, users are generally expected to assume responsibility for their systems. One CIO interviewed stated that his users owned the data. It was their responsibility to maintain the tables that were critical to running their R/3 system. Others surveyed echoed this sentiment. After years of concern in the IS camp for data integrity, IS has turned over this responsibility to the user community.

Some user groups will hire ex-programmers to provide systems support, maintain R/3 tables, administer local systems and applications, and set up procedures for system security and backups. In other cases, adept users will be assigned this responsibility.

13.2 Meeting the Four Challenges

An article in *Computerworld* summarizes the changes on the IS side. "Once you bring in SAP AG's R/3, your IS organization will never be the same. Old jobs will disappear, new ones will emerge, and some staff will become the department's golden children—to be handled with extreme care."[1]

Just as a company that has successfully implemented R/3 has identified the job and responsibility changes directed by the new system to train, manage, and motivate properly, so too does management need to pay attention to the changes in skills and perceptions inherent in the four challenges identified above. This attention will pay for itself in the most effective use of the individuals involved. It will also allow management to identify potential retention problems: and they are significant, as most companies have discovered. Individuals with even one project under their belts are frequently called by headhunters offering very high salaries.

Management will also need to define project roles and responsibilities more tightly. At least in the old days everyone knew who was in control of the project—IS. Today, with a mix of user departments playing strong roles in the design and implementation process, it is easy to see that political turf battles will erupt. And if each team member believes he or she understands the issues better than the next person, even with clear role definitions, problems can arise. The project leader will be the person directly in the line of fire, and therefore, as we have said, must be selected as much for his or her political astuteness as for the ability to discover the best technical solution to a business problem.

Finally, it is useful to understand that executive roles and perspectives will also shift with the introduction of R/3.

Executive management is generally (although not always) aware of the significant part information systems plays in the ability of the company to provide goods or services and to make a profit. IS used to be seen as an expense to be controlled. Today it is more likely to be recognized as a company asset that must be utilized properly to return value for the cost. The CIO should be positioned as the individual with the broadest view of the company processes and their various difficulties. He or she is likely to be found in the forefront of the drive for reengineering and automating to achieve business goals.

The CIO must be responsible to align the IS architecture with the company's strategic goals. Accomplishing this objective remains near

---

[1] Rochelle Garner, "SAPed!!" *Computerworld*, July 3, 1995, p. 59.

the top of the list of IS concerns. Inability to achieve alignment may be due to the historical views of IS often held by the peers of the CIO.

The CIO, then, is not the only executive who must shift perspectives. User executives, as well as BOD members, must begin to understand the nature of the potential inherent in well-defined and implemented information systems, as well as the difficulties inherent in these tools.

Mike Radcliff is the CIO of Owens Corning, a company deep into the process of implementing R/3. He offered some thoughts regarding the changes in mind-set for the IT professional. He suggests that the IT business has changed significantly and advises people to direct and control their own careers. Radcliff says "Boldly walk away from the past. Understand and master new competencies. View work as a series of assignments—life is a project. Become a generalist—which today means a specialist in multiple disciplines." And finally he suggests people focus on employability, not on employment.

Radcliff sees the role of the CIO as a corporate leader who delivers business outcomes and manages IT for the achievement of long-term goals. Further, he believes the CIO ought to develop the IT organization as an "incubator for the implementation of business change."

The role-change challenges described above are illustrated in the following case example.

13.3 *The Case of NEC Technologies*

NEC Technologies, Inc., a division of NEC Corporation, is in the computer and peripheral business in the US. Recently, it implemented nearly the full suite of R/3 capabilities across four marketing divisions, four distribution centers, and three manufacturing plants. The company's rapid growth had led to piecemeal systems and problems with excessive down time.

In the summer of 1993, the finance department began to assess various packages to replace its aging legacy systems and provide increased analytical capabilities. By April 1994 it had selected SAP. At the same time, the chairman had decided the company needed an enterprisewide information system and could gain value from a reengineering effort. The overall mission was to improve customer satisfaction.

By the fall of 1994, it was decided to begin by implementing R/3—Big Bang-style. In addition to making this contrarian decision, NEC Technologies decided to implement R/3 in a vanilla form and do the reengineering after the system was operational!

A core project team was formed consisting of eleven high-level users. The lowest level person was a manager; the highest level person was the assistant VP of sales. The members represented sales, manufacturing, distribution, finance, service, procurement engineering, and the SBUs. There was only one IS person on this team.

These individuals were removed from their day-to-day responsibilities and collocated in a war room to complete the R/3 configuration. Because of their levels in the company, they were able to make the hard decisions. There was no passing of requirements back to IS or delaying of decisions.

Placing these representatives of each element of the business together naturally led to a process view of the company and a breakthrough in their way of thinking about how an activity in one area has impact in another. They were forced out of their old *silo* mentality.

In eight months (September 1994 to April 1995) the team completed the design, configuration, testing, and training, and were ready for cutover to production.

They suffered from the system being down for most of the first ten days after implementation! When it came up, the speed was unacceptable. This was primarily because the basis technology that was used was not really proven at that point. In addition, there were some hardware failures (CPU boards), so SAP specialists were brought in to tune the system. Akira Isahai, the project manager, says that two factors were critical to their success at this point. The users were very tolerant. They didn't even ask to have the old systems brought back, says Isahai. This support was made possible by the fact that the entire executive team, including the chairman, was involved in the decision, and was motivated to fix the problems and get the system up and running.

After the first month and a half, the system was stabilized, although it still needed some optimization efforts to further increase line speed. At that point, the users could really focus on learning the ins and outs of the system. Today they are ready to explore ways to enhance the business processes using R/3 as a platform for change. Implementing the system, according to David L. Thomae, Vice President and CIO, is only the end of the beginning.

The company's experience in taking ownership for the system led to some organizational changes. A new department was formed—strategic operations management. John Bruni, the highest-ranking member of the project team, was promoted to vice president and now heads up this group. His responsibility is to discover ways to use the system to reengineer the company. Two ex-team members now report directly to Bruni, while the others went back to their old jobs or to promotions. In all cases, these individuals will continue to work with Bruni as representatives of their businesses.

At the same time, the old MIS organization was renamed *strategic systems* and has a new mission—to bring innovation, transformation, value, vision, and alignment of new technological enablers to the business. This new group understands it needs to be close to the business. The analysts, for example, are now business consultants, not technological resources.

This example illustrates some of the changes in the roles of IS and users in practice. It also illustrates how a company can be successful in implementing R/3 even when it operates contrary to accepted wisdom. The difference is in motivation. When a company is determined to make a solution work, it will. If they are ambivalent, it may work or it may not. In this case there was no ambivalence.

CHAPTER 14

Lessons Learned

14.1 The Case of Owens Corning   260

14.2 Summary of R/3 Implementation Issues   264

14.3 The Mature Installation   267

14.1 The Case of Owens Corning[1]

Owens Corning provides an excellent summary of lessons learned. The company is the world leader in building material systems and advanced composite materials, and recently launched a two-year (100-week) initiative—Advantage 2000—to reengineer its global operations to achieve its vision for the year 2000 and beyond. The chairman and CEO, Glen Hiner, defined the project's goals in a memo to all employees sent on August 30, 1995:

> Advantage 2000 *will redefine our business processes to be more common and global with an emphasis on speed and simplicity. We are investing in new business tool technologies (software and hardware) and new business processes to increase our capabilities and competitiveness providing:*

> - *Ability to be more responsive to customers for increased customer satisfaction.*
> - *Fast and easy access to global information; better information to manage our business.*
> - *More empowered employees.*
> - *More team-oriented work environment.*
> - *A paper-free work environment.*

The scope of Advantage 2000 includes the creation of a global business process model for all Owens Corning business units and the rapid replacement of over two hundred legacy information systems. A 10-person steering team was convened to guide the process of reengineering, and to develop a powerful business tool that would "empower the workforce to make decisions, be more responsive to our customers, and optimize operations." The team communicated electronically with employees globally via a weekly status update that gave progress highlights and answered online questions. In addition, employees received fact cards, electronic newsletters, presentations, and monthly *report out* events.

The steering team assembled full-time implementation teams representing the global operations to carry out the reengineering process

---

[1] I am grateful to Mike Radcliff for the material contained in this section. It comes from his presentation, a series of email memos sent out by the steering team, and personal conversation.

and to configure the new software system. There were 150 people involved at first, now 200. Of these, about one-third are business people and the remainder are a combination of IT and consultants. All teams employed full-time members having extensive business experience. Each team was aligned with a core business process, and consisted of various functional and process-oriented subteams, such as planning and communication, process innovation, architecture, technology application, release management, and support.

The consultants were used for two specific tasks: technical training, particularly in the SAP internals and the client/server environment as used by SAP, and early process design facilitation. Key to this process was the idea of knowledge transfer, where all necessary skills were transferred to Owens Corning employees by the end of the project. That way, the company could maximize the technical expertise of the consultants in the short term, and gain new capabilities internally in the long term. Owens Corning provided their own project management and change management talent.

The Owens Corning team began the reengineering project by creating a global supply-chain view that would apply to all business units. This approach provided the framework for multiple design teams to work in parallel, as well as a way to resolve integration issues across process boundaries. Each process team used a common reengineering methodology, received world-class benchmark data, and was facilitated by experts in R/3 and the specific business process under consideration

SAP R/3 was selected near the beginning of the process because it was a commercial off-the-shelf package that provided multilingual and multinational capabilities, real-time integrated information, and support for all core enterprise business processes. Designed to support an integrated supply chain model, SAP forms the basic context for reengineering. To strengthen the package, the teams identified external bolt-on solutions that would supplement the functionality gaps in SAP.

Target progress for each team was 1 percent progress from week to week. In this way the aggressive 100-week schedule could be met. The reengineering and implementation timetable allowed the team to conduct an initial pilot exercise followed by implementation of the system successively in each SBU. Additionally, the software was configured in a succession of releases. The development team believed this approach would mitigate the risk and provide rapid, cumulative team learning experiences. They would be able to validate the full project life cycle approach, including training and change management tactics and modify them as necessary for subsequent releases.

The two releases attempted only limited process redesign efforts. The first implemented the basic financial system at the corporate level for all SBUs' consolidation and financial reporting. The next release, in January 1996, encompassed a complete R/3 implementation for two divisions—22 locations simultaneously in Europe and the United States. In 1996, Owens Corning completed more extensive process redesign and upgraded to Release 3.0D. In the second wave of deployment, the original 22 locations received the results of both of these efforts. In addition, the technical infrastructure was replaced or upgraded to better support SAP and the goals of the reengineering effort. In 1997 two $1 billion plus businesses have been brought on line with SAP. A third is scheduled for October. Because the company continues to acquire businesses, it seems there is no end in sight for the SAP implementation team.

The Owens Corning steering team insisted that the project teams work to develop "good enough" solutions. By this, they meant to avoid the excessive time some teams spend on designing the perfect system. The emphasis was on speed and simplicity. The steering team warned employees very early in the process that the system would not meet all business needs at first. Business processes would continue to evolve as implementation progressed, and global process development would be tightly aligned with global systems capabilities.

One of the change management challenges was to assist employees in taking a corporate viewpoint, and to make processes more common and global. This initiative was carried out by the human resources team that was dedicated to the R/3 project; however, the R/3 steering team was necessarily invested in its outcomes. The selection of cross-organizational project team members and their focus on the best common approach for the corporation provided one vehicle to integrate this goal into the R/3 project. Employees were offered training in the basics of redesign and asked for their ideas regarding changes they felt were needed.

This focus on common systems—in contrast with unique business unit approaches—raised difficulties for some user managers. The project teams were asked to develop and optimize the business processes as a whole system. When trade-offs or loss of functionality were recognized, the team members attempted to resolve the gap and to work with the process owners to identify acceptable and unacceptable functionality gaps. In some cases the resolution added to the list of bolt-on solutions.

In response to these concerns the steering team published the following statement:

> *Despite the many benefits, SAP is not the perfect software solution. It will support all of our essential business needs and most of our other business needs, but it has limitations. Some of the limitations are in the standard software package. Other trade-offs may be self-imposed as we strive to make our processes more common and global.*

Thus, the trade-offs were deemed necessary to maximize the benefits of the SAP software, and to adopt a more common and global approach to avoid customizing the standard software.

The steering team summarizes its learnings as follows:

- Reengineer for implementation.
- Benchmark—find out what is world class.
- Design around enterprise supply-chain model.
- Focus on quantifiable business outcomes.
- Start small. Implement early. Learn by doing.
- Anticipate and address change impact early.
- You will underestimate training requirements.
- Compress the schedule. Don't allow time to admire problems. Force decisions and forward momentum.
- Support of top management is critical.
- Insist on full-time and diverse teams—getting the right people will be the biggest hurdle.
- Attitude wins!

Michael Radcliff, vice president and chief information officer, has been a leader of the Owens Corning Advantage 2000 effort and member of the steering team for its duration. He says that the major lesson at this point was in underestimating the training needed, including both business and computer literacy. The shift from a task to a process orientation means that employees need more information than ever before. In addition, they require a greater comprehension of the overall business process. The speed with which individuals become computer literate varied more than the team had estimated. Some become acclimated quickly; however, others have taken more time to become proficient in the window-based PC environment.

"The main thing though, is attitude," explains Radcliff. "Our employees are dedicated to achieving the growth goals the company has set forth, and they are committed to learning new ways of doing business in order to accomplish those goals. The enthusiasm we have seen in this project has energized the whole company. That is why it is a success."

14.2 Summary of R/3 Implementation Issues

R/3 can do almost anything asked of it if you understand it well enough. One consultant told a story of working with a customer to configure the sales and distribution modules. The customer wanted to process an order even when the price was missing, since in this particular business pricing might be determined just prior to shipment. The two puzzled for several days over ways to circumvent the system logic that insisted a price be entered. Finally they wondered if it would be possible to set up a series of tables that entered a price of zero but flagged the order for attention before shipping. They tried it out and were able to gain the result they wanted.

I have researched the process of implementing R/3, and studied in detail companies having compelling stories about their approaches. This book has presented the results of this research in three sections. First, we described the system and introduced the topic of when and how to accomplish the reengineering of whatever scale is required. Next, we identified the guidelines that experienced teams must follow. From this section, we learned that the system is both robust and complex, and that the implementation effort will be front-end loaded, with the greatest effort needed prior to delving into the system itself.

In the second section, we described a step-by-step process for implementation, complete with numerous real-life examples. This process is necessarily described in a linear way as though one step naturally follows another. Implementation teams, however, constantly stress the iterative nature of this process. A team will make a series of decisions and test them in the development environment. The net result may be to question the original assumption and reformat the work done to that point. This process continues until the system performs as needed.

The third section contains aspects of implementation that, if managed well, will both enhance the implementation process and guard against the pitfalls discovered by many implementation teams. Much of the challenge of forming and developing excellent teams, managing the political challenges, and managing in complex situations will fall to the project leader. It is essential to appoint someone who can skillfully navigate these potentially stormy waters.

At one company we studied, the project leader became frustrated with her users and began to think of them as wayward children to be disciplined and made to pay attention to the system. This set up an increasingly negative atmosphere. It seemed the project was headed for serious trouble until the steering team leader, in a difficult counseling session, pointed out what was happening to the project leader. She got the message and held a series of meetings with her users to listen to their concerns. She began to realize the stress faced by these managers who were facing a difficult situation because of a combination of reorganization and new regulations. These "grief" sessions became a normal part of the project leader's approach, and the users began to revise their opinion of her. Where once they thought of her as an enemy forcing yet another change upon them, soon they began to regard her as a colleague who wanted the company to succeed as much as they did.

This final section summarizes the larger scale issues identified by the appearance of SAP. Several conclusions from this study are obvious:

- Tackling R/3 is not much different from other large-scale IS projects—just more demanding. The risks are significantly higher than normal because integration starts at the beginning and not the end of the project. Failure is most likely to come from nontechnical sources.

- The payoff from R/3 is as much from the new behavior of people doing work as from the simplified, consistent workflow delivered by the software. Anyone who forgets that this is a human implementation should forget the whole thing.

- R/3 is an enabler of reengineering, and reengineering is a strategic process. Treat R/3 as a critical element of corporate strategy and consider its implementation in strategic terms. Implementing R/3 is not the traditional IS project of even five years ago.

- Communicate and force others to communicate. Change of any kind is scary and R/3 change can be some of the scariest. Extensive communication won't alleviate fears, but it will bring them out in the open and provide the greatest chance for building consensus and support for the new system.

- Don't shortcut the change management effort. If this is the soft stuff, managers ask, why is it so hard? When the implementation is seen as a major organizational change, early effort will be repaid many times over.

In addition to these clear lessons, a new view of business is beginning to emerge.

R/3 has changed the face of information technology forever. We now have the enterprisewide integrated system we only dreamed of a few years ago. Companies can now consider the automation of their basic business processes as if it were a utility like electricity or water. Hook it up and get back to the real challenging business at hand. However, you will find that just as a power outage or a break in the water main means a cessation of these basic elements, should R/3 be implemented poorly or not used well, you will not be able to conduct business until the system is fully functional.

The requirement for integrated change is clear and present.

IS is now a line management tool capable of being used well or of being misused. Some will ignore or misunderstand its power. Those who succeed in the next century will be the companies that recognize the power of integrating business strategy, information systems, and the potential of the individual employee.

The information age is merely in its infancy. We are rapidly moving into a global networking era (a mature and sophisticated version of the information era) with vast implications. The ability to conduct business instantly anywhere on the globe shifts business concepts of customers, vendors, inventory, even competition. We are able to share information across traditional boundaries of country, culture, monetary system and time.

These shifts mean business entities can assume a position of leadership for global connection and change. If businesses see the need for a cleaner environment or a reduction in weapons of war, these requirements will become part of the global consciousness with massive impact. This shift will only take place, however, when individual employees become aware of their power. This ability to influence and lead from any position in the company will be enhanced by the changing organizational forms (teams, networks, permeable boundaries, process orientation) and the application of integrated information systems to the business in a strategic way.

Ultimately, the value of R/3 is its ability to change people's minds. Information is useful only if someone can think about things in a different way—can conceive of a hitherto unseen process, product, or market. When the individual has a compelling vision of what the company can become and can convince others of its value, that company will shift its approach.

R/3 has the ability to allow companies to cease dealing with basic business information as a burden and consider it as a given.

14.3 The Mature Installation

The most mature R/3 installations are generally found in Europe. Often these companies implemented R/2 and have migrated to R/3. Employees skills and understanding of SAP grow over time and result in a greater ability to absorb changes in the system. The shift from R/2 to R/3 is not without difficulty since it typically means the adoption of client/server technology. A number of those interviewed mentioned having struggled with this shift in their computing approach. The Basis administrator in a Russian installation states that the "real abilities of the system don't correspond to its announced characteristics." This company is having to rely upon its headquarters to make decisions regarding the organization and sequence of implementation steps since the company is complex and distributed over a very large territory.

Others, however, began with the early releases of R/3. In many ways this was an easier transition because they began on a client/server platform, but there were growing pains as both SAP and its customers added functionality.

The Case of RTL Television

RTL Television in Cologne, Germany is a good example of a mature installation of SAP products. RTL operates a commercial nationwide TV station. It is the largest advertising medium in Europe with $1.9 billion in gross advertising revenue. It is the market leader in Germany with a target audience of people 14 to 49 years of age. The core business functions (news shows and magazines, program inventory management, and program scheduling) are supported by a combination of platforms including HP, SUN, DEC Open VMS, and several self-developed applications based on Windows and Sybase. These are integrated with a number of boutique vendors' offerings. All administrative functions are supported by SAP R/3.

In 1991 RTL operated a traditional IS department for small companies. There were four different application systems which were integrated by interfacing. In addition, there were many individually programmed software solutions, and there were numerous terminals each with point-to-point cabling. There was no network; in fact, there was no data center. The situation became untenable, and in 1992 a project was begun to evaluate alternatives. SAP was chosen early in 1993. All affected users were involved in the decision and all concurred that SAP would solve their problems.

Karin Schemmer was and still is the project leader for the SAP installation. In February through May 1993 the project team attended SAP training. In April an HP9000 was installed and on it SAP Release 1.2A. The team began to develop the specifications for FI, CO, and AM (now FI-AA). They upgraded to 2.0B before going live on January 3, 1994. Other modules were added in succession as the team also dealt with several upgrades. HR submodules, time management, and payroll were implemented, overlapping with the first phase, starting in 1993. By 1995, payroll was complete for both RTL employees and freelancers. This had required customizing and self-development for the latter.

In 1995, the team planned for both the optical archive and legal consolidation of FI and the TR module. By this time they had upgraded through 2.1G to 2.1L and installed SUN Sparc for all SAP servers, Archiv-Server (HP9000), Jukebox (HP OSAR), two scanners and barcode reading pens.

The optical archive went live in January 1996, while the legal consolidation went live in January 1997. Projects, by this time, were being implemented in six to nine months' time. The TR project was started in June 1995; however, the functionality RTL required was not available until Release 3.0D. The system was upgraded to this release in August 1996 and the project went forward.

RTL did not need reengineering to implement R/3. It did, however, carry out some redesign work. RTL typically starts up new (mostly small) companies. In January 1994 when it started the operational SAP system, it had 12 affiliated companies. Today there are 23, all of which use the FI, CO, and AM modules implemented by RTL.

Most of the original affiliates had their own bookkeeping systems, which were often outsourced. Most did not even have any controlling system, and typically the assets were managed by Excel spreadsheets. Today all those systems have been replaced by the RTL R/3 system. And it takes only one or two days to implement a new company in R/3.

There was some redesign work as a result of implementing the HR module. Two departments were fused together. In addition, many affiliated companies use the RTL R/3 system for payroll.

RTL is very pleased with the results of implementing R/3. It has replaced the accounting, assets management, cost control, and payroll systems with one integrated system. This has improved its effectiveness and ability to manage the business. Today RTL enjoys a well-established system with easy access to all relevant information. Schemmer says, "By implementing FI, CO, and AM, we replaced three different application systems. That meant interfaces for master data from three different systems and interfaces for actual data from at least three systems. And all this with programmers from three different software houses!"

She adds, "R/3 was implemented quite fast because everybody in the project team had sufficient competence and qualifications—and everybody was very, very motivated. ('This is my baby now—this is my chance to change things!') Very important—they all had the same goal."

Each module was assigned a team of four to six people plus the project leader and a consultant from SAP for one day per week. The user team members discussed all issues with their departments and returned with final decisions. In addition, these project members (called SAP opinion leaders) are responsible for the customizing of "their" module. When a module becomes productive, they remain responsible for all aspects of customizing, testing upgrades, creating IMGs and the like. In this way, RTL has built up a significant amount of SAP know-how across multiple departments.

All the users were so frustrated with the old systems that their response to the new was very positive. Of course, their first look at SAP resulted in comments such as the one reported by Schemmer: "Pooh, this is overwhelming and complicated! To book a bill I have to use three screens now and it was only one in the old system. This takes too long!"

This was rapidly followed by a second wave of reactions. "Wow, this system has a lot of functions the old system didn't have. I feel I can answer the creditors' questions much better and quickly on the phone than before. And, by the way, the old system made me just a data typist, but I'm a bookkeeper—now I feel I really can use all my knowledge!"

RTL and Its Relationship with SAP

As a mature installation, RTL has had considerable experience in dealing with SAP AG. Some of this experience has been difficult and some helpful. As one of the first customers of R/3, RTL has had a relationship with SAP for a number of years. SAP has used RTL as a reference account for several potential customers. This relationship was helpful to RTL even though it seemed for a time that it had been forgotten by SAP. We'll continue the story of RTL with their struggles over upgrades.

In the summer of 1996 RTL had to upgrade from 2.1L to 3.0D. This change had to be accomplished in a short time, RTL believed, because of an announcement from SAP in April that HR would no longer be supported under Release 2.1L and that all HR clients had to be at 3.0 by the end of 1996. This was a bit confusing because in 1995 SAP had announced that it was not necessary to upgrade to Release 2.2 and that there would be a quick upgrade from 2.1 to 3.0. On the basis of that information RTL stayed with 2.1 since everyone was happy with it.

When SAP announced RTL had to upgrade to 3.0 due to HR, RTL discovered that no one seemed to know about the earlier announcement regarding the quick upgrade. Time went by and finally RTL was told that there would be a quick upgrade but not to Release 3.0B or 3.0C, only with 3.0D—which was not released at that time. RTL had to wait for several months knowing that they had to accomplish the upgrade by the end of the year.

In July RTL started the quick upgrade as soon as it was released. The results were disastrous. Much of the functionality in 2.1L did not work any longer, and, via OSS, SAP sent corrections which destroyed functionality further rather than fixing it. RTL was also frustrated by the lack of information from SAP. The company felt that in certain situations it is necessary to receive important information, rather than to have to go searching for it. And finally, RTL team members were upset by the quality and tone of the answers to their problem calls. All in all, RTL was quite upset with its treatment by SAP.

The SAP board of directors reacted to this situation immediately. SAP has an escalation management system in place and RTL was rapidly renamed an "escalation client." SAP apologized and provided support for the eventual upgrade to 3.0E. This is certainly helpful since there have been many corrections issued for 3.0E (over 100) and RTL does not have the capacity to manage that many changes. So another help call has gone out to the escalation manager.

Like any relationship when both parties are growing and changing, there are disagreements. It is heartening to know that SAP has responded to this long-term and valuable customer in an appropriate way. However, this situation raises the issue of how to gain SAP's attention. Research results indicate that there are two major routes. One is a personal connection with the people in Walldorf and the second is membership in the local users group. Within the U.S., the ASUG, as stated earlier, is an active and useful point of contact with the SAP system developers.

APPENDIX A

Data Modeling Concepts

The concept of modeling a real world environment into abstract objects (called entities) connected through relationships was developed and first published by P.P. Chen[1] in 1976, based on research of E.F. Codd[2] in the late 1960s. Since then, the relational data model has been steadily developed and implemented in many database systems like Oracle, Informix, DB2 (IBM), and others. The purpose of a relational data model is to describe real and abstract things in our daily environment and define their data as entities and to give these things a

---

[1] Peter P. Chen, "The Entity Relationship Model—Toward a Unified View of Data," ACM Transactions on Database Systems, Vol. 1, No. 1, Association for Computing Machinery, Inc., March 1976.
[2] E.F. Codd was a researcher at the IBM laboratories developing data description languages. He is one of the fathers of SQL.

name. Entities are grouped into types in order not to create an infinite number of entities. A symbol (for example, a box) is used to document such an entity type on a piece of paper. The word *object* is used often in conjunction with the word entity. While an entity contains only data, an object contains data and the programs to manipulate that data. Since these words are often used in context with SAP they might be strange to somebody unfamiliar with data modeling.

An example of a real thing is a pencil (see Figure A–1). Examples for abstract things are vendor and color. In the real world pencils come in different sizes, colors, and may be supplied by different vendors. A particular kind of pencil is usually identified by a unique name (e.g., a material number). In this illustration the collection of pencils is described as an entity type which can have different colors and can be supplied by different vendors. The picture indicates this through the lines which are the symbol for a relationship. The arrow indicates that one can assign multiple items of the entity type to the related other entity type (e.g., a pencil might have several vendors).

To implement such a structure in a database, a table is defined for each entity type. A table (see Figure A–2) then stores a row of data for each entity. In this way, a table PENCIL can store a row of data for each of the different kinds of pencils which are all uniquely identified by their respective material number (e.g., PEN_DEF_12).

Each row of data is defined through data fields which are called attributes. In our example of the table PENCIL, the attributes are:

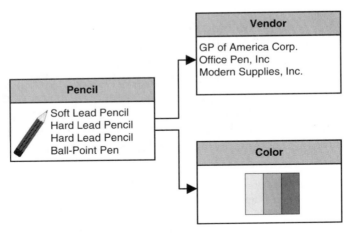

Figure A–1: Objects/entities

Table: PENCIL		
Material Number	**Material Description**	**Eraser**
PEN_ABC_12	Soft Lead Pencil	YES
PEN_DEF_12	Hard Lead Pencil	YES
PEN_DEF_14	Hard Lead Pencil	NO
PEN_GHI_12	Ball-Point Pen	NO

Figure A–2:   An Entity Table

material number, material description, and eraser. Each attribute has a domain which defines all the possible values for the attribute. The domain of the attribute eraser is YES and NO. No other values are allowed in our example.

In order to implement a data structure as a database it is necessary to create some redundancy. Certain attributes might be replicated throughout different tables. In the above example the material number will be reused in those tables which have a relationship with the table PENCIL. While the content is the same, the name of the attribute might be different in other tables.

To make clear that such an item has exactly the same meaning throughout all tables where it is used, it is called a data element. A data element is always unique. It can have representations in different tables under different attribute names.

Content and Structure of the SAP Data Dictionary

As we discussed, entity types and attributes are implemented as tables, rows, and fields. Relationships are implemented by using keys which are fields specially designed for this purpose (see Figure B–1).

To set up a relationship between the two tables PENCIL and VENDOR, the key field VendorNumber is also included in the table PENCIL when this table is created. Next, the purchasing department can fill the table PENCIL with all the descriptions and fill the table VENDOR with all the names and addresses. To build the relationship between a particular pencil and the supplying vendor, the VendorNumber is also included in the table PENCIL when this table is created. As a result, when looking up information about pencils, the

PENCIL			
Material Number	**Material Description**	**Eraser**	**VendorNumber**
PEN_ABC_12	Soft Lead Pencil	YES	VEN_01
PEN_DEF_12	Hard Lead Pencil	YES	VEN_01
PEN_DEF_14	Hard Lead Pencil	NO	VEN_01
PEN_GHI_12	Ball Point Pen	NO	VEN_02

Table Row

VENDOR			
VendorNumber	**Name**	**Address**	**...**
VEN_01	GP of America Corp.	12 Pen Street	
VEN_02	Office Pen, Inc	1 Rose Garden	
VEN_03	Modern Supplies, Inc.	100 Myrtle Ave.	

Figure B–1:   Entity relationships

program can use the VendorNumber in the table PENCIL to look up the vendor information in the VENDOR table.

It is very important to understand this concept since the entire configuration of SAP is stored in tables like these. The SAP software uses this table concept to remember what has been configured (which values the fields contain) and which relationships have been established between values of different tables.

A view is a collection of fields from one or more tables which can be maintained as a group by a user. Views are often used to present fields of different tables and maintain their data in a specific context without having the need to write a program for it.

In Figure B–2, a view is created to list all pencils which come with an eraser. We are using the tables PENCIL and VENDOR to select the fields which should appear on the screen and define the view with them. We name it Pencils_With_Eraser_View to indicate its purpose. A view can be processed like a table even though it is not a real table. For this reason there are also limits to manipulating the data within a view. The technology to create and use a view is provided by the database system (e.g., Oracle, Informix) on which SAP resides.

A match code is similar to a view but more sophisticated. The technology for match codes in this case is designed and implemented by SAP in its software. A match code is a search path to data where

Pencils_With_Erasers_VIEW

Material Number	Material Description	Eraser	VendorName
PEN_ABC_12	Soft Lead Pencil	YES	GP of America Corp.
PEN_DEF_12	Hard Lead Pencil	YES	GP of America Corp.

PENCIL

Material Number	Material Description	Eraser	VendorNumber
PEN_ABC_12	Soft Lead Pencil	YES	VEN_01
PEN_DEF_12	Hard Lead Pencil	YES	VEN_01
PEN_DEF_14	Hard Lead Pencil	NO	VEN_01
PEN_GHI_12	Ball Point Pen	NO	VEN_02

VENDOR

VendorNumber	Name	Address	...
VEN_01	GP of America Corp.	12 Pen Street	
VEN_02	Office Pen, Inc	1 Rose Garden	
VEN_03	Modern Supplies, Inc.	100 Myrtle Ave.	

Figure B–2: Pencils-with-Eraser View

often many fields like name, address, title, and so forth are provided for input by a user. If the user knows the address but not the name or title, then the match code will find all names with titles which are listed under the address the user entered. A match code can span many tables, giving a user extensive options for a search path. Match codes are defined in the ABAP/4 data dictionary. Since match codes are so important for the end user, we describe working with them in greater detail in Chapter 4.6.

Locks contain information about how to handle situations when two or more users compete over accessing the same row in a table. This could happen if, let us say, two purchasing clerks want to update the address of the same vendor at the same time. If the system did not provide a mechanism to protect the data entry of one person against concurrent changes from another, the second person would change the data without the first person knowing it. This would result in a great deal of confusion since the first clerk would be convinced his or her changes took place when in fact they did not. While companies often take care of this type of situation through organizational means (for example, one clerk is responsible for vendors A through C while another is responsible for vendors D through F) there are many situations where the system has to provide the mechanism of protection, that is, the counter for the last issued order number. If this counter is unprotected during a concurrent update the same number could be given out twice. Locks are one mechanism among others to protect the integrity of data in the SAP database. They are embedded in the ABAP/4 program code by the programmer who has to make sure that concurrent update situations are handled properly.

APPENDIX C

~~~~~~

The Development of ABAP/4

The development of the ABAP/4 (Advanced Business Application Programming) language began in the mid-1970s by SAP. At that time SAP needed a simple language to generate list reports from the data files of the standard software system they were developing. It was called *Allgemeiner Berichtsaufbereitungsprozessor* which can be translated to *common report writer*. With further developments of the SAP system the requirements for the programming language grew, and with it the command set of this language, making it today one of the leading fourth-generation programming languages. The command set is the list of programming keywords which a developer is allowed to use when writing the program code. It determines and/or limits the ability of any given program to manipulate data in the system.

SAP developed the ABAP/4 into a fully featured programming language supporting client/server environments and with Version 3.0 of

R/3 started to support the object-oriented programming paradigm. With the changes of system architecture (first R/2 on mainframes, then R/3 on client/server systems) the command set is changing and evolving. Some ABAP/4 commands which were used in the mainframe environment of R/2 are now obsolete and no longer supported in the client/server environment of R/3. New commands were added such as those to provide support for Microsoft's OLE technology.

The ABAP/4 programming language itself has a unique structure. The code is developed in program modules, which allows the developer to structure the code better. A program file typically contains several program modules. These modules are called from the screens with which the user is interacting, for example, in a order processing transaction when entering order information.

SAP predefines a general processing logic for screen interactivity. Developers have to learn this type of programming before they can create a new transaction. The program structure is based on the interaction with a user during run time. A user works with the graphical user interface (screen) which contains fields, menus, buttons, pop-up windows, etc. The interaction is controlled by a program logic called DYNPRO (DYNamic PROgram). A DYNPRO consists of four parts of which two must be coded by the developer: Process Before Output (PBO), Process After Input (PAI), Process On Help Request (POH), and Process On Value Request (POV). POH and POV are optional.

PBO is executed before the screen is displayed with its fields, buttons, and so forth. This section of the program calls ABAP/4 program modules which contain the actual processing logic to manipulate the business data. In the PBO part, data can be retrieved from the database (for example, to initialize the field content of the screen) and manipulated by the ABAP/4 program. The PBO part is concluded with displaying the screen. Then, the user interacts by entering data into the fields and finishes by pressing the ENTER key on the keyboard or using the mouse to select a button or entry.

After this, PAI is executed and ABAP/4 modules to manipulate and store the entered data are called. The ABAP/4 modules react to events which are encountered during runtime and which are triggered by the user or the SAP runtime system itself. An example of an event is when a user presses a function key or when a new page is started during list output. An event is coded within the ABAP/4 program by the developer using the appropriate ABAP/4 command. This allows further structuring of the program and makes it more readable.

Within ABAP/4 a developer can also define functions which are blocks of ABAP/4 code stored in a special function library. Functions are used when a generic piece of ABAP/4 program logic is needed. Typical functions are calendar functions and conversion functions (currency, time, date, etc.). Functions allow the developer to reuse program logic. SAP R/3 comes with an extensive function library which can be used by developers.

A developer uses the ABAP/4 editor to write the ABAP/4 code. Before creating the program, the developer has to specify the program name and its development class. A development class is used to group programs which belong together. It is important for developers to use special naming conventions when creating programs in order not to conflict with the ABAP/4 programs SAP delivers. Since all SAP modules (FI, MM, SD) are written in ABAP/4, none of them should be changed or overwritten. SAP provides naming space for custom developed reports and online transactions. Custom program names have to start with the letter Y or Z in order to comply with the rules. If developers do not stay within this naming space, upgrading the SAP software becomes a hazard and can be very costly since SAP might overwrite custom programs during the upgrade process.

Relational Database Concepts

In order to understand relational database concepts used in R/3, let us look at a simple example.

We want to create a standard software package for an architect. For our architect, the software (see Figure D–1) must be able to

Figure D–1:   The architect's software package

capture and process data of family home designs such as (1) and calculate their cost. This includes variations of this type including (2).

The way we start is to gather all the attributes which are necessary to describe the houses our standard software shall support. As discussed in Chapter 3, attributes become data fields once the data model is implemented in a database system. Table D–1 is a list of attributes to describe the type of houses we want to design.

Table D–1: Architect's attributes

Attributes	Value
Location of house	New Canaan, Conn.
Number of walls	4
Angle of roof	30 degrees
Number of windows on west side	2
Number of windows on east side	2
Number of windows on north side	1
Number of entrance doors	1
Number of entrance doors on south side	1
Color of west wall	red
Color of east wall	red
and so on...	

As we add attributes, we are able to describe our subject in more detail and accuracy. More attributes also make the house design more flexible so that the architect can offer a greater variety of designs to his/her customers. At the same time, increasing the number of attributes results in growing complexity, making it more difficult to keep an overview and understand the overall model.

In the next step (Figure D–2) we transform our list of attributes into the data model. We do so by classifying the attributes associated with the house by its important components, for example, the walls and the roof. These components as well as the house are known as entity types.

The choice of grouping the attributes and naming the resulting entity types (HOUSE, WALLS, and ROOF) and relationships depends on the view of the person who creates the data model. Different people can create different designs and all might be correct. Therefore,

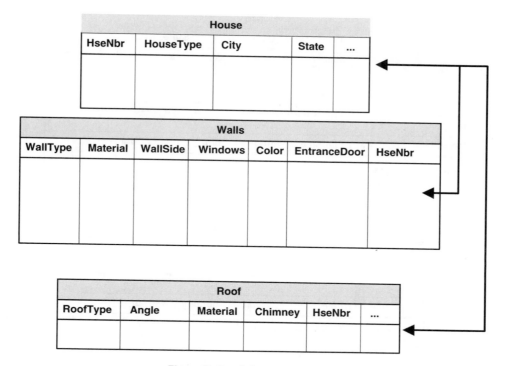

Figure D–2: A data model

the software which processes the data will also be different. In addition, we have added attributes which are not in our list because they are needed for purely technical reasons. These attributes are used as keys to represent the relationships between the entity types. To build a relationship, the same attribute is included in the two entity types which are related. In the above example, the entity types HOUSE, WALLS, and ROOF are related through the attribute HseNbr. This is indicated in the data model with connecting lines and arrows.

This data model can now be used to create the database. For each entity type a database table is created. The attributes are used to create the table fields. A relationship is created by including the same field in two tables. Database systems utilize a programming type language called Data Definition Language (DDL) to create the database with all tables, fields and relationships.

Now we can build software which will allow the architect to enter house design data into the database (see Figure D–3). For this purpose

House				
HseNbr	**HouseType**	**City**	**State**	**...**
4711	Saltbox	New Canaan	Conn.	
4712	Cape	Ridgefield	Conn.	
4713	Cape	Wilton	Conn.	

Data Row → 4711 Saltbox New Canaan Conn.

Walls						
WallType	**Material**	**WallSide**	**Windows**	**Color**	**EntranceDoor**	**HseNbr**
Wall_1	Brick	East	2	red	no	
Wall_1	Brick	West	2	red	no	
Wall_1	Brick	South	0	red	yes	
Wall_1	Brick	North	1	red	no	
Wall_2	Wood	East	2	white	no	5327

Roof					
RoofType	**Angle**	**Material**	**Chimney**	**HseNbr**	**...**
Angled	30 degrees	Shingle	yes		

Figure D–3: Design database

we would create data entry screens which allow us to enter data for each of the tables. We would start with the table HOUSE and enter the type and address of the house as well as a unique number (HseNbr 4711) for identification. In the next table, WALLS, we would enter the descriptions of the walls, which material and color to use, how many windows need to be accommodated per wall, and so on. Then we would enter the data for the roof into the ROOF table.

As shown in Figure D–3, for each house we created one row of data in the table HOUSE, four rows of data in the table WALLS and one row of data in the table ROOF. After completing data entry of our description, we have to tell the system how all the parts relate to each other. In their configuration guide, SAP describes this process as assignment. We assign a wall to a house. We also assign the roof to the house. In our example we enter 4711 as the house identifier into the field HseNbr of the table WALLS for every wall that belongs to our house in New Canaan. We also enter this identifier into the table

ROOF for the roof that belongs to it (Figure D–4). From our data model we can now describe our house 4711 as one of type Saltbox with 4 red walls, 5 windows, and one door. It also has a chimney and an angled roof.

Now we want to calculate the cost to build the actual house. We would have to add some cost information to the database for the materials, create some tables describing vendors providing the materials and contractors who can build the house at the proposed location

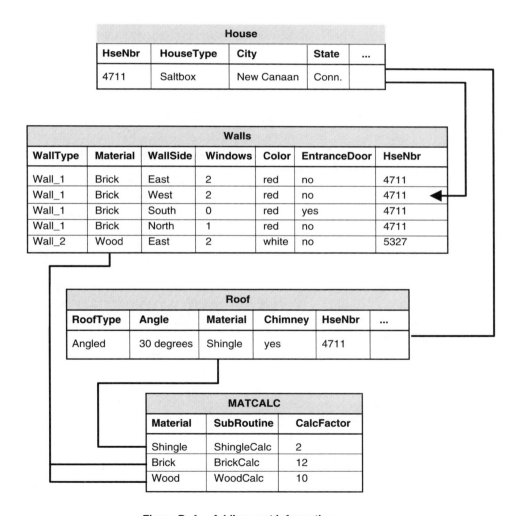

House

HseNbr	HouseType	City	State	...
4711	Saltbox	New Canaan	Conn.	

Walls

WallType	Material	WallSide	Windows	Color	EntranceDoor	HseNbr
Wall_1	Brick	East	2	red	no	4711
Wall_1	Brick	West	2	red	no	4711
Wall_1	Brick	South	0	red	yes	4711
Wall_1	Brick	North	1	red	no	4711
Wall_2	Wood	East	2	white	no	5327

Roof

RoofType	Angle	Material	Chimney	HseNbr	...
Angled	30 degrees	Shingle	yes	4711	

MATCALC

Material	SubRoutine	CalcFactor
Shingle	ShingleCalc	2
Brick	BrickCalc	12
Wood	WoodCalc	10

Figure D–4: Adding cost information

289

with their cost. We would need to have a different cost calculation for each material. For this purpose we added an entity type MATCALC. This table will give us additional flexibility since it allows us to configure our software by determining which calculation program (SubRoutine) to use when a specific material is requested. In order to configure the software, we enter the names of the programs used to calculate the cost for building a house using a specific material. The calculation program can also use various input parameters for the calculation. For example, we might use CalcFactor as indicated in Figure D–4 to be used for a conversion to metric standards.

Now assume the architect wants to calculate the cost for our house. The house is built from bricks. The software looks up the table MAT-CALC and takes the program name which it finds in the row of the material "Brick" which is called BrickCalc. The main program of our standard software then retrieves the calculation program BrickCalc from a library which is also part of the database and executes it.

To *configure*, in this example, means to enter the name of the appropriate calculation program into the field SubRoutine. The name of the calculation program is a parameter for our software. A *parameter* is a variable which is submitted to the main program in order to make it perform a certain function. In our case the main program executes the calculation program whose name it finds in the field SubRoutine. If we entered BrickCalc into the field SubRoutine for the material "Wood," the wrong calculation program would be executed when calculating the cost for a wooden wall, leaving us with wrong results. We can also have an entity type which allows us to define the sequence of data entry screens to be used when creating an invoice (e.g., first screen: customer bill-to information, second screen: customer ship-to information, etc.). By changing the sequence in the configuration table, one could influence whether the screen for bill-to information or ship-to information appears first for data input. This then also influences the flow of the work process of invoice processing in this business.

Tables like MATCALC are called configuration tables while tables like HOUSE, WALLS, and ROOF are called application data tables. The configuration tables are the key to setting up the functionality of the SAP system for your company. Configuration tables are used to control basically every aspect of the way SAP functions when it runs in productive mode in your company.

BIBLIOGRAPHY

~~~~~~

R/3 System Online Documentation, SAP AG, 1994.

R/3 System Summary of New Application Functions in Release 3.0, SAP AG, 1995.

Bancroft, Nancy, *New Partnerships for Managing Technological Change*, John Wiley & Sons, New York, 1992.

Buck-Emden and J. Galimow, *The Client/Server Technology of the SAP R/3 System*, Addison-Wesley, Harlow, Essex, Eng., 1996.

Cameron, Bobby, and Stuart D. Woodring., "Choosing Client/Server Core Apps," *The Forrester Report*, Volume V, Number IX, Forrester Research, Inc., Dec. 1994.

Chen, Peter P., "The Entity Relationship Model—Toward a Unified View of Data," *ACM Transactions on Database Systems*, Vol. 1, No. 1, Association for Computing Machinery, Inc., Mar. 1976.

Dallas, James, "Maintaining Proper Communication, Focus Key to Information System Implementation," *Pulp & Paper*, Feb. 1995.

Davenport, Thomas H., *Process Innovation: Reengineering Work through Information Technology*, Harvard Business School Press, Boston, MA, 1993.

Forrester Research, Inc., *The Software Strategy Report*, Vol. V, No. IX, Dec. 1994.

Garner, Rochelle, "SAPed!!" *Computerworld*, July 3, 1995.

Hammer, Michael and James Champy, *Reengineering the Corporation: A Manifesto for Business Revolution*, HarperBusiness, N.Y., 1993.

Myers, Marc, "The Trouble with Off-the-Shelf-Apps," *Network World*, Oct. 9, 1995.

Rotman, Laurie, Margaret Spinner, Julie Williams, "The Draper Gopher: A Team Approach to Building a Virtual Library," *Online*, Mar./Apr. 1995.

Scheier, Robert and Wendy Pickering, "When Business Suites Don't Fit, Tailoring Can Be Costly," *PC Week*, May 15, 1995.

Scheier, Robert L., "Tailor Made," *PC Week*, June 12, 1995.

Sinneck, Michael, "It's All in the Implementation," *InformationWeek*, Dec. 12, 1994.

GLOSSARY

~~~~~~

ABAP/4

ABAP/4 Development Workbench (BC-DWB)

Advanced Business Application Programming/4.
SAP's fourth generation programming language. ABAP/4 is used to develop dialog applications and to evaluate databases.

ABAP/4 Repository

ABAP/4 Development Workbench (BC-DWB)

All development objects of the ABAP/4 Development Workbench are stored in the ABAP/4 Repository. These development objects include ABAP/4 programs, screens, documentation etc.

agent

Workflow (WF-WF)

Executor of a work item. This can mean people as well as mechanical processing units and software programs.

Application Link Enabling

Application Link Enabling (CA-ALE)

Application Link Enabling (ALE) supports the creation and operation of distributed applications. The basic concept is to guarantee a distributed, but integrated R/3 installation. This involves business-controlled message exchange with consistent data on loosely linked SAP applications.

Application integration is achieved not via a central database, but via synchronous and asynchronous communication.

ALE comprises the following three layers:

- application services
- distribution services
- communication services

application programming interface

Basis (BC)

A set of routines used by an application program to request and carry out lower-level maintenance services performed by the operating system.

application server

Basis (BC)

Processes on a host system consisting of a dispatcher task and one or more work processes.

The dispatcher manages the queues of processing requests generated by users and work processes.

Work processes carry out the requests.

application toolbar

GUI and Graphics (BC-GUI)

The application toolbar is the area in the upper part of the window which covers the entire window width below the standard toolbar. In this area, the push-buttons are displayed side by side in a pre-determined order.

ARIS Toolset

Business Navigator (CA-MOD-NAV)

Set of tools developed by IDS Prof. Scheer GmbH. The set consists of the following:

- Navigation component
- Modeling component
- Analysis component

The ARIS Toolset modeling component was used to create the contents of the SAP R/3 Reference Model.

attribute

Business Navigator (CA-MOD-NAV)

Characteristic feature of an object in the R/3 Reference Model.

In the R/3 Reference model, attributes are given values for objects used in business process modeling where this may be of help in the context of an R/3 implementation. For functions, these may include:

- the processing type (online, batch, central, local)
- the transaction code
- the release level

A number of other attributes are available for documentation and project results. However, attributes can be maintained only in the PC version of the R/3 Reference Model using the ARIS Toolset.

Workflow (WF-WF)
Property of an object type in the workflow object type catalog.
Attributes of object types are defined as part of the object type definition. Conditions can be formulated in the workflow definition using attributes. The attribute values are read at runtime and used to control the workflow.
The respective descriptions of the attributes are inherited by the child object types from the parent object type.

attribute type
Workflow (WF-WF)
Classification of attributes of an object type.
Three attribute types are used to distinguish the attributes of an object type. They differ, in particular, with regard to the implementation of the read access.

- virtual attribute
- database attribute
- status attribute

bridge
Basis Services (BC-SRV)
Computer that links two LANs with each other.

client
Cross–Application Functions (CA)
Legally and organizationally independent unit on the highest level of the R/3 System, for example, a group or corporation.

Data Dictionary

Basis (BC)

Central catalog that contains the descriptions of an organization's data and provides information about the relationships between the data and its use in programs and screens.

The data descriptions in a Data Dictionary is also called metadata, i.e., data that describes other data.

Data Dictionary, active

ABAP/4 Development Workbench (BC-DWB)

Data Dictionary where each piece of metadata is stored once.

New or changed metadata is immediately transmitted to all system components concerned.

Thus, for example, application programs and screens are always supplied with up-to-date information.

EDI

Workflow–EDI (WF-EDI)

Electronic Data Interchange.

Companywide electronic interchange of structured data between business partners at home and abroad. Hardware, software, and communication services may differ.

event

Business Navigator (CA-MOD-NAV)

Event (in the R/3 Reference Model).

In the R/3 Reference Model, an event is a status that has business relevance. Example: Standard order received.

At the time it arises an event can trigger one or more functions, and it can be the result of a function.

Personnel Administration and Payroll Accounting (PA)

Series of infotypes that are added, changed, completely or partially deleted or delimited in the HR System, for the reason specified (hiring, change in cost center, withdrawal, etc.).

The sequence of the infotypes that are edited using these events is defined in the HR System.

Production Planning (PP)

Factor, the effect of which on SOP data cannot be deduced from historical patterns.

Events complement the planning results derived from the forecast. Deals, promotions, and market intelligence are all examples of events.

Workflow (WF-WF)

Events are defined as a collection of attributes of objects in the workflow object type catalog and they describe the change in the state of an object.

A publicized event is "announced" throughout the system by a special function module that can be called up by any application or system program (the event creator).

Information (the event parameters) is transported from the user who created the event to the receiver in the event container. This ensures that the events are linked to run time–dependent data, which is then available to the receiver and can be used for event-driven control and communication mechanisms.

Which function module should be called up as an event receiver is determined in linkage tables flexibly and independently of the application that initiated the event.

function

Business Navigator (CA-MOD-NAV)

In the SAP R/3 Reference Model, a function is a business task.
Generally, input data in the form of entities is required to process a function, and the output is also generated as entities.
Examples of functions:

- Define accounting rule
- Send invoice

GUI and Graphics (BC-GUI)

Functions can be started by selecting the entry corresponding to it in a pull-down menu, its function key or its push button. The corresponding processing is then carried out by the system.

gateway

Basis Services (BC-SRV)

Intelligent interface that connects dissimilar networks by converting one protocol to another.

For example, a gateway converts the protocol for a token ring network to the protocol for SNA.

The special computers responsible for converting the different protocols, transfer speeds, codes, etc., are also usually considered as gateways.

GUI status

Basis (BC)

In ABAP/4, a development object that describes the elements that appear in a screen's menu bar.

inheritance

Workflow–SAPoffice (WF-OFFICE)

Transfer of a character attribute.

When a character attribute in the font attributes of the paragraphs is taken from the next highest hierarchical level due to the identifier "*", this is referred to as inheritance.

instance

Basis Services (BC-SRV)

An administrative unit, in which components of an R/3 System that provide one or more services are grouped together.

ISO

Workflow–EDI (WF-EDI)

International Organization for Standardization.

Organization which develops international standards to support commerce, science, and technology.

logical operators

Business Navigator (CA-MOD-NAV)

Symbols that represent logical relationships in the R/3 Reference Model.

There may be logical relationships between events and functions in process chains. These relationships are represented by logical operators. The following logical operators are used in the Reference Model:

- And-operator
- Exclusive-Or-operator
- Or-operator

main menu level

GUI and Graphics (BC-GUI)

The main menu level is the first level of the R/3 System directly after the logon. You select your required application here.

main screen

Materials Management (MM)

Screen for a user department or for a particular view in a material master record such as Engineering/design, MRP, or Sales.

menu

GUI and Graphics (BC-GUI)

Control element to select options.

Menus are control elements offering the user a range of options which, when chosen, initiate the execution of an action by the system. An action can be the opening of a subordinate pull-down menu.

There are two types of menus, the menu bar and the pull-down menu. The layout of the menu or the pull-down menus has been defined for each of the levels of the R/3 System.

Menu options are selected either with a single mouse click or by positioning the cursor and by pressing the ENTER key.

menu bar

GUI and Graphics (BC-GUI)

Menu on a screen/window.

The menu bar is located directly below the title bar and above the work area of the window.

When you choose a menu option, you open the relevant pull-down menu below.

"Menu bar" also refers to a function that activates the menu bar. After the activation, you can position the cursor on the required menu option using the arrow keys and start the required function by pressing ENTER.

model

Quality Management (QM)

The first parts or products that have been manufactured using the equipment, processes and conditions intended for use in the manufacture of the final production series.

These items are the result of an initial production run or technical changes made to existing parts or products.

These items are normally subjected to a very intensive model series inspection.

The results of the model series inspection are typically documented in prescribed model series inspection reports.

Special Purpose Ledger/Controlling (FI-SL/CO)

A one-dimensional predefined reporting structure which can be inserted in the rows and/or columns of a Report Painter report.

object

External Services Management (MM-PUR-ES)

Criterion which determines the processes of data collection and data reduction in the Logistics Information System (LIS). Examples of such criteria are sales organization, purchasing organization, plant, and material.

Objects form part of the information structures in the Logistics Information System. It is with reference to objects that performance measures are cumulated here at defined intervals.

Every object has object values. For example, the object "sales organization" may have the values "sales organization South" and "sales organization North."

organigram

Business Navigator (CA-MOD-NAV)

A type of diagram (organization chart) in the R/3 Reference Model.

An organigram shows SAP organization units, such as company code, production storage location, and a fund manager.

You have to use the ARIS Toolset to create a company-specific organigram.

organizational unit

Implementation Guide (CA-IMS-IMG)

SAP key term, with which the organizational structure of a customer is represented, with respect to the SAP applications in use.

Organizational units can:

- all belong to one application
  (for example, sales organizations in SD)
- belong to different applications
  (for example, company code in FI and AM, plant in MM and SD)

The representation of customer-specific organizational structures is a prerequisite for the correct application-specific system settings made in Customizing.

Personnel Planning and Development (PD)

An organization unit represents any type of organizational entity found within a company, for example, subsidiaries, divisions, departments, or special project teams. Organizational units are one of the objects that make up organizational plans.

productive session

Basis Services (BC-SRV)

A batch input session that is recorded and processed at a later time. Changes to the database are only made when the session is processed. A productive session can only be processed once.

R/3 Analyzer

Business Navigator (CA-MOD-NAV)

The product name of the R/3 Reference Model for display on a PC. R/3 Analyzer comprises the navigation component of the ARIS Toolset and the R/3 Reference Model. You can display the information contained in the Reference Model using R/3 Analyzer, but to work with the Reference Model you also need the full ARIS Toolset product.

R/3 Reference Model

Business Navigator (CA-MOD-NAV)

Representation of the functional capability of the R/3 System, expressed in business terms as a model.
The R/3 Reference Model is a wholly graphical, detailed representation of all aspects of running a business, including, for instance, information flows, data and organization structures, the chronological sequence of tasks, and how all of these are implemented in the R/3 System. A model can be created of the whole operation of a specific company using the R/3 Reference Model as a basis.

routing

Production Planning (PP)

Describes the sequence of processing steps required to produce a material or provide a service without reference to an order.

The major objects of a routing are the routing header, operations, material allocations, production resources/tools, and inspection characteristics.

Together with specific dates and quantities, routing data forms an important part of the order.

SAP Hierarchy Graphics

Business Graphics (BC-GUI-PGR)

SAP Hierarchy Graphics allow you to present data in hierarchical structures.

This program includes a number of options. You can, for example, design hierarchies with different distances and angles, color the nodes according to different presentation criteria or edit numeric values of items.

scenario

Business Navigator (CA-MOD-NAV)

Class of processes in the R/3 Reference Model process selection matrix.

Each process selection matrix is divided into typical scenarios that reflect the tasks in the particular business application concerned. One example would be 'order types' for sales and distribution.

A scenario has its own column in the process selection matrix, containing all processes that belong to that scenario.

A process chain is assigned to the scenario icon. This process chain contains the functions of all processes in the scenario column in a summarized form. The individual processes can be called either from the scenario process or from the process selection matrix.

screen

ABAP/4 Development Workbench (BC-DWB)

SAP-specific term for a screen and its flow logic.

A "DYNPRO" includes not only the screen itself, but control statements for processing the screen.

scroll bar

GUI and Graphics (BC-GUI)

Window element.

You operate the scroll bar with the mouse which allows you to perform a range of scrolling options (including absolute and relative scrolling, forward and backward). The scroll bar extends across the entire length of the object you want to scroll, either vertically to the right of the object, or horizontally directly under the object.

server

Basis (BC)

Data station in a local network, which performs particular functions in the network.

Depending on the type of server, it can, for example:

- grant and withdraw authorizations (domain server).
- manage common data.
- manage print output on a connected network printer (print server).
- manage all connections to the host (communications server).

table

ABAP/4 Development Workbench (BC-DWB)

Array of data in table form.

A table consists of columns (data values of the same type) and rows (data records).

Each record can be identified uniquely by one or several fields.

table field

ABAP/4 Development Workbench (BC-DWB)

Field in a database table.

table section

Logistics–General (LO)

Section of a chart in the planning table that contains information identifying and describing the capacity requirements displayed in the diagram section, for example, all the requirements that are dispatched to a work center.

table structure

ABAP/4 Development Workbench (BC-DWB)

Comprises a complete listing of table fields and a statement on which fields constitute the primary key.

TCP/IP

Basis Services (BC-SRV)

Transport Control Protocol/Internet Protocol.

A software protocol developed for communication between computers.

title bar

GUI and Graphics (BC-GUI)

Area that displays the window header and symbols for controlling the window size.

The title bar is located at the top of every R/3 System window. The title of the window is displayed in the center of the title bar.

transport

Basis Services (BC-SRV)

Transfer of development environment objects from a source system to a target system.

In general, transports are carried out via transport requests.

view

ABAP/4 Development Workbench (BC-DWB)

Groups together tables according to particular viewpoints.

When a table is created, a key is allocated according to technical (program) viewpoints. The fields contained therein may be unnecessary for solving an accounting department task, or they may be insufficient. In this case, a view can be created via several tables or parts of tables.

Consolidation (FI-LC)

In Consolidation, you can have various views of data: plan, actual, forecast, as well as different hierarchies, to reorganize the aforementioned data types for different views of the data.

Materials Management (MM)

Groups together all the data on a material that a particular department (for example, Purchasing) creates in a material master record.

The individual views can be processed separately.

Windows

GUI and Graphics (BC-GUI)

Windows is a Microsoft graphical user interface (GUI) for computers using the MS-DOS operating system. The Windows NT version competes with UNIX and can be used on different platforms.

workflow

Workflow (WF-WF)

Execution of a predefined workflow task at runtime.

A workflow consists of a sequence of work items, which are processed by human agents or mechanical processing units.

The time and logical sequence of work items (linked to the evaluation of conditions) is handled by the workflow manager and controlled flexibly by event-related response mechanisms.

INDEX

A

ABAP   126
ABAP/4   22, 28, 31, 174
    Development Workbench   31, 40
ABAP/4 Query   31
ABAP/4 Repository   55
ABAP/4 Workbench   54
ABC   33
access sequence   98
ADP   201
ALE   9, 32
American Cyanamid   8
Analyzer   42
Application Program Interface (API)   22
application servers   57
architectural elements   79
archiving
    by document   65
Aris Toolset   42
as is   168
assignments   88
ASUG   51
asynchronous update   60
attributes   275
authorization profile   63
Autodesk   141, 158, 160, 197

B

basis   174
basis technology   22–27
    system configuration   23

Battco   130–132, 134, 136, 137, 138,
    147, 162
Baxter Healthcare Corp.   172
Big Bang   145
BPR   116, 117, 123, 168, 178
bridge   19
business application   54
Business Navigator   40, 54
business objects   65
business process redesign. *See BPR*
Business Workflow   14, 29, 40

C

change management   9, 136–137, 148
    key principles of,   219–225
Chevron   208
client   18, 175
client/server   18, 174
client/server architecture   19
client-oriented   77
Common Programming Interface-Communi-
    cations (CPI–C)   24
communication   146, 148, 190, 205,
    220–221
    Monsanto   220
company code   88
componentization   6
Computervision   144, 158
condition type   97
configuration   80
configuration team   80

construction   195
correction and transport system   30–31
critical success factors   133
    begin process change   134
    commitment   139
    communicate   135
    complete process change
        Pickering, Wendy   135
    Dallas, James   134
    methodology   138
    project manager   136
    superior championship   136
    team   137
    training   138
    understand corporate culture   134
CSC   124
CSC/Index   180
customization   81

D

Data Definition Language   287
data dictionary   21, 27
data migration   198
data model   70, 273
data repository   27
departmental definition   14
determination procedure   94
development system   62
Development Workbench   14
Digital Equipment   169
Dispatcher   57
distribution channel   88
division   88
document   82
    number   104
domain   275
DYNPRO   68, 282

E

encapsulation   6
entities   273
Ernst & Young   180, 183
event–driven process chain (EPC)   41

F

field   27
Forrester Research   7

G

gateway   19, 26
GUI functions   39

H

Hill's Pet Nutrition   120–122, 124
Hydro Agri North America (HANA)   209

I

IBM   139, 197
IMG. *See* Implementation Management Guide
implementation   205–206
Implementation Management Guide
    (IMG)   40, 47–48
information technology   135, 173, 174
    as team members   137
    data dictionary   252
    implementation process   126
    objects   252
    role change   126
    role of,   122–127
inheritance   6
instance   25, 26, 174, 197
    data population   197–198
integration mechanisms   159–161
integration system   62
interfaces   201
IS. *See* information technology
IT. *See* information technology
IXOS   201

K

keys   277

L

LAN   18
levels   96
line items   104
Locks   280

M

managing change   127, 216–232
    key performance indicators (KPIs)   224
    Monsanto   216, 219, 224
    reengineering   114
master data   82

match code 107, 279
match code IDs 107
Mentor 183
middleware 19
Monsanto 136, 153, 160, 216–219, 220, 221, 224
Myers, Mike 8

N

NEC Technologies, Inc. 125, 153, 206, 256

O

object 30, 274
OLE 7
operation 104
order document 106
Owens Corning 158, 256

P

PAI 282
PBO 282
performance 99
plant 87
POH 282
polymorphism 6
POV 282
preventive maintenance 142
Procedure Model 40, 43–47
production system 62
project leader 156
project team 144, 157–159, 171, 179, 189, 190, 196
    IS 253
    training 175
    users 253
protocol 20
prototyping 184, 189

Q

quotation document 106

R

R/3 4, 5–11, 14, 25, 38, 117, 122, 124, 127, 140–144, 152, 184, 254
    application menu 38
    hierarchy 179
    object-oriented design 6
    OLE 7
    risks 5–11
    toolbar 38
    user menu 39
    window 38
R/3 modules
    financial accounting 32–33
    human resources 33
    manufacturing and logistics 33–34
    sales and distribution 34
reengineering 9, 114, 115–120, 125, 128, 222
    Battco 222
    Champy, James 115
    Davenport, Thomas H. 115
    Hammer, Michael 115
    Hill's Pet Nutrition 120–122
    information technology 122–127
    Monsanto 222, 223
    when 123–126
Reference Model 40, 41–43, 48
reinvent 116
relationships 273
report display variants 110
reports 109
response time 59
router 19
row of data 275

S

SAIC 118, 141, 146, 158, 162, 173, 198, 201
sales organization 88
SAP 4, 175
SAP AG 254
SAP Implementation Guide (IMG) 54
SAP Knowledgeware 23
Sapphire xx
scale/magnitude matrix 118, 123, 168
scenarios 182–184
Scheier, Robert L. 8
Scientific Applications International Corp. See SAIC
scripts 182–184
Semico 191
server 18

session manager   39
Small Bang   146
Steelcase   139, 155, 158, 173, 179
steering committee   152–153, 156
streamline   116
Symmetrix   115
synchronous update   58
system administration   54

T

tables   27, 28–29, 52, 182–184
    application data tables   29
    control tables   29
    prototyping   184
    system configuration tables   28
team formation   234–246
    project leader   236
        diplomacy   238
        discipline   236
        performance management   240
        structure   237
    project teams   240, 244
    training   244
testing   201
    Early Watch group   203

integration testing   202
    stress test   202
    unit testing   202
    user testing   203
to be design   179
training   48–51, 140, 143–144, 148, 205,
    221
    Monsanto   221
    project team   175, 244
    SAIC   221
transaction data   82
transport stack   19
transport system   61

U

update process   57
user
    acceptance   180
    role change   126
    support   206
users group   51

W

workbench organizer   60
workstation   21